THE BEST I EVER ATE

BOOKS BY JUNE PLATT

June Platt's Party Cook Book 1936
June Platt's Plain and Fancy Cook Book 1941
June Platt's Dessert Cook Book 1942

The Best
I Ever Ate

A PRACTICAL
HOME COOK BOOK

**RECIPES BY
JUNE**

Platt

**READING BY
SOPHIE**

Kerr

*The difference between
good and bad cooking is civilization.*

RINEHART & COMPANY, INC.

New York   Toronto

Grateful acknowledgment is made to the following magazines for permission to reprint excerpts from their publications:

Country Life, *Doubleday & Company, Inc., Garden City, New York, for permission to reprint "A Home for a Greedy Person."*

House and Garden, *New York, N. Y., for permission to reprint "As Good As Bread," copyright, 1944, by The Condé Nast Publications Inc.; "Begged, Borrowed, Maybe Stolen," copyright, 1945, by The Condé Nast Publications Inc.; "Dinner at Eight for Eight," copyright, 1946, by The Condé Nast Publications Inc.; and "Why Not Turn Your Christmas Dinner into a Picnic?" ("Christmas Dinner from a Basket"), copyright, 1947, by The Condé Nast Publications Inc.*

The New York Herald Tribune Sunday Magazine, *for permission to reprint "Dinners To Which We Are Not Invited."*

The Saturday Evening Post, *Philadelphia, Pa., for permission to reprint "The Best I Ever Ate," copyright, 1952, by The Curtis Publishing Company; and "Pie American Style," copyright, 1928, by The Curtis Publishing Company.*

Vogue, *New York, N. Y., for permission to reprint "Gourmet My Eye," copyright, 1948, by The Condé Nast Publications Inc.; "Menus for Moderns," copyright, 1951, by The Condé Nast Publications Inc.; and "La Quiche Lorraine," copyright, 1945, by The Condé Nast Publications Inc.*

A WORD FROM THE AUTHORS

This book is made up of informal essays on food designed to stimulate interest in fine cooking and appetite for fine eating. Exact recipes for the dishes mentioned follow each essay, recipes which have been worked out to the least detail and in the most practical way for professional, amateur or novice cook. Old-fashioned dishes as well as ultramodern are described herein and a few intricate foreign specialties are included for the cook who longs to try something unusual.

We heartily wish you all "Bonne cuisine et bon appetit!"

June Platt—Sophie Kerr

CONTENTS

ONE   The Best I Ever Ate
3

TWO   Dinners to Which We Are Not Invited
26

THREE   Pie—American Style
50

FOUR   Begged, Borrowed, Maybe Stolen
76

FIVE   La Quiche Lorraine
101

SIX   As Good As Bread
115

SEVEN   Vegetables Needn't Be Dull
138

EIGHT   Home for a Greedy Person
157

NINE   Dinner at Eight, for Eight
175

TEN   Christmas Dinner from a Basket
by June Platt
180

ELEVEN   Menus for Moderns
189

TWELVE   Gourmet, My Eye
220

Index of Recipes
225

THE BEST I EVER ATE

The Best I Ever Ate

Scientists have revolutionized practically everything from stockings to entertainment but are not yet satisfied. More and more they are insinuating their efforts into a realm where I for one, regret to see them—the realm of food. They ask us if we have had today our health quota of iron, calcium, phosphorus, riboflavin, niacin, expletiva, flinkor, omigollirinum and whuffle and they ask it so constantly, so accusingly that many of us have begun to wonder, begun to worry, begun to look at our meals solely as chemical compounds and not as agreeable adventures with the taste buds and the appetite.

So far as I am concerned this is desperately wrong, and a betrayal of one of the five senses. The question the scientists have forgotten to ask—and so have many eaters—is: Does this taste good? Does it make us linger over each bite, scrape up the last bits, salvage the last drops of gravy or juice with a bit of bread and finally, when the meal is over, remark with a dreamy satisfied smile: "That was the best I ever ate!"

One of our best American authorities on cooking, Mrs. Sheila Hibben, recently has had the courage to come out publicly with a statement that a streamlined, begadgeted kitchen is no guarantee of good cooking. No doubt this is heresy to the moderns. Though be it heresy it is also the gospel truth. Many of the most delicious meals I ever ate were concocted in dark, unhandy, unimplemented kitchens and cooked on cranky old wood-burning ranges without heat gauges, pressure tops or thermometers; the mixing spoons and forks were twisted and battered, the pots and pans heavy to handle and hard to keep clean. A domestic economist of today would give shrill screams of horror at sight of such a kitchen, yet out of many and many such kitchens came a steady supply of magnificent meals, planned and cooked by women who never heard of niacin, riboflavin et al.

Now don't mistake me. I am all for a convenient, up-to-date kitchen and I have spent far more money than I should on buying tricky widgets and thingumbobs to circumvent the more tedious parts of cooking. I don't even object to my food being reckoned in chemical formulas if the final result is exceedingly palatable. But—but—and again, but—science had better stay away from my door if it is going to hand me food without flavor, charm or morishness.

As I look back over a long and fairly serene life there are certain high spots in eating which linger gratefully in my memory. I remember Mrs. Doctor Smithers, a substantial Eastern Shore of Maryland matron of agreeable manners and easy hospitable ways. It was my privilege to know her when I was a young thing not easily impressed by good cooking because we had plenty of it in my own home, just as in most Eastern Shore homes of that era before science got going so sternly. Mrs. Smithers' kitchen had no gleaming tiled surfaces, no gas or electric stove, no enamel tables and cabinets, no shining *batterie de cuisine*, no fancy beaters, mixers or whatzits. The worktable was wood with a shabby dark oil-cloth cover, the shelves and closets were also wood, there was no red geranium on the window sill and no eye-alluring red and white curtain at the window. The lighting was an oil lamp sitting high in a metal bracket. A dingy sort of hole, in fact today it would be called a truly underprivileged kitchen.

Yet when Mrs. Smithers drifted into it in her casual way, tied an apron over her black silk dress and busied her plump and pretty hands with a few utensils, there would soon appear on her table such Fried Oysters as never were before and never will be again. She casually whisked up a thin batter of egg and flour and milk and some of the oyster liquor, plenty of pepper and not too much salt. She rolled into finest dust some old-fashioned soda crackers. She set an ancient black iron frying pan on the stove and laid into it a plenty of pure white leaf lard bought from a near-by farm. She put a couple of sticks of pine wood and one of oak into the old stove. Then—magic! Each large lean oyster, tonged that morning from the Bay, was dipped in the dry mixture, then in the batter, then again in the dry and at the proper moment dropped into the sizzling lard. A piece of brown paper—probably part of the bag that had held the crackers—was laid on a pan, the pan set on the stove shelf, and when each oyster reached exactly the right stage it was fished out with a disreputable two-tined fork and laid on the paper that any lingering drop of grease might be absorbed. Mrs. Smithers put no more than three oysters in the fat at one time but she kept a steady rotation, and as one came out, another went in. Each oyster was cooked through, juicy, soft and luscious inside, with a frail evenly brown shell on the outside. They came to table in a hot dish and were eaten by the dozen with beaten biscuit and mustard pickle, and nobody, but nobody, ever ate anything better. It was in fact an accepted local saying: "Mrs. Smithers's fried oysters are the best I ever ate." If anyone had suggested that Mrs. Smithers would do better with a scientific kitchen or had asked if her fried oysters contained the right chemical elements there would have been Homeric laughter and Homeric rage and the caviler would have been labeled as of unsound mind.

As I have said, Mrs. Smithers's Fried Oysters were usually accompanied by mustard pickle and her mustard pickle was very good indeed. It was not, however, the best I ever ate. That accolade must be given to the mustard pickle made by my Aunt Susie, my mother's younger sister, whose mustard pickle was five-star. Her recipe, just as she wrote it some fifty years ago, lies on my desk. Since Aunt Susie was a schoolteacher the writing is neat, the spelling correct. Here it is:

"One gallon good vinegar; one-half pound yellow mustard; six green peppers chopped; six small red-hot peppers cut in slivers; two tablespoons salt; one pound sugar or to taste; one gallon green tomatoes cut fine; two dozen small cucumbers; one quart lima beans; one dozen ears corn cut from cob and cooked three minutes; one head cauliflower cut fine. Cook all vegetables until about half done. Put vinegar on fire, mix mustard and when vinegar is hot stir it in, then add salt and sugar, cook a few minutes, then add all the vegetables cooked and drained. After simmering a while take from fire and add five cents worth of turmeric, one-quarter pound white mustard seed, one-eighth pound celery seed. Stir well and can while hot."

What a hopelessly amateur recipe with its "five cents worth of turmeric," its "after simmering a while," its "one pound sugar or to taste!" How inexact, how ridiculous! Nevertheless, that pickle was a wonder. Its color was dull gold from the mustard and turmeric and the ribbons of red-hot scarlet pepper laced through it beguilingly. The flavor was subtle, for each vegetable retained something of its own and yet had something of the spices cooked with it. There were no onions, for Aunt Susie thought onions too overpowering. If Susie had not married a well-to-do husband and lapsed happily into complete domesticity, she might have put her pickle on the market in a big way and become one of the early career women of this century. Those who tasted her pickle invariably cried for more and she complained that she had copied the recipe so often she was getting cramps in her fingers. Her kitchen was just as inconvenient, just as out-of-date, as Mrs. Smithers's! I must add that it held a battered mahogany sideboard of excellent design which was used as a pot cupboard while her dining room was furnished in the shiniest and most rococo of golden oak. My Aunt Susie had stylish tendencies and in her day old mahogany was out and golden oak was in.

Among my friends on the Eastern Shore there was one who was generally conceded to make the best pocketbook rolls and the best beaten biscuits in the whole nine counties. She was very temperamental but when she was in the mood she would offer some of her delectable breads for sale, at which time the world certainly beat a path to her door. Her name was Mrs. William B. Griffith but in our friendly Eastern Shore way she was generally called Miss Lucy. Slender, small-boned, feverishly active, rapid of speech, she would have been pretty if she'd had any personal vanity, but she screwed her hair on top of her head and wore clothes fashioned for utility not adornment. Her temper was sharp and so was her tongue, she loved and hated with violence, her tastes and prejudices knew no shades of black and white. This did not affect her cooking nor the essential kindness of her heart. If anyone in the neighborhood was sick, he or she was sure to find a plate of Miss Lucy's pocketbook rolls among the dainties brought by neighbors to tempt his appetite. Because she cooked by inspiration and instinct, it was hard for her to define her recipes and it was only by a lot of finagling that I got the formula for those rolls in writing. A proper Bostonian once told her that they should be called Parker House Rolls and Miss Lucy's gray eyes flashed. "I have called them pocketbook rolls since the day I was born," declared Miss Lucy grandly, *"because that is their name."*

Miss Lucy's recipe for pocketbook rolls is as amateur in form as my Aunt Susie's recipe for mustard pickle. It is aimed at those who know how to cook and are accustomed to translate indefinite terms into definite accomplishment. Here it is:

"Scald two cups milk, dissolve in it two tablespoons each of butter and sugar. Cool and add one teaspoon of salt, one yeast cake dissolved in a little lukewarm water and sufficient flour to make a thin batter. Beat well, cover and stand in a warm place until light, add flour enough to make a very soft dough and knead until smooth and elastic. Set aside again until light, then make into balls the size of an egg and let rise on the bread-board covering with a cloth. When light, roll down half of each one until quite thin, brush with soft butter and fold over the thick side. Place an inch apart on greased pans, brush with milk, let rise for fifteen minutes and bake." I asked Miss Lucy how hot the oven ought to be and she replied: "Put your hand in and try it until it is just right for rolls."

I felt pretty funny about this last until one of the judges in a recent national cooking contest—where stoves and all other equipment were the last word in modern efficiency—told me that she had seen many of the young contestants disregarding the thermometers and gauges to try the ovens by hand. Perhaps the human hand is after all the most reliable heat indicator a cook can have. As for Miss Lucy's rolls they were always lightly soft inside with a pale-brown sweet crust of flaky brittleness, and had the flavor of perfect bread, which is sun-ripened golden wheat, pure butter and milk, combined with the magic of leavening to form a true staff of life.

Miss Lucy's beat biscuit were as much a triumph as her rolls. They were small, roundish, with a top as crisp as a toasted cracker, an interior of flaky layers which literally melted in the mouth and a bottom crust a bit irregular and just firm enough to hold the biscuit together. There are no such beat biscuit today—why people actually put baking powder into them! The only legitimate ingredients for beaten biscuit are flour, lard, salt and cold water, mixed into a stiff rough dough which must be put on a breadboard or biscuit block and pounded with a heavy iron hammer or the back of an ax for forty-five minutes. I mean pounded! No light taps, no loving little rappings, but beat-beat-beat, hard, regular, moving the dough now and then, doubling it over and turning it so that no crumb be overlooked. At the end of this bout the dough will be smooth, elastic and resilient from the air which has been beaten into it.

Now comes the "making out" or shaping of the biscuit. The dough is pulled into a long narrow piece and from this pieces approximately the size of a small egg are broken off. A smart cook can break the dough so accurately that all the finished biscuit will be the same size. The broken-off pieces are picked up, one by one, and kneaded in the hands, pinching together, molding, rolling with a special motion which must be studied and isn't easy. When the finished biscuit is properly shaped, it is given a last quick circular roll which makes it into a ball and it is then set down on the breadboard. When all the biscuit are molded and set in rows each one is slightly flattened by a dexterous quick pressure from the right wrist of the cook, then as a finishing touch they are pricked three times with a four-tined fork, set in a shallow baking pan half an inch apart and baked in a hot oven. Such a biscuit is a unique and unequaled hot bread. Break it open and slosh it with butter and honey or peach preserves, or lay the two halves on your plate and cover with fried chicken gravy or red ham juice. What a dish!

The beat biscuit is good cold, buttered or plain, it is a grand lunchbox or picnic bread. It renews its pristine freshness if you dunk it in cold water and reheat it in the oven. And if there should be any left over it makes a marvelous stuffing for roast fowl or fish. Of course it is a lot of hard work to make beat biscuit and no one today seems to want to do it. Gone are the days when the banging on the biscuit block echoed from every Eastern Shore kitchen every weekday morning and a plate of the piping hot little brown darlings came in with the breakfast coffee, eggs and ham. The modern palate is the loser.

But this is not a prolonged look into past culinary glories nor a lament for the same, but a tribute to those skilled cooks of the past who, without being students of chemistry or possessors of modern equipment, went into the kitchen and produced masterpieces of good food which linger, oh so pleasantly, in memory. As for instance my Aunt Eliza—on the paternal side—who made a special peach pie beyond compare. She would line a pan with rich pie dough and fill it with halves of ripe peaches, laid cavity side up. She would sprinkle these with what she considered enough sugar (and she was never wrong), dust it lightly, very lightly, with flour, fill the pie dish to overflowing with sour cream, add a lattice top of piecrust, pinch the edge decoratively, and bake in a moderate oven. The cream cooked into the peaches, the peach juice cooked into the cream, the sugar blessed the whole affair, the piecrust lattice and edge turned an enticing ecru, and the pie, hot or cold, was a poem in appearance and flavor, the best I ever ate in peach pies, and no cook I ever had could duplicate it. It was Aunt Eliza's specialty and hers alone.

Back in my mother's family there was my Cousin Jennie who made a plus-ultra poundcake but never gave away the recipe. My Cousin Jennie, actually a second cousin of my mother, was a stout elderly widow who with house and garden free and clear lived comfortably, contributed to church and to charity, dressed neatly and enjoyed local social life to the full on an income of fifty dollars a month. Now and then she made her poundcake, and when I was in college and my mother was sending me a box of special goodies, she would sometimes contribute a small loaf to the package. It was baked an even color all over except for a pale streak down the top; within it was pure gold of finest texture. It sliced evenly, broke lightly in the hand, and the aroma that came from its slices was like candy, fruit and flowers combined. There is no poundcake like this now and there was precious little of it then, for fifty dollars per month did not run to extravagance in butter and eggs even at the turn of the century and poundcake cannot be made without extravagance. It is a luxury cake, not for the small budget. I am not really sorry that Cousin Jennie would not part with her recipe for I know very well I could not have made cake as good as hers no matter how hard I tried. She had the magic touch.

I once knew another woman who had the magic touch for spongecake. Her name was Mary and she was the sister-in-law of my wonderful cook, Julia Hunt, who was with me for over twenty-five years and never made a poor or indifferent dish. Mary came to me when Julia was sick and she was, to understate it highly, spirited, in fact so spirited that at the end of our first week together I had to reason with her. "If you're sick," I said, "go home and go to bed. But if you're simply peevish because of unexpected company don't bang things around and don't scowl and don't snap at me, for I'm the only one in this house privileged to have a bad temper."

This statement had such an effect on her that she went right to work and made me a spongecake and it was the best I ever ate, bar none. Its superior flavor was not its only claim to distinction—it didn't dry up after cutting as most spongecakes do. When it had been duly praised, Mary confided that it was just an ordinary three-egg recipe but that she always added the grated zest of a lemon or small orange, whichever was handy, and sometimes a spoonful or so of the fruit juice.

If I have been dallying with recollection of cakes and bread and fried oysters it's not because I want to slight the best I ever ate of meat dishes but because I can offer no more than the sketchiest hint of how to reproduce them, since these meat dishes were made of the very best meat and the very best meat is hard to find and costs like fury when it is found. Where one could now buy a proper saddle of mutton I do not know, outside of one place in New York where I hear it is occasionally offered, but people don't want mutton, they say, they won't eat anything but lamb. Yet Saddle of Mutton with Breton Beans at the old Carlton Hotel in London was a dish of the greatest distinction.

The beans were boiled, seasoned, puréed and placed at the end of the noble platter which held the mutton. The roasting was just right, meat done all the way through, yet when the long thin slices were carved by the head captain's razor-sharp knife, they were brown on the edge shading in to an appetizing *cooked* pink, juicy, tender and not a bit greasy. Three slices were laid on the diner's plate overlapping like a job of fine roofing; the puréed beans were placed at one side; a little thin pan gravy was spooned over the meat, tart ruby currant jelly was offered. No meat dish I have ever eaten, either in America or on the Continent, equaled this Carlton Hotel mutton, which seemed so simple but was in reality a combination of skilled selection of the meat and complete finesse in cooking. Simple? Maybe.

Beyond this special mutton the best meat dishes I have ever eaten are two and both were French. The roast partridge at the old Montagné Restaurant in Paris, and the fried chicken with brandy at that famous inn, La Providence, in the village of Jouy near Chartres. For a good many years after the Second World War, Prosper Montagné exercised his art at the corner of the Rue St. Honoré and the Rue de l'Échelle. From the outside his establishment looked very modest; and inside there was no chi-chi or dolling up, just a low-ceiled double room in old-fashioned style, but at the back of the first room there was a niche which connected with the kitchen at one side. In that niche there was a big flat-topped stove and presiding over that stove was Prosper Montagné, a short, ruddy, bright-eyed man with gray hair and a clipped gray mustache. Many Americans went there for the word had got around that Montagné served roast beef and good coffee, both of which were, and still are, hard to find in Paris. There was a large, heavy, pear-shaped *maître d'hôtel* who seated customers and presided over the fruit table and was a genius with the big melons that lay there in cracked ice. He'd cut a hole in the top of one, take out the seeds, spoon out most of the flesh and return it bathed in a mixture of liqueurs selected to artfully enhance but not destroy the taste. Then the delectable mixture lay inside the melon shell waiting to be served.

Montagné's had other distinctive features: one was a deep brown pot of boiled potatoes which, swathed in white linen, was offered with almost every meat and fish dish, not only once but for second and even third helps as appetite demanded. Monsieur M. himself made the coffee and it was without chicory, served in hot cups, black, fresh, its scent celestial. Montagné's roast beef was as simple as the Carlton roast mutton, but it, too, was the best meat, hung just the right number of days and, as with the potatoes, the customer was invited to have seconds and no extra charge.

But it was with game that Montagné's art reached its acme. Venison he prepared with magic, and all the game birds passed into his hands to become sublimated temptations to greediness. He did a special dish with pheasant in which the meat was taken from the birds, pounded together, shaped in a big sausage roll with the giblets in the center, the whole wrapped in piecrust and baked—well, it had to be seen and eaten to be believed. Yet for my own taste I found the Montagné roast partridge best.

The partridge had apparently been plucked and drawn and then covered, first with a couple of big grape-vine leaves, then with a thin slice of salt pork, and oven-cooked under this double blanket. At the last moment leaves and meat were removed and the bird gently, thoroughly, crisply browned. The giblets, which had been cooked in the same pan, were chopped, spread on a small slice of toast, and on this the bird was laid and rushed to table, meltingly tender, just right in every way. Sometimes one of the cooked vine leaves was laid over it to keep the heat in, perhaps, or just for style. Then came the jar of hot potatoes, and a salad of *mâche* and beets, and afterward the cold, sweet, spicy melon and the scalding black coffee.

Montagné smiled genially when the clients went over to the stove and said how wonderful it all was, but he accepted the praise as natural. And the client went out knowing that though the bill was high he had received full value for his cash. Montagné, I am told, spent the profits of his restaurant for a fine chateau near Biarritz and also in reckless playing the races. I hope he had a good time.

The fried, or to be exact, *sauté* chicken with brandy at La Providence was in its own way as delicious as the partridge of Montagné's. Everyone going from Paris to Chartres stopped at this famous inn which was, when I first went there, owned by M. Delaunay, formerly one of the chefs to King Edward VII of England, a hearty but discriminating royal eater. In compliment to his late employer, M. Delaunay had a short pointed Edwardian beard, and wore English tweed cutaway suits, and since he combined the regal styles with wooden sabots the effect was piquant.

La Providence was unostentatious, just a group of two- and one-story small buildings ranged around a courtyard full of bright flowers. Tables were set out there when the sun shone, but for dark or rainy days there was a dining room at the left of the entrance. At the back there was a delightful vegetable garden, a chicken yard and also a building for wine storage, and over all there was an air of order, peace and industry well managed.

M. Delaunay's son-in-law was the head chef and a skillful one as well as a most intelligent and sympathetic man. In 1949, the last time I was there, he said that since the old Delaunays and also his wife had died he meant to turn the restaurant over to the faithful staff that had been there so long. I hope he taught his successor to make that *sauté* chicken. He would put a lavish lump of butter in the frying pan, drop in pieces of chicken, turn them constantly until they were lightly browned all over, add salt and ground pepper and about two jiggers of brandy, clap the lid on the pan and let the chicken cook through at reduced heat, and uncover again for a final browning and crisping. One of his minions would meantime be deep-fat-frying potatoes, another was tossing together a salad just picked from the garden, and the hungry client who had been watching all this and nibbling at simple hors d'oeuvres and sipping cold dry vermouth could sit down among the flowers of the courtyard and lunch in leisurely beatitude. After the chicken and the salad and the potatoes, he might be served a bit of Brie or Pont l'Évêque, or a slice of apple tart graced by a tang of orange zest and a sprinkling of toasted crushed almonds. The coffee came from the kitchen in the pot in which it had just been made. No one ever said anything about niacin, calcium, iron or phosphorus on the Delaunay premises.

So it seems to me that we shouldn't get too set on making eating nothing but an exercise in science. Let the dietary experts stay, but if it comes to a choice between them and the real cooking experts I will vote for the cooking experts every time. For people in good health, this classifying what we eat only according to its chemical ingredients can be carried right on into an awful finicking hypochondria. But if we *must* ask the exact amount of animal, mineral and vegetable elements in our food, let us ask first that great basic question: "Does it taste good?" If it doesn't, don't eat it. Food without flavor is an abomination, a byword and a hissing!

The following are the
recipes for dishes mentioned in this article

Fried Oysters
(*for 6–8*)

Buy 3 dozen fresh shelled oysters and be sure they have some juice with them. When ready to cook them, strain the liquid through cheesecloth, and save ¼ cup of it. Wash the oysters and drain well. Have ready a deep iron frying pan or deep fat fryer in which you have melted 1 pound fresh leaf lard, but do not heat to smoking point yet.

At this point, beat 2 whole eggs in a bowl and mix into it the ¼ cup oyster juice and season with ½ teaspoon salt and the same of coarsely ground black pepper. Spread a sheet of waxed paper out onto the kitchen table and place on it a generous pile of cracker meal. Place the oysters in a bowl conveniently near by, then place the fryer back on a moderate flame and heat until the lard becomes smoky hot, or registers 350° to 375° F. by a deep fat thermometer.

Now roll a few oysters at a time first in the cracker meal, then dip into the beaten egg mixture and roll again in the cracker meal and drop a few at a time into the smoky hot fat. Watch out, for they may splatter a bit. Cook 3 to 4 minutes or until a rich golden brown. Fish them out of the fat with a long two-prong fork and drain on paper towel. Keep warm while you repeat the process until all the oysters are cooked, then serve at once, in a hot serving platter, accompanied by homemade mustard pickle (see page 5).

Pocketbook Rolls
(for 6–8)

Scald 2 cups milk by putting it into a little saucepan on the fire and bringing it just to the boiling point. Remove from fire and dissolve in it 2 tablespoons butter and the same of sugar. Cool until lukewarm, then add 1 teaspoon salt and 1 yeast cake dissolved in ¼ cup lukewarm water. Stir well.

Sift 2½ cups all-purpose flour into a big bowl and stir into it the liquid mixture, using a big wooden spoon. Beat until smooth and well mixed. Cover with a tea cloth and place in warm place away from draft, until it has doubled in bulk, or for about 2 hours. At this point add 3 cups flour gradually kneading it in with your hand right in the bowl. Then transfer to floured board and knead until smooth and elastic or for about 5 minutes, adding more flour if necessary, but not more than ¼ cup of it. Shape dough into a smooth ball and place in clean bowl, cover with cloth and place in warm spot to rise again, or for about ¾ hour.

Have ready 2 well-buttered cookie sheets. Break the dough into pieces about the size of an egg and shape into smooth balls. Place on floured board and cover, and let rise again for the third time, for about ¾ hour. Now, using a rolling pin, roll down half of each ball, until quite thin. Brush with melted butter, and fold the thick side down onto the thin side, and place on cookie sheet about an inch apart. Brush with milk, and let rise again for the fourth time, for about 15 minutes. Place in preheated 375°–400° F. oven and bake for about 25 minutes. This recipe makes about 2½ dozen rolls.

Maryland Beat Biscuit
(for 6–8)

These are definitely fun to make. Sift together 2 cups pastry flour with ½ teaspoon salt. Work into it with finger tips ⅓ cup fresh leaf lard. Add gradually just enough ice water to make a very stiff dough, or not more than ⅓ cup. Use a fork for this process. Gather it all into a rough ball and place it on a lightly floured heavy breadboard, or carving block, on a sturdy table and beat as hard as possible, with a smooth heavy mallet or heavy wooden potato masher, for at least 45 minutes, occasionally doubling the dough 3 times over. When it is smooth and elastic in consistency, and when you have given it the last beat and are worn out, give it a final doubling up to form a long sausage shape and with the fingers, press together and stretch it out until about 14 inches long.

Have ready a cookie sheet lightly greased with lard, and a preheated hot oven set at 450° F. Break off pieces of the dough approximately the size of small eggs, and shape into balls smooth on top. Place about 1 inch apart on the cookie sheet, and when they are all done, press with your right wrist to flatten to ½-inch thickness. Prick each one 3 times with a four-prong fork, and place in hot oven. Bake 15 to 20 minutes, or until a pale golden color. Serve immediately. No use worrying about what to do with any leftover ones, for there won't be any.

Aunt Eliza's Peach Pie
(for 6–8)

First prepare the pastry. Sift together 2½ cups pastry flour with ¼ teaspoon salt. Work into this with the finger tips 6 tablespoons vegetable shortening and 6 tablespoons butter. Moisten with 3–6 tablespoons of ice water. Form into 2 balls, one slightly larger than the second. Wrap in waxed paper and chill for at least ½ hour.

When ready to make the pie, roll out the larger ball and line a 10-inch Pyrex pie plate with the pastry. Now remove the skins from 8–10 large, ripe, freestone peaches by plunging them into boiling water for a second or two before peeling. Cut them in half, remove pits and place cut side up on the pastry. Sprinkle with 1 generous cup granulated sugar, and sift 1 scant tablespoon flour over the sugar. Now spread evenly over the whole, 1 cup extra heavy cream, which you have soured by adding 2 tablespoons lemon juice. Roll out the small ball of pastry and cut it into thin strips the size of the diameter of the pie. Lay them crisscross across the pie to form a lattice, having first moistened the edge of the pie slightly with cold water. Trim and roll up the edges to secure the lattice, then crimp the edges prettily. Place in preheated, hot 450° F. oven and bake until the crust begins to brown around the edge, then decrease the heat to 375°–400° F. and continue cooking until the syrup boils up and the peaches are done or for about 50–60 minutes in all. Serve hot or cold.

Poundcake
(for 6–8)

Wash ½ pound butter in cold water, working it with your hands until smooth like putty. Place it in a clean cloth and pat dry. Place in refrigerator for 5 or 10 minutes. Remove from refrigerator and place in a big bowl. Separate the yolks from the whites of 6 eggs. Measure 1 cup sifted granulated sugar. Sift some flour and measure out 2¼ cups of it.

Cream the butter until very creamy, then add gradually the granulated sugar. Beat well until very light. Beat the yolks with rotary beater until light and creamy and add to them the grated rind of 2 lemons and the juice of ½ lemon and 1 teaspoon vanilla. Add this to the butter and sugar and beat very well. Now stir in the flour into which you have mixed about ½ teaspoon grated nutmeg, adding it little by little. Beat the whites with rotary beater until stiff enough to form a peak but not dry and fold them into the batter ⅓ at a time. Place in bread tin 4½ by 8½ by 2½ inches deep which you have buttered first, then lined with typewriter paper and buttered again. Place in preheated 325° F. oven and bake for 1 hour and 15 minutes, or until it is a light golden brown and until an inserted cake tester comes out clean. Allow to cool in the pan.

When cake is cold it may be wrapped in clean napkin wet with brandy and set away in cake-box.

Spongecake
(for 6–8)

Sift ¾ cup of granulated sugar. Sift some pastry flour and measure out ¾ cup of it. Add pinch salt and sift again. Separate the yolks from the whites of 3 eggs. Beat the yolks with rotary beater until very light, then beat in the sugar a little at a time. Stir in the grated rind of 1 lemon using the fine side of the grater, and add 1 tablespoon strained lemon juice. Now beat the whites until stiff with a wire whisk. Fold into the egg mixture ⅓ of the sifted flour, then fold in ⅓ of the whites, another ⅓ of flour and another ⅓ of the whites, the last ⅓ of the flour and the remainder of the whites. Place gently in a well-buttered angel-cake tin and place in preheated 325° F. oven and bake for 40 minutes or until it tests done. Turn out immediately onto cake rack to cool. When serving, tear apart with fork rather than using a knife.

Saddle of Mutton or Lamb
(for 6–8)

Ask the butcher to prepare a saddle of lamb or mutton for roasting. He should remove part of the center bone, and he should remove all the skin that covers the fat and part of the fat and he should make deep incisions in the fatty surface, and remove the kidneys and most of the fat from the underside and trim the flanks and roll them under and tie it all firmly with strings, so that it will keep its shape. If it is lamb, it will weigh about 5½ to 6 pounds when trimmed. Mutton will weigh more. In any event, it should be cooked for 10–12 minutes per pound, depending on whether you like it really rare, or nice and pink inside. I prefer it to be cooked 12 minutes to the pound. In other words, a 5½ pound roast would take about 1 hour and 10 minutes. Only practice will make perfect. Salt and pepper the roast slightly on the inside only between the flank and under part of roast. Place it fat side up in your roasting pan, on a rack. Place it in a preheated 500° F. oven and roast for 15 minutes at that temperature, then reduce the heat to 400°–450° F. and continue roasting, basting it every 15 minutes. Salt and pepper the roast on the outside about 20 minutes before it will be done. Ten minutes before it will be done, transfer the roast to the top part of your roaster and pour over it all the fat, endeavoring not to include any of the brown residue in the bottom of the original pan. Place the roast back in the oven while you make some clear gravy by adding ¾ cup of consommé to the brown residue and 1 teaspoon of Bovril. Let this all boil down a minute or two until syrupy, and transfer it to a little saucepan to facilitate heating it, when you are ready to serve the roast. Place the roast on a hot platter, garnish with parsley and send to table to be carved and served. It should be sliced in thin slices lengthwise following the back bone. The clear gravy should be served separately in a little sauceboat, and a purée of boiled dry white marrow beans should accompany the roast.

Purée of Dried Marrow Beans
(for 6–8)

Wash and soak for 8 hours, 3 cups dried white marrow beans. Drain off the water and cover with about 3 quarts cold water. Bring very slowly to boiling point, skim carefully, add 2 small white peeled onions, reduce heat, cover, and simmer gently for about 2½ hours or until the beans are tender throughout. At this point add 2 cups of peeled-diced potatoes and cook until potatoes are done. It may be necessary to add additional boiling water once or twice during the cooking process, but 2 additional cups should be enough in all. Drain but save what little juice remains. Push the beans and potatoes while hot through a fine sieve using a wooden spoon or potato masher. Add about ¼ pound sweet butter and season to taste and heat well, incorporating just enough of the bean water to make the purée the right consistency, like mashed potatoes. Place over boiling water in top part of double boiler and stir frequently until ready to serve. Place in hot serving dish, sprinkle with chopped parsley and serve at once.

Partridge Wrapped in Grape Leaves and Bacon
(for 6–8)

Select 8 choice tender partridges. Have the poultryman clean them, leaving them whole. Clean them carefully yourself and wipe them clean inside and out with a damp cloth. Have ready 8 fine grape leaves, well washed, dried and heavily buttered both sides. Cut 8 strips of bacon in half. Butter a roasting pan lightly. Salt and pepper the birds well inside. Soften ½ pound butter and stir into it the juice of 1 lemon. Place 2 tablespoons lemon butter inside each bird. Tuck the legs neatly into the little slits left by the poultryman in the apron. Cover the breast of each bird with 1 buttered grape leaf and lay 2 half-strips of bacon over each. Tie leaves and bacon in place with thin string. Place the birds in the buttered roasting pan, breasts up.

Preheat your oven, setting the control at Hot, 500° F. Place the birds in oven and roast, basting occasionally for about 25 minutes or until lightly browned. Salt and pepper lightly, reduce heat to 375° F. and continue roasting, basting occasionally until the birds are almost done or for about 10 minutes longer. At this point remove the grape leaves, let the bacon slices stay in bottom of pan. Add 2 cups stemmed and washed small seedless white grapes, and continue roasting about 10 minutes longer. Remove from oven and pour over the birds ½ cup good brandy which you have heated slightly. Light the brandy, being careful not to burn yourself, and keep ladling the brandy and pan-butter over the birds until the flames die out naturally. Increase heat of oven again to 500° F. and roast for 5 minutes longer or until birds are delicately browned. Place birds on hot platter and surround with the grapes.

Reduce the juice in pan until syrupy by boiling it rapidly over a good fire, then pour this hot gravy into a separate dish. Garnish the birds with a little chopped parsley and serve at once, accompanied by the clear gravy.

Hot Pâté of Pheasant
or Chicken or Guinea Hens
(for 6–8)

The day before the party make some puff paste in the following manner. Wash ½ pound butter in a bowl of cold water, working it with your hands until softened to the consistency of putty, soft and pliable. Squeeze it in a piece of clean linen to extract any water there may be left in it. Now sift some cake flour and measure out 2 cups of it. Add ½ teaspoon salt and sift it into a bowl. Work into this with the finger tips, 1 tablespoon butter, then add gradually ¾ cup of ice water, still using your hands to mix it. Knead it lightly on a slightly floured pastry cloth or board, roll out to about ⅜-inch thickness into a rectangular piece about 6 by 12 inches. Place the dough horizontally in front of you, shape the remaining butter into a slab about ⅓ the size of the dough, and lay it in the center. Fold the flap of dough on the left to cover the butter, then fold the right-hand flap over to the left. The butter should be completely covered and out of sight, and the whole secret of the puff paste is to see to it that the butter never breaks through to the surface. Roll the paste away from you to make a rectangle again. Give it a turn, which means to place it horizontally again before you and fold the left side over to the right, and the right side over to the left, forming a square again. Press lightly with the roller. Wrap in waxed paper and place in refrigerator (not in the freezing compartment, however) for 20 minutes. Remove from refrigerator and place it before you as it was before, and roll away from you again as before. Give it a turn and fold in 3 again, wrap in paper, place in refrigerator again. Repeat this process every 20 minutes until you have rolled and folded it 8 times. Wrap well in waxed paper and then in a cloth and keep in refrigerator until ready to use. So much for the pastry part of this dish.

The next step is to prepare the filling which may be made from the breasts of chickens, guinea hens, or pheasants. In any case, you will need 2 plump birds. Ask the butcher or poultryman to clean and cut them up as for fricassee. Wash the livers and wrap in waxed paper and place in refrigerator until ready to use. Clean, singe, wash and dry the pieces of bird and place in a deep enamel saucepan and pour over them just enough hot water to barely cover. Place on low flame and stand by and skim very carefully. Do not allow the birds to really boil. When no more scum comes to the surface, add 2 peeled carrots, 2 peeled onions, a branch or 2 of celery and watch carefully again until it comes to boiling point, and skim again if necessary. At this point season to taste with salt and add a bouquet garni of parsley, 1 pinch of thyme and 1 small bay leaf. Simmer until tender or for about 1½ hours if the birds are tender, or longer if necessary. Remove from fire and cool in their broth. Place in refrigerator until ready to assemble the pâté.

Now put the gizzards in a little pan, cover with cold water, add a little salt, and cook gently until tender, or for about ¾ hour. Cool in their broth. In the meantime, peel 6 shallots and chop fine. Place in small frying pan with 3 tablespoons butter and cook slowly until the shallots just begin to brown. In the meantime, peel 8 firm fresh mushrooms, remove tough part of stems, wash if necessary, and chop not too fine. Add them to the shallots and cook until they form their juice and cook down again. In a separate little frying pan, brown the livers quickly both sides, in a little butter, then pour over them 1 tablespoon of good brandy, stir, re-move from fire, and chop coarsely. Add this to the mushrooms, likewise the gizzards also cut into small thin pieces, discarding all the tough part. Now season highly to taste with salt, coarsely ground black pepper, a pinch of cayenne and a dash of mace or nutmeg. Put aside until ready to use.

Now place the cooked birds on low flame just long enough to melt the jelly. Drain and save the broth. Pick the white meat only, from the bones, and put it through the meat grinder once, using the medium-sized cutter. You should have 2 cups or more of meat. If you haven't, add some of the dark meat, but it's better with only white meat. Season highly to taste with salt, pepper, mace, a few celery seeds, and a pinch of cayenne.

Place 2 cups broth in a little pan and let it boil down rapidly, until re-duced to 1 cup.

It is now time to make the mushroom sauce which should accompany this fancy dish. Peel, wash, dry, and chop very fine, 1 pound mushrooms discarding the tough part of stems. Peel and chop fine 8 small shallots. Cook them slowly without browning for 5 or 10 minutes in ¼ pound butter, then add the mushrooms and cook until they make their juice and boil down and are about to brown, then add 2 or 3 tablespoons of good brandy, and the cup of reduced broth. Continue simmering for about 10 minutes. Season to taste with salt and pepper. Just before serving, heat to boiling point and stir in 2 or 3 tablespoons heavy cream.

Now you are ready to make the pâté. *This is the fun part. Have ready a little bowl containing 1 egg beaten together slightly with 1 tablespoon cold water. Also have ready a shallow baking pan at least 12 inches long. A cookie sheet with sides will do.*

Now assemble the ground-up breasts of bird (to be known henceforth as farce), the liver, mushrooms, and gizzard concoction, a lightly floured pastry board, and rolling pin, a diamond-shaped cookie cutter, and a pastry brush. Light your oven and set it at 450° F.

Place the puff paste dough on the board and roll out to a rectangle, approximately 14 inches by 9 inches and about ⅛ inch thick. Place it horizontally before you. Trim off a 2-inch strip from one end and with the diamond-shaped cookie cutter make 4 diamonds. Cut these again into 4, making 16 small diamond-shaped pieces. Put these aside for the moment. Now spread half of the ground-up farce down the center lengthwise. Make a little trough in it and fill with the liver and mushrooms. Cover with the remainder of the farce, shaping it into a nice neat roll, leaving a little space at either end. Roll the far side of the pastry up and over onto the farce and moisten the edge, then roll the near side up and over, but not too tight, then press it gently to stick the two sides together. Moisten both ends and roll up and press gently to seal. Now rinse the baking sheet in cold water and transfer the pâté, *placing it bottom side up with care, in the center of the pan.*

Make three crosslike incisions in the paste, spacing them evenly. Paint the entire surface with a thin coating of the beaten egg. Now lay 5 of the small diamond-shaped pieces around each incision, making a decoration of 3 stars. Paint the stars with egg, and poke your index finger down into each hole, to make a good vent. Place in preheated 450° F. oven and bake for about 5 to 8 minutes or until it begins to brown lightly, then reduce the heat to 375° F. and continue cooking for about 30 minutes longer. Garnish with fresh parsley or watercress and serve at once, accompanied by the mushroom sauce, in a separate sauceboat. Cut at table in 1-inch slices with a sharp knife.

Chicken Sautéed in Butter and Brandy
(for 6–8)

Buy 2 fine plump frying chickens, cut in 6 pieces each, or if you prefer, 4 or 5 whole chicken breasts cut in half, making 8 to 10 pieces. Clean, singe, wash quickly in cold water, and dry thoroughly. Have ready an iron frying pan, hereafter called a cocotte, *in which you have placed ⅛ pound sweet butter. Place in warm place so that butter will melt and the* cocotte *will heat gently through, but so that the butter will not brown.*

In a separate iron frying pan, melt ¼ pound sweet butter, and place over moderate flame. When the butter is sizzling hot, add the chicken and brown lightly both sides, turning the pieces over constantly so that they will brown evenly all over. This should take about 20 minutes. Transfer the pieces, one by one, to the iron cocotte *removing wings and breasts first, allowing dark meat to cook a little longer. When the chicken has all been transferred to the iron* cocotte, *pour about ⅛ cup of water or chicken broth into the big frying pan and stir well, to melt all the nice brown residue into a spoonful or two of rich syrupy clear gravy. Pour this carefully over the chicken in the* cocotte *and place the* cocotte *over a moderate flame. When you hear it sizzling, sprinkle lightly with salt and coarsely ground pepper and pour over it 2 or 3 jiggers (about ⅓ cup) of good brandy, and clap the cover on immediately, so that all the flavor remains in the* cocotte. *Reduce the flame slightly and continue cooking about 15 minutes longer, or until tender through. Remove lid, and increase heat slightly and cook about 5 minutes longer, turning the pieces over so that they all have a chance to brown and crisp up a bit. When done, place pieces attractively on hot, round, deep platter, add ⅛ cup water or chicken broth to the juice in the* cocotte, *stir and pour over the chicken. Garnish with parsley, or crisp watercress and serve at once.*

Two Apple Tarts
(for 6–8)

First blanch ½ cup shelled almonds by pouring boiling water over them. Let stand 5 minutes and pinch off the skins. Wash and dry and cut in thin slivers. Place in moderate oven on a tin for 5 minutes to dry out. Next make a paste by sifting together 2⅔ cups pastry flour with 6 tablespoons granulated sugar. Work into this with finger tips ½ pound sweet butter. Moisten with 2 tablespoons vinegar. Form into a flat ball, wrap in heavy waxed paper and press it all over gently. This will make all the odd bits stick together and facilitate rolling later. Place in refrigerator for 1 hour.

In the meantime, peel 16 small winesap apples, and cut in quarters and core, dropping them in cold water as you go along. This is to keep them from getting dark. When they are all done, drain well, and slice fine. Melt ¼ pound sweet butter in a great big frying pan and add the sliced apples. Cook slowly for 10 minutes, shaking the pan occasionally to keep the apples from sticking and browning. At this point, add 2 generous cups granulated sugar, and sprinkle with the grated rind of 1 lemon and 2 small oranges. Cook for a minute or two, then pour over the apples the strained juice of the 2 oranges and 1 lemon. Continue cooking for about 15 to 20 minutes longer, watching carefully, shaking the pan frequently. If the apples do not seem to be turning transparent evenly, cover them for 5 minutes or so. The steam will help cook them through. Remove lid toward the last and be sure the juice has boiled down enough to be nice and syrupy but don't let it boil down too dry. When done, remove from the fire and cool.

When ready to finish the tarts, roll out half of the pastry at a time on a lightly floured board, endeavoring to make a neat circle 12 inches in diameter. Roll up on rolling pin, and unroll over an 8-inch tart or pie tin, allowing the pastry to hang over about ½ inch. Trim if necessary and roll the overhanging edge under, and crimp prettily. Repeat the process and line the second pan. Fill the 2 pans with the apples and juice, dividing them equally, keeping out a little of the juice. Sprinkle the slivered al-

monds over the surface of both pies and pour over them the juice which
you have saved out.

Place in preheated 425° F. oven and bake for about 25 minutes or until
the syrup is bubbling up well and the pastry is a lovely brown, and until
the almonds have browned lightly. Remove from oven and serve hot, or
lukewarm.

TWO

The Dinners
To Which We
Are Not Invited

Every housekeeper in good and regular standing has certain special menus which are reserved for guests and great family feasts; they are not, for obvious reasons, offered at everyday commonplace dinners. The caviar *blini*, the turkey stuffed with Brazil nuts and garlanded with tiny spicy sausages, the crown roast of lamb with its ceremonial white frills, the guinea hen *suprême*, the squab chicken with white grapes, the lobster or crab meat soufflée, the green turtle soup, the rice *Espagnol*, the artichoke bottoms pyramided with minted fresh peas, the pistachio ice cream, the marshmallow marguerites, the pecan and date tartlets, the *marron surprise*—no, they certainly do not appear on our tables save when we're giving a party. Most of us consider our housekeeping bills, also the tempers and talents of our cooks; or if we're doing the cooking ourselves, we must consider our own culinary limitations. Likewise we have the hospitable desire to set before our guests something to make a special fiesta of their presence in our home.

Personally I have been fortunate enough to have a series of good cooks, most of whom have stayed with me for years, none of whom ever left me because of poor cooking. They have all had that cook's sixth sense which is an appreciation of flavor. I remember eating a proud dinner in a proud house where every dish served was an enigma and a dull one. I couldn't tell what the soup was made of, the fish—well, it was *fish,* I knew that, but no more; the roast had no taste whatsoever and the vegetables and salad were equally flat. I recognized the ice cream only because it was cold and looked like ice cream. Never in my life, before or since, have I eaten a meal like this where there was practically no definite taste in anything. It was a very strange, a bewitched dinner, I thought, and a mighty poor sort of magic.

Of my various cooks I can say with simple admiration and no brag that what they cooked was not tasteless and dull but full of flavor and savor and toothsomeness.

So when I ask people to dinner I am fairly sure that if the butcher and the grocer do not send low-grade material, if the stove does its duty, and the guests are reasonably prompt, the meal will be worth eating.

And yet—and yet—I have often reflected as I sat at dinner alone, how much more interesting the food is than when I am giving my very grandest party. French fried onions, for instance, crisp golden wisps of incomparable pungency—I do not offer these at parties and yet I know that if I did most of the company would shout for joy. Suppose I gave a dinner at which there was nothing but a great platter filled with ground beef patties, crusty brown outside, and juicily, temptingly pink within; a mountain peak of French fried onions; a gallon of cole slaw dressed with a sauce of cream and lemon juice and celery seed; and afterward an enormous dried-apple-and-raisin pie and large cups of devilishly black hot coffee. It sounds wonderful and it would taste even better. But do I ever give a dinner like that? No, not to anyone but myself and perhaps one or two people who regard French fried onions as I do, the most delicious way in which a most delicious vegetable can be served. Furthermore I am never invited to this sort of dinner, though I know many of my friends must have them.

There are other dinners to which no one is ever invited. What, never? Well, hardly ever. For instance, corned beef and cabbage, the meat rose-tinted and sweet, the cabbage youthfully green, and accompanied by the proper accessories, ruddy carrots, and little new potatoes boiled in their tender jackets. Some plain mustard, please, with the corned beef, for my taste no vinegar on the cabbage, but let there be plenty of peppercorns cooked with this dish.

If you can achieve old-fashioned cornmeal dumplings to be boiled with the cabbage and served instead of potatoes, you will have something extraordinarily good and as rare as ptarmigan these days. They should be made of white water-ground meal, patted into shape by hand and cooked watchfully else they will disintegrate and turn the cabbage liquor into mush.

For dessert after a corned beef dinner there should be something very light—pears stewed with lemon peel and served with soft custard, or perhaps a lemon snow pudding or some chilled slices of fresh pineapple, refreshed with kirsch.

As a special favor I was once invited to the home of a friend whose cook makes probably the best fish balls in the whole world. We had cups of hot madrilene for a first course, then fish balls and cole slaw and hot rolls, and then a half grapefruit, cold as snow with sugar optional. The fish balls were not very large, the fish and potatoes were blended together into a cream—probably by the cook's own hand—and fried dry and brown and lightly crusty and served as soon as they came from the frying kettle. They were no longer mere mundane mixes of salt fish and spuds but a true *bonne bouche*. The cole slaw was made of fresh-sliced young cabbage, over which had been poured a scalding highly spiced cooked dressing, with bits of sweet red pepper and a handful of celery seed to vary the texture and color of the dish. The lesson is clear—if you or your cook can make any dish, however plain, superlatively well, you have the basis for a dinner which will be appreciated and remembered by those lucky enough to share it.

Fresh pork is an item which has never had much standing as a company dish. When I am having a feast of fresh sparerib or tenderloin or even plain pork chops with gravy, do I ask the world to come and pleasure itself with me? No, I do not. But imagine a dinner of pork chops crackling brown on the outside and as sweet and tender as chicken breast within, all sloshed over with plenty of gravy full of succulent pan-scrapings, inevitably accompanied by sweet potatoes baked in their jackets, fried apple rings, and plenty of frail tiny green and white scallions on the side, followed by lightly sugared slices of orange smothered in fresh grated coconut, yes *fresh*—and perhaps an almond cookie or oatmeal macaroon or a rolled brandy snap. Who would not come gratefully to such a dinner? And go away refreshed and lightened in his imaginations?

Or spareribs! Dream up a platter of roast spareribs and a sheet of crisp, thin spider bread and a bowl of kale or turnip greens, a side dish of black-eyed peas and another of tart applesauce with a touch of nutmeg. No dessert, just coffee and a cigarette—any sweet would be a superfluity. But who gives such a dinner? Where may it be found? Nowhere, I suppose, unless some dweller in the deep country might be inspired to offer it to a group of city guests ravenous from a long hike or a vigorous ride through the winter woods, for it is certainly a cold-weather dinner for hungry people.

As I write this I am struck by the fact that the articles of food most often omitted from company dinners are those of the highest flavor— onions, cabbage, turnips and kale for example; and also what are called hearty dishes, such as dried beans and peas, fresh pork, dumplings of all sorts, steamed puddings. We might have more faith in the self-control of our guests. We might trust them not to overeat even if the food we offer them is most often associated with gourmands, not gourmets, although I have noticed that hearty eating, even too-hearty eating, is apt to follow the serving of good and unaccustomed hearty dishes.

And it would be hard not to overeat if you were invited to a dinner of old-fashioned chicken pie, baked in a deep pan with a crust below and above and at the sides, the crust shortened with the fat of the fowl itself which has been cut up and stewed gently with mace and bay leaf and salt and peppercorns and tiny cubes of salt pork or slivers of lean ham until half an hour before dinner time; then the stewed chicken with all its delicious gravy poured into the crust-lined pan, the top laid over all, slashed to let the steam escape, and the masterpiece set in the oven and baked until the crust is exactly done. Asparagus straight from the garden goes with this chicken pie, or sweet corn if in season, or that mix of beans and corn to which the aboriginal Indians gave the euphonious name of succotash. My belief is that even the woman most determined to be a sylph would put on two pounds of weight at this dinner and glory in her downfall! She would even eat the huge brandied peach with two spoonfuls of thick cream which came out of the icebox for dessert.

Before we get too far away from the subject of chicken, let me rise to inquire why no one ever serves plain stewed chicken and dumplings at anything but a family dinner? We all know the travesty of stewed chicken served in many wayside inns and roadhouses with two skinny leathery rectangles of waffle on the side. But I don't mean that sort of stewed chicken. I mean chicken that is not tough or strong of flavor, but tender and delicate, that has been stewed and gravied by someone who knows the last word in stewing and gravying, and that comes to the table surrounded by a ring of large, light dumplings cooked in that creamy yellow gravy, steaming, delectable. And there should be fresh young green peas all oozy with butter, or maybe lima beans just as young and just as well buttered, and there should be spiced watermelon rind or sweet pickled plums, and maybe some large ripe tomatoes sliced with onions standing by. Dessert? Ah, this is the moment for a ruby-bright cranberry or cherry tart with a crisscrossed top.

Another perfect stew, with or without dumplings, which is seldom or never allowed to come before guests, is a lamb stew with carrots and potatoes and again the insinuating onion. Lamb stew with hot biscuit may not be as stylish as crown roast but most people would welcome it more gratefully. Remember, plenty of gravy, even though it is not according to the etiquette books to sop it up with a crust held in the fingers—if you use a fork the pleasure of the process is ruined, for there is an artificiality, a stiltedness about chasing gravy over the plate in any way but with a hunk of bread. And what a shocking sight it is to see good gravy going back to the kitchen uneaten! When my sister and I were very young we made a dyke of mashed potato and filled the space behind it with a lovely lake of whatever gravy was offered, then, blending together the inner edges, we ate zestfully but carefully until both dyke and lake had vanished, the trick being to come out even with the last taste. Alas, with advancing years we were obliged to forego this geographical degustation. It was impressed upon us that gravy is not elegant. And so grew up the taboo of oceans of gravy at company dinners barring not only the pork chops, lamb and chicken stews aforementioned but also the whole delicious tribe of pot roasts, goulashes and their kind.

Today, because so many hostesses must needs also be cooks, there is a distinct rise in the gravy tide, for casserole dishes are the easiest, the least expensive and tastiest of main courses and a casserole dish of any kind connotes gravy. A casserole of veal can be called *Blanquette de Veau,* a casserole of beef becomes the far-famed French *Daube*—though I wouldn't advise any amateur cook to tackle the making of either of them. *Poulet en Casserole,* with toasted rolls, a plain or vegetable salad, an icebox dessert—now there is a delicious, satisfying meal for a servantless home and one not without a flavor of fashion, too. Hitch a toasted sardine canapé or half an avocado filled with shrimp mayonnaise on the front of this dinner and serve black coffee afterward and you may feel as smart as you please. It's distinctly a company meal for most of us even if it isn't in the grand tradition of squab turkey and duckling *bigarade* and *filet mignon bordelaise*.

But ordinary stews are not for guests, even when we put a French name on them. Neither are dinners of oyster pie or clam pie or baked beans—with grape catsup and steamed brown bread—or corned beef hash, or fish chowder! Yet in almost every household there is a plain menu which is done to perfection and is enjoyed by the family alone until it becomes a secret rite of kinship. In my own family my father, not a very hearty eater, was absurdly, passionately, fond of a marvelous dish which consisted of nothing but dumplings and apples, the fruit stewed very slowly with sugar to a glorious rich rosiness, the big round dumplings cooked to a light moist fluff, the whole served hot with thick cream. When we had this he would eat nothing else, though I'm bound to say that my mother, sister and I didn't follow him in this exclusiveness. My mother always made it herself and it was truly a wonderful dish— but I cannot recall that we ever had it when there were guests present. No doubt my mother felt it would label us locally as peculiar—and it would have. Guests were special and must be feasted with turkey and baked ham and ice cream and chocolate cake, not stewed apples and dumplings.

All the same, all the same—it would be rather nice if now and then we would all break out and share the homely *specialités de la maison* with friends! It might in time set a new fashion in hospitality, and it surely would be a blessing to the groaning food budget.

Broiled Beef Patties
(*for 6–8*)

Buy 3 pounds of lean raw beef, preferably top round. Ask the butcher to put it through the grinder twice. Shape into 16 balls of equal size, enclosing in each one a small lump of butter. Handle them as little as possible. Flatten the balls, and place on rack of broiler pan which you have rubbed with a piece of bacon. Preheat your broiler and set it at 500° F. Place the pan as close to the flame as possible and broil 5 minutes, turn and broil second side 3–5 minutes depending on how rare you like your meat to be. Salt and pepper and place on hot platter. Dot each pattie with a small dot of butter. Sprinkle with chopped parsley and serve at once.

French Fried Onions
(for 6–8)

Peel 6 Bermuda onions and slice crosswise in ¼-inch slices. Place in bowl and cover with cold milk. Soak at least ½ hour, drain off the milk. Have ready a paper bag containing 1½ cups flour seasoned to taste with salt and pepper. Separate the rings, place the onions in the bag with the flour and shake well. Have ready 3 pounds vegetable shortening in a deep fat fryer. Heat the fat to smoking hot 370° F. and drop a good handful of the onions in at a time and cook until a golden brown.

Fish them out with a long fork and place on paper towel to drain and keep warm in oven while you cook the rest in the same manner. Serve as soon as possible.

Cole Slaw with Hot Boiled Dressing
(for 6–8)

Shred very fine 1 small tender young head of cabbage. Chop fine 1 large sweet red pepper and combine the two.

Place in a small enamel pan, 2 teaspoons granulated sugar, ½ teaspoon salt, ½ teaspoon prepared mustard, and ¼ teaspoon of coarsely ground black pepper. Mix together and stir in ½ cup of mild cider vinegar, and ¼ cup water. Place on low flame and simmer for 1 minute or 2. In the meantime, cream together 1 tablespoon butter and 1 teaspoon flour, and stir into it the boiling hot vinegar. Cook gently for 5 minutes until thickened, then pour it gradually onto the well-beaten yolk of 2 eggs. Pour while hot over the cabbage and peppers and sprinkle generously with about 2 teaspoons celery seed. Mix well and add gradually 1 cup heavy cream. Chill and serve.

Dried Apple and Raisin Pie
(for 6–8)

Place ½ pound dried apples in a great big pot and pour over them 5 cups cold water. Place on low flame and cook, stirring occasionally, for about 30 minutes, then add ½ pound black seedless raisins and continue cooking for 15 minutes longer. At this point add 1 teaspoon ground cinnamon, ¼ cup granulated sugar and ⅜ cup light brown sugar. Continue cooking for about 5 minutes longer. Cool and place in Mason jars in refrigerator until ready to use for pie. This quantity makes 1½ quarts or sufficient for 1 large and 1 small pie. For a large pie, mix some plain pastry as given on page 58, and roll half of it out and line a large Pyrex pie plate. Stir into 4 cups of the apple and raisin mixture, 4 tablespoons Calvados (brandy made from apples). Fill the shell with this, and dot with ⅛ pound butter. Roll out the remainder of the pastry, cover the pie, trim the edges, roll under and crimp the edges prettily. Make several gashes in the top, and place in preheated, hot 450° F. oven and bake until the crust is a golden brown or for about 30 minutes. Remove from oven and cool. In the meantime, make some hard sauce in the following manner:

Cream ¼ pound sweet butter and beat in gradually 1¼ cups powdered sugar. When well blended and fluffy, flavor with a pinch of nutmeg and 1 teaspoon vanilla and sufficient Calvados to make it soft enough to spread easily, or about 2 tablespoons.

When your pie is completely cooled off, spread the hard sauce carefully over the entire surface. Serve at once to be cut into 8 even-sized pieces. Note: *The remaining apple and raisin mixture may be put in the refrigerator for a week if necessary.*

Boiled Corned Beef Dinner with Cornmeal Dumplings
(for 6–8)

Soak for 1 hour in cold water, 5–6 pounds properly cured brisket of corned beef. Drain, cover with 6 quarts cold water, bring to boiling point, skim carefully, reduce heat, and simmer gently for about 4 hours. In the meantime, peel 8 carrots, 8 parsnips, 8 onions, 8 white turnips (or substitute 8 pieces of yellow turnips), leaving them all whole. Also cut into 8 pieces a fine tender white cabbage, leaving the core attached to hold the leaves together. One hour before the meat will be done add all the vegetables, excepting the cabbage, and continue cooking until just tender. Thirty minutes before the meat will be done, drain off into an iron cocotte *3 quarts of the pot liquor, and add the cabbage. Cover and cook until just tender or for about 20 minutes. At this point, lift it carefully into a small pan and add just a little of the juice to keep it moist until ready to reheat for serving, while you cook the dumplings in the iron* cocotte *in the remainder of the juice. The dumplings should, by the way, be mixed and shaped while the cabbage is cooking.*

Beat 2 eggs well, add ½ cup milk, and 2 tablespoons melted butter. Stir in 1 cup white cornmeal. Sift together 1 cup all-purpose flour, with 1 scant teaspoon salt and 2 teaspoons baking powder, and add it to the first mixture. This will make a very stiff dough. Shape with your hands into 16 balls. Roll them in more white cornmeal and place them in a collander. Drop them all at once into the cocotte, *containing the remainder of the pot liquor, now flavored with cabbage. Clamp on the cover immediately and allow the dumplings to simmer gently for 15–20 minutes, without removing the cover. Fish out with sieved spoon and place in hot serving dish and serve at once, garnished with a sprinkle of paprika, along with the rest of the dinner which should be served all together on a great big platter, meat in the center, vegetables around the edge not forgetting the cabbage, all garnished with a bunch of parsley. Serve with this boiled dinner a pot of English mustard and some horse-radish in cream, preferably freshly grated.*

Corned Beef Hash with Caramelized Onions
(for 6–8)

Prepare 3 cups chopped cooked corned beef. Peel 6 or 8 medium-sized potatoes and boil them until almost tender through. Drain well and chop them coarsely in a wooden chopping bowl. You should have about 3½ cups of them. Add them to the beef and add ½ cup finely chopped onion. Season to taste with salt and a little coarsely ground black pepper.

Melt ⅛ *pound butter in a heavy iron frying pan and add to it ¾ cup
rich milk. Spread the hash evenly in the pan, dot the top with an additional 6 tablespoons butter, cover tightly, place on low flame and cook
slowly for about 30 minutes. Watch carefully so that it doesn't burn on
the bottom. Lift up a little corner of it and if it has formed a crusty bottom, remove from fire and carefully run a spatula knife under the whole
to loosen it from the pan. Fold half of it over onto itself and turn out
onto a hot platter. Garnish with boiled caramelized onions done in the
following manner:*

Peel and boil 8 medium-sized onions until almost tender through.
Drain well. Melt ⅛ pound butter in a frying pan, add the onions and
sprinkle with a little salt and 1 teaspoon granulated sugar. Place on low
flame and cook, turning them over and over until a pale golden brown.
Place around the hash, add a spoonful of water to the pan and stir and
pour over the hash. Garnish with chopped parsley and serve at once.

Lemon Snow Pudding
(for 6–8)

Mix 4 tablespoons gelatin with 2 cups sugar, add 1 cup cold water and
1½ cups boiling water. Stir over the fire until thoroughly dissolved. Add
1 cup lemon juice, and 3 cups cold water. Strain and mix well. Set in the
refrigerator to cool.

When it begins to congeal, whip until frothy and fold in the well-
beaten whites of 4 eggs. Pour into 8 individual molds which have been
rinsed in cold water.

Make a liquid custard of 6 egg yolks, 3 cups milk and 4 tablespoons
sugar. Flavor when cool with 1 teaspoon lemon extract and serve poured
around the gelatins which have been turned out on a deep dessert plate.

Stewed Pears with Custard Sauce
(for 6–8)

Moisten 1½ cups granulated sugar with 1½ cups cold water. Place on
fire, and bring to a boil and boil 3 minutes. Have ready 8–10 ripe Bartlett

pears, peeled, halved and seeds removed with a little potato scooper. Place in cold water containing the juice of 1 lemon until all are prepared. The lemon is to keep them from turning dark. Place the pears in a large pan and pour over them the syrup and add 8 thin slices lemon peel. Boil gently for 5–7 minutes or until the pears are done. Don't overcook. Place in pretty serving dish and chill before serving.

To make the custard sauce, heat in top part of enamel double boiler, over boiling water, 3 cups milk sweetened with 6 tablespoons granulated sugar. Beat the yolks of 6 eggs with a rotary egg beater, but not too long. When the milk is scalding hot, add a little of it to the egg yolks and stir, then add the yolks gradually to the rest of the milk, stirring constantly. Cook, stirring constantly until the custard thickens enough to coat the spoon, about 5 or 6 minutes. Be careful not to overcook. When cool, flavor with 1 teaspoon vanilla.

Roast Loin of Pork
(for 6–8)

Buy a 6-pound loin of pork nicely trimmed. Wipe it with a damp cloth, and dry. Rub it well with the following mixture of seasoning: 3 teaspoons salt, 1 teaspoon pepper, 1 teaspoon thyme, ½ teaspoon mace or nutmeg— all rubbed together to a powder.

Place the roast in enamel or earthenware roasting pan and place around it, 2 carrots sliced in ½-inch pieces, 2 onions peeled and sliced thin, 2 large cloves garlic crushed, 4 whole cloves, and a bouquet—a large bunch celery leaves, a large bunch parsley and 3 bay leaves tied together. Pour over the roast, ½ cup dry white wine and ½ cup consommé.

Place in preheated 450°–475° F. oven and roast for about 20 minutes or until a golden brown. Reduce the heat to 350° F. and continue roasting slowly, basting occasionally, until well done, or for about 3–4 hours. Fifteen minutes before it will be done, transfer the roast temporarily to another pan and squeeze over it the juice of ½ lemon. Place back in oven while you make the gravy from the residue in the first pan.

First pour off all the fat, then add to the pan ¾ cup consommé and ¾ cup white wine and ½ cup water. Boil this down rapidly, scraping the brown part down from the sides and bottom of pan and cook until thick and syrupy, or until you have only about 1 cup clear gravy left. Serve, garnished with parsley, with the sauce in a separate gravy dish.

Roast Spareribs
(for 6–8)

Buy 3 sides fresh young spareribs, weighing in all about 6 pounds. Wipe them with a cloth and salt and pepper their both sides. Ideally they should be cooked in separate shallow pans so that they can brown evenly all over. Place in preheated 350° to 375° F. oven and roast, basting occasionally with their own fat, for at least 1½ hours. If they are not brown enough at the end, turn the heat up to 450° F. the last 10 minutes. Place on large hot platter, garnish with parsley and serve at once.

If you wish to make gravy, pour off all the fat from all the pans, saving, however, 3 tablespoons of it. Soften the brown residue in the pans by adding a little boiling water to each. Combine all the clear gravy and reduce by boiling until syrupy. Now place the 3 tablespoons fat in a little pan, add 3 tablespoons all-purpose flour, stir and cook for a minute or two, then add 1 cup hot milk gradually to make a smooth gravy. Add the clear gravy and a little more milk if too thick. Season to taste with additional salt and pepper if necessary and serve in sauceboat.

Spider Corn Cake
(for 6–8)

Light your oven and set it at 450° to 500° F. Heat a heavy 12-inch iron frying pan by placing it in the oven.

Sift together 1½ cups white corn meal, 1 tablespoon granulated sugar, 1 teaspoon salt and 1 teaspoon baking soda. Beat 2 whole eggs and beat into them 2 cups buttermilk. Add the flour mixture, sifting it in all at once and beat with spoon until smooth. Stir in 1 generous tablespoon melted butter. Remove the pan from the oven and rub it well with vegetable shortening. Spread the batter evenly over the entire surface and place immediately into the preheated oven. Bake about 30 minutes or until a golden brown. Serve at once cut in pie-shaped pieces.

Kale
(for 6–8)

Remove coarse stems and imperfect leaves and the tough part of the center ribs from 5 or 6 pounds of kale. Wash thoroughly in several waters, until you are sure it is free from sand, then wash it once more just to be sure. Cover with boiling water and bring to a boil, then drain well. Cover again with more boiling water, sprinkle with salt and cook for about 20–30 minutes or until tender. Drain well. Chop coarsely, add plenty of butter and serve.

Black-Eyed Peas
(for 6–8)

Pick over carefully 1 pound or about 3 cups black-eyed peas, and wash them thoroughly in several waters. Place them in a large pan, and cover with 8 cups cold water. Soak overnight. Put them on to cook right in the water in which they soaked and add 1-pound slice tenderized ham cut in 2-inch squares. Add 1 bay leaf and several sprigs of parsley, and 1 teaspoon thyme and 1 clove garlic tied in a little bundle wrapped in cheesecloth. Also add ½ teaspoon salt and about 8 whole peppercorns and 2 small onions into which you have placed 2 whole cloves. Place on low flame and bring to a simmer, skim carefully and cook about 2½ hours. Remove the cheesecloth bag. Sprinkle peas with chopped parsley. Serve at once with cornbread.

Fish Cakes
(for 6–8)

Wash 8 ounce package of Gorton's Salt Codfish in running lukewarm water for 5 minutes, then place in pan and pour over it 2 cups cold water, and soak overnight or for about 12 hours.

Pour off the soaking water, cover again with cold water, place on fire, bring gently to a boil, and simmer for 1 hour. In the meantime, peel 6 or 8 old potatoes, cut in quarters, and cook in boiling water until tender. Drain thoroughly and mash with potato masher, but do not add any butter or milk. Drain the fish when it is done and while the potatoes are still hot, add the fish and beat the two together vigorously until light and fluffy, adding one by one 3 raw eggs. Season to taste with salt and pepper.

When ready to fry the cakes, have ready a deep iron pan containing at least 1 pound melted vegetable shortening. Heat to 375° F. or to the smoking point and drop the fish and potato into the fat by spoonfuls and cook, turning them over once carefully so that they will brown to a golden brown all over, or for about 3 or 4 minutes. Drain on paper towel and serve immediately on hot platter, accompanied by chili sauce, heated in a double boiler. Makes 15 large cakes.

Chicken Pie
(for 6–8)

The day before the party, clean 2 fine plump fat young fowl. Singe and wash the birds inside and out and place them in a large, rectangular 8-quart-sized enamel pan (the vegetable container from your refrigerator is ideal provided it has a cover). Pour over the chickens 3 quarts warm water. Not hot, not cold. Place on fire and bring slowly to boiling point. Stand by and skim off carefully any foam that may come to the surface, but do not skim off the fat and be careful not to allow the water to really boil. Turn light way down, and cover the pan, leaving a crack for the steam to escape. Cook ever so gently for 1 hour, then add 6 peeled onions left whole, 1 bunch celery carefully washed and from which you have removed as many strings as possible, a sprig parsley, ½ bay leaf, 12 whole peppercorns, and 4 teaspoons salt. Continue simmering until the chickens are done and falling apart, or for about 3 hours, counting from the time the water boils again after the vegetables are added. Remove from the fire and cool in their broth, turning them over so that they are kept moist. When cool enough to handle, remove all the meat from the bones, discarding all skin and unattractive bits keeping the meat in as large pieces as possible. Now skim off and keep as much fat as possible from the broth, then wring out a clean cloth in ice water and line your strainer *with it, and pour the broth through this, leaving whatever fat there is in the cloth. This should then give you a generous 2 quarts of clear strong chicken broth, and if your birds were nice and fat you should have about 2 cups of chicken fat. Before putting the fat in the refrigerator to chill, strain it through a fine sieve. You will be using part of the fat to make the crust and the sauce for your pie, and it should be very cold and solid when you use it. Pour the broth over your chicken and place in refrigerator overnight or until ready to make your pie.*

Allow 2 hours for making and assembling the pie, before baking. First make the sauce. Place the chicken and the broth on a low flame just long enough to melt the broth. Do not allow it to boil. Now make a roux *by melting 4 tablespoons chicken fat and 4 tablespoons (½ bar) butter in the top part of an enamel double boiler. Place on low flame and stir in 10 tablespoons flour, cook, stirring constantly for about 1 minute, then add gradually 3 cups hot chicken broth, stirring constantly to make a thick smooth sauce. Season to taste with coarsely ground black pepper and additional salt if you think it needs it. Place over boiling water and stir in gradually 1 cup cream. Remove from fire and cool by placing over cold water.*

Now make the pastry, which is really a biscuit dough. Have ready a 2-quart-sized round Pyrex baking dish. Sift some pastry flour and measure 4 cups of it into the sifter. Add 1 teaspoon salt and 8 teaspoons baking powder and sift it into a big bowl. Cut into this 10 tablespoons sweet butter (1¼ bars), and work it into the flour with your finger tips. Then work in 8 tablespoons cold solid chicken fat. Moisten with about ¾ cup cold milk. Toss out onto well-floured cloth or board and knead for just ½ minute or so, to make a smooth dough, then wrap in waxed paper and chill for at least ½ hour. When ready to complete the pie, take a generous half of the dough and roll it out to make a circle big enough to line the inside of the Pyrex dish bottom and sides, and lie over the rim a bit. Now comes the only difficult part of making the pie. Roll the paste lightly up onto the rolling pin and unroll it over the dish so that it will fall down into the dish without breaking. If it does break, don't be alarmed, just do the best you can with it, patching it if necessary, until the sides and bottom are covered with a thin coating of dough. Lay in this all of the chicken, placing the finest white pieces on top, being sure that it divides into at least eight pieces of white meat. Now pour over it all of the sauce, or enough to fill the dish level full. Now roll out the rest of the dough

*into a circle just large enough to amply cover the dish. Roll the over-
lapping edge under the bottom overlapping crust, and using your finger
crimp it prettily all around. Cut about 6 slits in the top, and place in refrigerator until ready to bake. Have the oven preheated and set at 450° F.
and 25 minutes before you will be ready to serve the pie, place the dish
on a cookie sheet and place it in the hot oven to bake to a golden brown.
The top crust should rise up and look beautiful like biscuits. Watch carefully toward the end of the baking and if it is browning too quickly, reduce the heat a little. Serve the minute it comes out of the oven, and
accompany it with buttered fresh peas, and buttered boiled white onions
garnished with parsley.*

Note: *A delicious soup may be made of the vegetables cooked with the
chicken, by placing them in a Waring mixer with a little of the
broth and reducing the whole to a pulp, thinning to desired consistency with additional broth or with half broth and half cream.*

Chicken Fricassee with Dumplings
(for 6–8)

*Buy 2 tender young fowl weighing about 5 pounds each, cut up as for
fricassee. Melt ¼ pound butter in a pan and cook in it 8 tablespoons flour
without browning, then add 1 quart boiling water slowly to make a
smooth sauce.*

*Melt ¼ pound butter in a large frying pan and add the chicken and
brown very lightly on both sides. Place in an iron* cocotte *and add ½
cup water to the frying pan to dissolve the brown residue and pour it
over the chicken. Add the white sauce and 4 peeled and sliced white
onions, 1 teaspoon salt and a little coarsely ground black pepper. Cover
and place on low flame and simmer gently for about 2½ hours or until
the second joint may be pierced with a fork. Stir occasionally.*

*Make the full recipe for baking powder dumplings as follows, and drop
them into the pot. Cover tightly and don't open the pot for 15 minutes.
Remove cover, tie a pretty napkin around the* cocotte, *place on serving
platter, garnish with a bouquet of parsley and serve at once, accompanied
by plain boiled onions and mashed potatoes.*

Baking Powder Dumplings
(for 6–8)

Sift together 1½ cups flour, with 3 level teaspoons baking powder and ¾ teaspoon salt. Cut into it 2 tablespoons butter. Add enough milk, about ½ cup, to make a soft dough. Drop from a spoon, dipped in water, into the stewpot and cover tightly and cook steadily, but gently and without lifting the cover, for 15 minutes. Serve at once.

Lamb Stew
(for 6–8)

Buy a whole shoulder of lamb weighing 5–6 pounds. Persuade the butcher to trim off as much fat as possible, and have him cut it up for stew in not-too-small pieces, bones and all.

Have ready 16 little white onions peeled and left whole, and 2 pounds small new potatoes (about 16) peeled and left whole. If you have to substitute old potatoes, peel and quarter 8 large ones and cut off the sharp angles, as the potatoes should be a pretty oval shape. Peel 8 big carrots and cut them in two. Peel 8 white turnips and if large cut them in two and shape the same as the potatoes, cutting off the sharp angles. Place all the vegetables in separate pans of cold water, until ready to use, excepting the onions, which should not be put into water as it makes them come apart. Open a small can of Italian-style, pear-shaped tomatoes and drain off the juice, or substitute 4 fine ripe garden tomatoes, peeled, quartered, and as many seeds removed as possible. Make a little bouquet of parsley, 1 bay leaf and ½ teaspoon thyme, and peel 1 clove garlic. Open 2 cans of chicken consommé and add 4 cups boiling water. Put 4 tablespoons flour in a little cup.

Have ready an iron cocotte *containing a small lump of butter. You are now ready to make the stew. It will take about 3 hours in all, so time it accordingly. Place ¼ pound butter in a large, heavy iron frying pan. Spread your meat out on a large platter and sprinkle it lightly with salt and coarsely ground black pepper, and 1 teaspoon granulated sugar. The sugar is to help brown the meat to a pretty color. Melt the butter in the frying pan and when sizzling hot add all the meat and brown not too fast, so that the butter doesn't burn. Stir with a wooden spoon so that the meat browns on all sides. Turn the light down progressively, as the meat browns, and when browned to your satisfaction, sprinkle over the meat 4 tablespoons all-purpose flour and turn the light way down and stir continuously until the meat is coated on all sides with the flour, then add gradually the 1½ quarts consommé and water, which should be hot when you add it. Stir well while it is boiling, then transfer the meat and gravy to the* cocotte, *which you have placed on an asbestos mat on a low flame. Now add the bouquet and the clove of garlic which you have crushed, and the prepared tomatoes. Cover and cook gently for 1¼ hours, stirring occasionally, while you prepare the onions. Brown the onions slowly in a separate frying pan in 2 tablespoons butter, sprinkling them with 1 scant teaspoon sugar, to help caramelize them to a golden brown. Remove from fire temporarily. Now tilt the* cocotte *and skim off as much fat as possible from the stew and remove the bouquet. Add the peeled carrots and turnips and cook ½ hour stirring occasionally, then add the browned onions and potatoes and cook ¾ hour longer. Taste and add more salt and pepper if necessary and serve at once, garnished with parsley.*

Fried Pork Chops
(for 6–8)

Select 8 or 10 rib pork chops, center cut, about ¾ inch thick. Salt and pepper them lightly. Place 2 tablespoons butter in a large heavy iron frying pan and heat. When the butter is sizzling hot, add the chops, and fry quickly for about 5 minutes on either side, being careful not to allow the fat to burn. At this point, cover the pan with a heavy lid, reduce the heat, and cook slowly for 35–45 minutes, depending on the thickness of the chops. Remove the chops and keep warm. Drain off all but about 4 tablespoons of the drippings, being careful not to lose any of the brown part. Stir into the remaining fat in pan, 2 level tablespoons flour and stir and cook for 1 minute or 2, then add gradually 2½ cups milk. Continue cooking, stirring constantly until smooth and moderately thick. Season to taste with a little coarsely ground black pepper and additional salt if necessary. Garnish the chops with parsley and serve at once with the gravy in a serving bowl.

Orange Ambrosia
(for 6–8)

First prepare the freshly grated coconut. Unless you have a kitchen aid or a rotary cheese grater, the process of preparing the fresh coconut is tedious but definitely worth the trouble. Buy 2 large coconuts. Shake them to be sure they have plenty of milk in them. One coconut is plenty, but it is wise to have a spare one on hand, in case the first one cracked open proves not to be a good one. First pierce the 3 soft spots with an ice pick and place the coconut over a pitcher so that the coconut milk will come out, and not be lost. Once emptied, give the coconut a good whack with a heavy hammer to break it open. If it smells sweet and has no spots and if the milk tastes good, the coconut is good. The next process is to remove the meat in as large pieces as possible from the hard outer shell. After that the thin brown skin next to the meat must be pared off carefully with a sharp knife. Be sure that the knife you use has not been used recently for paring onions. To be doubly sure, wipe the knife with a section of lemon, as coconut quickly takes on the flavor of anything it comes in contact with. As you prepare the coconut, place the meat in ice water to prevent discoloration. Once it is all prepared, drain, and wipe the pieces dry, and if you are fortunate enough to have a rotary cheese grater or a kitchen aid grater, reduce the coconut to shreds. Otherwise just patiently grate it on the medium side of your hand grater. Cover with waxed paper and chill while you prepare the sliced oranges for the ambrosia.

Select 8 large navel oranges and using a sharp knife cut off all the orange and white part of skins, leaving the oranges free from either one. Now remove the pulp from the oranges in perfect pieces by cutting away from tough membrane, cutting down into first one side of section, then the other. Sprinkle the oranges as you cut them with a little powdered (not confectioners') sugar. When it is all prepared, arrange the sections in alternate layers in a glass serving bowl, starting with a layer of oranges then a layer of coconut, more oranges and ending up with coconut. Cover with waxed paper and a plate and chill before serving.

Blanquette of Veal
(for 6–8)

Soak 3 pounds solid breast of veal, cut in inch squares, in cold water to cover, for 2 hours. Drain off all the water. Place the meat in a deep enamel pan. The top part of a large 3-quart enamel double boiler is ideal. Pour over it 1 quart fresh cold water, or as little more as possible, so that the meat is well covered with water. Add 1 teaspoon salt, place on low flame and bring very slowly to the boiling point. This is a slow process and will take about ½ hour. Stand by and skim very carefully. Add 1 small onion in which you have stuck a clove, and 1 large carrot cut into chunks, also a little bouquet securely tied of a few celery leaves, parsley, ¼ teaspoon thyme and 1 small bay leaf. Cover partially and simmer gently for 1½ hours.

In the meantime, remove the stems from ½ pound small white mushrooms. Wash them carefully. Have ready an enamel saucepan containing ¼ cup cold water, the juice ½ lemon, and 1 tablespoon butter. Peel the mushrooms one by one and quarter them and place them immediately in the saucepan containing the water, lemon and butter. When all are prepared, place the pan on the fire, cover and bring to a brisk boil. Cook for 4–5 minutes, shaking the pan occasionally. Watch carefully, so that they don't boil dry. Remove from fire and keep warm.

Now place 12 little white onions of uniform size in a sieve and dip the sieve down into a pan of boiling water. Let it stay for 1 minute. This is to facilitate the removal of the outer skin. Drain and with a little knife cut off as little as possible from each end of the onions and peel. Place the onions in a little pan just big enough to hold them comfortably, then add 1 tablespoon butter and ¼ cup broth from the veal. Cover and place on low flame and cook gently for about 35 minutes or until just tender through. Watch carefully and add a spoonful of hot water if necessary to keep them from boiling completely dry.

When the veal is done, remove the bouquet and carrots and onion, and strain off most of the broth into another little pan. Dot the meat with butter, place over boiling water, cover and keep warm while you make the sauce.

Melt 8 tablespoons butter, add 8 tablespoons flour, cook together 1 minute or 2, stirring constantly to make a white roux, *then add the hot broth gradually of which there should be 3 cups. If there is not enough, add boiling water to make up the difference. Now add the mushrooms and their juice and the onions and their juice to the meat. Chop fine some parsley. Break 2 egg yolks into a little bowl, add ¼ cup heavy cream, beat together and add to it gradually a little of the hot sauce, and in turn add it gradually to the sauce. Do not allow it to boil. Season to taste with salt, coarsely ground black pepper, 1 pinch nutmeg and the juice of about ½ lemon. Also drain into it all the remaining juice on the meat. Pour the same over the meat and pour it into a deep serving platter. Garnish with chopped parsley and serve at once accompanied by a big bowl of flaky white rice.*

Beef Stew
(for 6-8)

Brown slowly, in a little butter, ½ pound scalded salt pork cut in little squares. Transfer the pork to a stewpot and in the remaining fat brown lightly 4 pounds chuck of beef cut in little squares. Add this to the stewpot. Add to the first pan 1½ dozen small onions, sliced fine, cook slowly for a minute or two, then add 2 cans hot consommé in which you have dissolved 2 spoonfuls beef extract. Stir well and pour over the beef. Season to taste with salt and pepper and add 1 tablespoon paprika. Cover tightly and simmer gently for about 1 hour, then add 3 pounds potatoes peeled and cut in squares. Cover and simmer about 1 hour longer. Avoid stirring once the potatoes are in so that they will retain their shape.

Fried Apples
(for 6-8)

Take 6 large tart apples, wipe clean, cut in crosswise slices about ½ inch thick. Heat 4 tablespoons fat in pan—bacon or ham fat is very good for this—and fry slices slowly until brown on both sides. Drain, serve hot with pork, ham or sausage. Some people like to sprinkle the cooked slices lightly with sugar and cinnamon, but a well-flavored apple doesn't need it.

Oyster Pie
(for 6–8)

Make some biscuit dough in the following manner: Sift some pastry flour and measure out 4 cups of it into a sifter. Add 1 teaspoon salt and 8 teaspoons baking powder. Sift this into a big bowl and with your finger tips work into the flour 8 tablespoons lard and 8 tablespoons (1 bar) butter. Moisten with about 1 cup milk. Toss out onto a lightly floured board and knead for just a minute or so, to make a smooth dough, then wrap in waxed paper and chill for at least ½ hour. When ready to complete the pie, take a generous half of the dough and roll it out to make a circle big enough to line a 2-quart-sized baking dish, bottom and sides, preferably an earthenware one with slanting sides. Be sure the circle of paste is large enough to lie over the rim a bit. Now comes the only difficult part of making the pie. Roll the paste lightly up onto the rolling pin and unroll it over the dish so that the paste will fall down into the dish without breaking. If it does break, don't be alarmed, just patch it as necessary. Lay in this, 1½ quarts raw oysters, sprinkling them as you go along with salt and coarsely ground black pepper, dotting with plenty of butter (about 8 tablespoons or 1 bar in all). Sprinkle the top with about 2 tablespoons flour and pour over all the oyster juice. Now roll out the rest of the dough into a circle large enough to cover the dish and hang over the edge. Roll this up as before on the rolling pin and unroll it over the pie. Roll the overlapping edge under the bottom overlapping paste, and using your floured fingers, crimp it prettily all around. Cut 2 or 3 big slits in the top crust to let steam out.

Have the oven preheated and set at 450° F. and about 25 minutes before you expect to serve the pie, place the dish in the hot oven to bake until a golden brown. The top crust should puff up and look like beautiful biscuits and the under crust should be crisp on the bottom but there should be a gelatinous top to the under crust inside. Serve at once.

Note: *If there should happen to be any little oyster crabs swimming around in the oysters when you get them, leave them in.*

Dr. Walter Taylor's Favorite Clam Pie
(for 6–8)

Chop fine 1 quart clams. Prepare 1 heaping tablespoon finely chopped onion, and the same of celery, and the same of sweet green pepper. Make the whole recipe for plain piecrust on page 58. Roll out slightly more than half of it and line a large 10-inch Pyrex pie plate with the paste. Place temporarily in refrigerator while you make a thick, rich cream sauce.

Melt 6 tablespoons butter and cook in it for 1 minute or 2 the chopped vegetables. Add 4 tablespoons flour, and cook together over low flame without browning for 1 minute, then add gradually 1⅓ cups hot milk, stirring constantly to make a smooth sauce. Season to taste with a little salt and coarsely ground black pepper and add the clams and whatever juice they may have. Mix well and cool, before pouring it into the pastry-lined pie plate. Roll out the rest of the paste into a circle large enough to cover your pie. Roll it up onto your roller and unroll it over the pie. Turn the overlapping edges under the overlapping under crust, crimp the edges prettily, cut 6 slits in the top, and place in preheated, hot 450° F. oven and bake until a golden brown or about 25 minutes.

To give the authentic Taylor twist omit celery and green pepper and add 2 diced medium potatoes, 2 diced carrots and 1 cup fresh green peas.

Old-Fashioned Grape Catsup

Buy 10 pounds Concord grapes, wash, drain and stem. Pinch off skins from 2 cups of them and save skins in separate dish. Place the rest of the grapes and the pulp from the skinned grapes in a deep kettle. Crush slightly. On low flame, very gently, bring to boiling point, stirring constantly. Cook until soft or about 25 minutes. Rub through a fine sieve. Now add the saved-out skins (they make the catsup more interesting in texture) and add 2 cups light brown sugar, 3 pints red wine vinegar, 3 tablespoons allspice, 6 tablespoons ground cinnamon, 4 teaspoons ground cloves, 2 teaspoons powdered mace, 1 generous teaspoon cayenne,

3 teaspoons salt. Simmer until thick, stirring very frequently; it will take about 45 minutes. Place in sterilized pint jars, adjust rubbers, and seal. Wipe jars clean and keep in a cool dry place. Makes 3 pints, and is a perfectly wonderful accompaniment to baked beans and steamed brown bread.

Peggy's Halibut Chowder
(for 6–8)

Buy 3 pounds fresh halibut cut in 1-inch-thick slices. Trim off, but save, all of the skin and bones and cut the fish in 1-inch pieces. Cover the bones and skin with 3 cups water and bring to a boil and simmer for about 10 minutes, then strain. Place in a large enamel fish pan, 1 2-pound 4-ounce can of Italian-style plain tomatoes. Add 3 cups diced old potatoes and 2 cups chopped onions, 2 teaspoons salt and a dozen whole peppercorns, 3 small bay leaves and a can of chicken consommé. Also add the strained fish broth. Simmer for ½ hour or until the potatoes are done, stirring frequently. At this point, add the fish and reduce heat and simmer gently until the fish is opaque and done through or for about 15 minutes longer. Remove from fire and stir in ¼ pound butter and 1 cup heavy cream and 2 cups milk which you have heated in a separate pan. Season with additional salt and coarsely ground black pepper if necessary and serve at once in a big soup tureen.

THREE

Pie—
American
Style

These remarks on a delightful subject somewhat neglected by the world's best literature do not pretend to be a scientific or an exhaustive treatise. They are made entirely in the amateur spirit, both as a pie maker and a pie eater. I do not claim professional merit, professional skill, but I do claim a considerable experience with and an undying appreciation for a properly made American pie.

I say American pie because observations in other countries have forced me to the belief that America is the only habitat of the real honest-to-goodness pie, both two-crust and lattice-top. In Great Britain if you ask for apple pie you receive a modicum of stewed apple, watery and insufficiently sugared, hiding under a crust which seems to be singing the national ballad about possessing a heart of oak. This description goes for any British fruit pie. They don't even call them pies but tarts! The many delectable forms of pie which are known to the lowliest American menu card have never been heard of in Great Britain. True, but incredible.

On the continent there are even fewer pies than in Great Britain. The only real pie I ever met in France was an eel pie, and a most delicious one, which was served to me at an inn in Mâcon, as the fish course. But one eel pie does not, cannot make a pie-ish nation and the little tarts heaped with fruit which the French *patisseries* offer have as much relation to a magnificent woozy blue-purple huckleberry or blackberry pie as a Basque beret has to a Western ten-gallon sombrero.

In Spain pie is unknown—so now we have the primary reason for the voyage of Columbus. In Italy I have met a dish which was called pie but which actually was a saccharine and pasty cake decked in white icing and decorated with endless scrolls and sprays and dots and dashes of pink and green. Any intelligent New England pumpkin pie would have laughed itself into a custard at the idea of calling this object a pie.

No, pie is America's own. Years of intensive baking by ardent housewives have given it its present shape, its infinite variety, its toothsomeness and its overwhelming popularity. Pioneer women picked wild fruits and berries and made pies and when all else failed they invented mixtures known as vinegar pie, sometimes called maigre pie, crumb pie and shoo-fly pie, sweetened with sorghum, thickened with flour, crude, perhaps, but still pie. When Johnny Appleseed's first harvest was gathered, we may be sure that apple pie reigned supreme in every home fortunate enough to have a share of the fruit. In my opinion it has reigned supreme, king of the pies, ever since that happy day.

It is hard to imagine anything better to eat than a first-rate apple pie. It must be sweet but not too sweet, and there should be a suggestion of crisp sugariness here and there in the fruity innards. It must be juicy, but not too juicy, and the juices must have cooked to a pinky amber and run out slowly, rich and thick. The crust must be delicately brown, and if the juice has boiled up through it here and there in carameled sweetness, these little crisp spots only enhance its charm. And now we come to the vexed question of cinnamon.

Two distinct schools of thought have arisen on the matter of cinnamon in apple pie. The pro-cinnamon school contends with rabid intolerance that an apple pie without cinnamon is like an egg without salt, flat, stupid, *sans* all flavor. The anti-cinnamon school with equal vehemence insists that to put cinnamon on good pie apples is to make them fit for none but the undiscriminating palate, spoil all their delicacy and ruin them so far as the epicure is concerned. Families and friends are divided, homes broken up wherever this controversy breaks out. The craven straddler who says he loves apple pie with or without cinnamon is set upon by both parties and murdered. For my part I will say, fearlessly, that if the apples are not fine of flavor I think a dash of cinnamon helps. But not too much, oh, not too much.

The apple pie is made in many variations, all of them pleasing. It may be of dried apples or fresh, of applesauce or apple butter. The fruit may be cooked in the pie or separately. There may be paste on top or criss-cross slats or it may be left open face, and for the deep dish variety, paste over the top alone and no bottom crust. Cheese may be served with it, and apple pie *à la mode* with a great dollop of rich vanilla ice cream topping the fresh-baked pie has a legion of admiring devourers.

For me there is one apple pie par excellence. You must have the earliest, littlest, spiciest green apples, and from these make a slow-cooked applesauce, strained smooth and sweetened. Then make a rich piecrust by any rule you choose, and line the pan with care. Pour in the applesauce and close with an upper crust with some hieroglyphic V-shaped cuts in a jolly pattern and crimp neatly around the edge. Bake as usual and cool. Then, just before the pie goes to the table, take a sharp pointed knife and cut carefully round the upper crust, inside the crimped edge, and lift it off. Add half a cup of the richest, thickest, most creamy sweet cream and stir it in with the lightest, most gentle hand. Put back the upper crust and send to table and cock your ears for the loud cries of joy and rapture.

There is no article of diet which is such a universal standby as apple pie. It may be dessert or it may be a whole meal, any meal, from breakfast on to the midnight snack. It may be eaten by anyone of any age always provided that it is a first-class apple pie and not one of the deleterious second- or third-raters sometimes seen. It is good hot, cold or tepid. I have never tried frozen apple pie but I believe it would be very tasty. I don't know whether apple pie would be good buttered or dipped in gravy, but I doubt if anything save basely adulterated ingredients can make it wholly inedible.

Ask anyone what is his favorite pie and you'll be told "cherry" or "peach" or "blueberry"—most people don't mention apple. But say, "What about apple?" and the answer comes ninety-nine times out of a hundred, "Oh, I mean my favorite after apple," in a tone indicating that apple pie is taken for granted as premier.

Cherry pie, as years go on, seems to be becoming extinct. Time was when everyone had plenty of small scarlet sour cherries to can and preserve and pickle and plenty more to make into pies, but today the big sweet cherries seem to have crowded out the sour varieties, and big sweet cherries though luscious indeed lack the tang of the sour ones for pies.

If Billy Boy's girl-friend was doing a bit of busy work in her kitchenette these times she probably wouldn't be baking a cherry pie because she'd find it difficult to get the right cherries. What a fraud that song is! Anyone who has ever taken on the tiresome soppy task of pitting cherries knows full well that a cherry pie cannot be baked as quick as a cat can wink her eye—no, not even by the smartest young thing who cannot leave her mother.

Most men adore cherry pie, but I know one New York editor whose favorite is another and rarer sort—red raspberry pie! If any contributor should send him a manuscript accompanied by a fresh-baked red raspberry pie I believe that he would accept it, be it ever so badly written. Another literary gentleman of my acquaintance dotes on currant pie, and this is a very fine pie indeed, but at his home is the only place I have ever eaten it.

Personally I prefer my currants in jelly, and I once spent a whole laborious day removing the seeds with a pin from two quarts of currants to make some real Bar-le-Duc. It was a quick successful job after the seeds were out but the seed-removing was a terrific chore. As for red raspberries, I think it is a shame to put them in a pie when they are so incomparable *au naturel*. A dash of sugar, a spoonful of *eau de vie de framboise* may be added to them, but after that even cream, either sweet or sour, is unnecessary.

But blueberries! Or blackberries! There's another story. Many years ago on the Eastern Shore of Maryland we used to buy water pails full of fresh low-bush and high-bush blueberries—we called them all huckleberries—brought to the door, and the price of a pailful was fifty cents. This meant huckleberries for breakfast with cream and sugar, huckleberry pie for dinner and huckleberry muffins for supper, with several quart cans stored away for winter use. The fault of most huckleberry pies is that the juice is too thin or too thick and the berries not properly cooked, leaving a smack of acidity. The berries should be slowly cooked with the sugar beforehand and let stand while the crust is made, and when the fruit is put into the lower crust a dusting of flour should be added with the nicety of Solomon's judgment. Too much flour makes a gummy juice, too little leaves it thin. When it is just right it is food for Olympians.

Blackberry pie is almost as good. On my father's fruit farm we had a huge, soft, juicy berry which seemed foreordained by nature for the piepan. Bees and wasps and peppy little yellow jackets hung round the clusters of berries, so that picking was not without its adventures. Blackberries should be treated like blueberries, cooked before putting into the crust and with a dusting of flour to make the juice the right consistency.

Strawberries and plums are wonderful fruits but they were not specially created for pies. Nor for that matter was the pear, though now and then you meet a pear pie maker who turns out a product of genius, no less. But the peach pie is something else again. Peach pie is hard to spoil even by a novice cook, and when an expert makes one, then is the moment when the epicures and gourmets and the gourmands likewise, like morning stars, sing together in ecstatic chorus.

I like my peach pie with the fruit (and a couple of kernels from the peach pits) peering warmly reddish gold through an inviting crisscross of crisp sugary slats, and I resent with a bitterness which hates to see fine things degraded and greatness debased the horrid little peach tarts offered on many restaurant pastry trays—half a peach, upside down on a spoonful of sticky savorless custard, all riding in a measly little shell of alleged puff paste and masked with a vanilla-flavored sugar syrup. This is nothing to eat, worse than nothing! To begin with, who among peach-pie eaters could possibly be contented with one-half peach? The answer is exactly nobody!

No one, I feel, should use fresh ripe apricots in any cooked form—they are much too good eating just as is. But dried apricots and canned ones make a superb pie at its best with a top crust only, deep-dish style, and for a last little touch serve it with whipped sweet cream to which has been added a few drops of bitter almond extract. This is only for those who don't mind being stylish stouts. It has no place in a reducing diet.

Prunes make good pies, though not imaginative ones. Raisins make marvelous pies, simply marvelous. On this comes a culinary note from the land of the Pennsylvania Dutch. I had a school friend whose father was a minister of a Lancaster County church, and it was she who first told me of raisin pie, because, if you please, they were invariably served at the big funeral dinners in her father's parish, and she, piggy little moppet, always begged to go along when her father was called to preach a funeral sermon knowing they would be asked to stay for the dinner and she could get her fill of raisin pie. Probably the bereaved family thought it was sweetly sympathetic of the preacher's little daughter to insist on coming with him. So are ignoble motives sometimes nobly interpreted.

A pie for winter, half raisins and half cranberries, tastes far better than it sounds, and the all-cranberry pie has almost as many devotees amongst the male sex as cherry pie. Thrifty housekeepers frown on cranberry pie because of the sugar it takes, but I am told that by first cooking the berries in a double boiler without any water the sugar required is much less. The same holds true of rhubarb, first of the springtime pie fruits and wearing proudly in many localities the very name of pie plant, as if there could be none other. Rhubarb cooked without water in a double boiler requires only about half the usual amount of sugar, and rhubarb must always be cooked before it goes into a pie, cooked to a fair rosy hue, the lengths of stalk melting lusciously into thick bland syrup. The mean acid-green filling seen in far too many rhubarb pies is a disgrace to the baker.

That popular group of pies loosely headed "custard" embraces many worthy varieties, plain custard pie, coconut, chocolate, cream, maple, lemon, orange, caramel, coffee—and many many more, but of them all Old-fashioned Cheese Custard stands firm as the pie sublime. Let no dark-browed alien waiter offer you a slice of a dry and crumby cheese cake and tell you that it is cheese custard pie. He lies in his teeth! Cheese custard pie is delicately flavorous, with a distinctive smooth subtlety—a most more-ish tasting pie! It is at its best when made on a farm where the chickens and cows have liberal habits and eggs and cream and butter are therefore still lavishly in supply. I have an old, old, old recipe for cheese custard pie which I will write down here that those with long memories may read and feel a deep nostalgia for such cooking extravagance: Cream one-half pound of butter with one-half pound of sugar, add two wine-glasses of wine and two of brandy and the yolks of four eggs beaten light. To a large dipper-ful (about a pint) of cottage cheese, add a pint of cream and beat together, then beat into the first mixture. Stir in a pound of stale cake crumbs, whites of eight eggs beaten very stiff, one small nutmeg grated, cinnamon and grated lemon rind to taste. Note: Go very light on cinnamon, heavy on the lemon rind. Bake in a single crust very slowly.

Now there was a pie for you, none of your hanky-panky weak-kneed affairs, but a pie for stalwart men and buxom, rosy-cheeked women. And speaking of substantial, also delicious pies let no proud Northern wight sniff at the sweet-potato custard made on its native heath by one who knows. Rich with butter and cream, sweet with its natural sugar, thinned and lightened by eggs aplenty, given zing with lemon and baked in a crisp fluted crust, the sweet-potato custard becomes a pie for company and not a mere family fill-up. A whiff of nutmeg adds to its distinctive merit, but don't overspice it.

Don't overspice pumpkin and squash pies, either. I have eaten these pies when their rightful flavor was lost in strong cinnamon, ginger and clove but they should not—definitely—be turned into a Roman holiday for the spice box. Better not make pumpkin pies at all than treat them so unworthily.

There is one noble and difficult pie which I have left unmentioned until now—lemon meringue pie. Even the most reliable, the most experienced of cooks cannot guarantee success with lemon meringue pie, yet when it is successful it is incomparable. The crust must melt in the mouth (and not be soggy), the lemon underpinning must be tenderly a-quiver and not tough and leathery, nor yet so soft that when cut it bleeds itself into attenuation; the meringue must hold itself high and haughty, all snowy fluff inside with a top of golden beige beaded here and there with amber drops of utter sweetness. Such a lemon pie is as rare as a perfect pearl. In taste it should be piquant, without roughness or any under flavor of acidity. One point more: the perfect lemon meringue pie must not be a thin and shallow affair, no, it must be at least three inches in height from crust to meringue top with the filling and meringue fifty-fifty in proportion. So far as my observation goes the Middle West leads in perfect lemon meringue pie production. There is something in the air of the Mississippi Valley which seems to conduce to skill in making this pie.

I can't name the region of this country which excels in making that outstanding institution of the winter dinner table—mince pie—for everywhere it is made well. Mince pie is a tradition, a household rite. It is not so very long ago when every responsible housekeeper made her mincemeat in the autumn at the same time she baked her fruitcake, and stored it away in tall stone jars to ripen and coalesce. Suet and lean boiled beef were first chopped fine, then raisins were seeded, huge fat raisins, wine red in color and winy in fragrance. Apples were pared and cut into little cubes and citron, candied orange peel, currants, sugar and spice were measured with care. The kitchen smelled like Christmas. After everything had been simmered for perhaps two hours the mincemeat went into tall stone jars and cooled its tropic heat. Then the lady of the house would unlock a Certain Closet where there were Certain Bottles, and choosing one would go to the kitchen and pour upon the mix a generous libation of a Certain Liquid, pale tinted and with a heady fruity bouquet, and blend it and stir it until the whole rich mass was permeated with its felicity.

After this the mincemeat sat in its stone jar and aged and mellowed and refined its flavor until the first snowfall when the first mince pies were made. There are not many more glorious moments in the life of a young barbarian than the day of the first snow and the first mince pie, and the young barbarian's elders also reacted visibly to the festal occasion.

In my native town there were certain mince-pie makers who stood out for individuality. One always cut up preserved watermelon rind in her mincemeat. Another thought a glass of wild-grape jelly gave it a superior flavor. A third used no sweetening but rock candy, the white kind that comes on strings. (N.B. She took out the strings.) But my mother had no whim about her mincemeat save to put in it a minimum of suet because she thought the flavor coarse.

Today we buy our mincemeat in cans, and very good it is, a little better perhaps if you add some fresh chopped apple, a bit more sugar, an extra handful of raisins and a couple of jiggers of brandy. Yet it has not the taste of the mincemeat scooped from the deep stone jar, for that mincemeat was flavored with something unique, unbuyable. It was flavored with Home.

The name of the genius who invented pie is unknown. No statue has ever been erected to his or her memory. In old manuscripts of centuries gone by there is mention of pyes and pasties of various sorts, probably pasty indeed considered by our standards, but as ancestor to one of today's most popular and delightful dishes there is no need to sneer at their simplicity or their crudity. It is enough that pie in many forms, in many lands has long had an honored existence. For my part I hope this existence will continue down the ages, always with the slogan, "More and better Pies, Down with all Substitutes and Imitations."

Plain Pastry for One Pie

Sift together 2½ cups all-purpose flour with 1 teaspoon salt. Add to it, 6 tablespoons vegetable shortening and ¾ bar (6 tablespoons) sweet butter. Work the shortening into the flour lightly, using your finger tips. When mealy in consistency, moisten with not more than 6 tablespoons ice water. Form into 2 flat balls, wrap in waxed paper and chill until ready to use.

Puff Paste

Put 1 pound sweet butter into a bowl of cold water and work it with the hands until it is of the consistency of putty, soft and pliable, squeezing it in a cloth to extract any water there may be in it. Now put 4 cups flour in a bowl with 1 teaspoon salt. With the finger tips work into this lightly 2 tablespoons butter, then add gradually 1½ cups ice water, still using your hands to mix it. Knead it lightly until it makes a smooth ball. Toss onto a lightly floured board and roll it out to about ⅜ inch thickness in a rectangular shape, about 15 to 20 inches. Place the dough horizontally in front of you, shape the butter into a slab about 6 by 12 inches, lay it perpendicularly in front of you on the center of the dough. Fold the flap of dough on the left to cover the butter, then fold the right-hand flap over to the left. The butter is now completely covered and out of sight, and the whole secret of the puff paste is to see to it that the butter never breaks through the surface. Roll the paste away from you to make a longer rectangle. Give it a turn, which means to turn it so that it is horizontally before you. Fold the dough so as to form a square, flopping the left-hand ⅓ to the right, and the right-hand ⅓ to the left.

Press lightly with the rolling pin and place in refrigerator to rest for 20 minutes. Then take it out, and be sure to place it before you the way it was before. Roll away from you as before, until you have a rectangle 3 times as long as its width. Be careful not to roll it too thin the first 2 or 3 times. Place it carefully horizontally before you and fold from left to right and right to left, as before, to form a square. Let it rest again for 10 minutes, and repeat the process until you have rolled and folded it 8 times. Place on ice to chill thoroughly until ready to use.

Apricot Pie
(for 6–8)

Make half the recipe for plain pastry (page 58). Chill for ½ hour or longer. In the meantime, wash thoroughly 2 boxes (11-ounce size) quick-cooking dried apricots and soak them in 4 cups cold water for 1 hour. Place on fire and cook until tender or for about 10 minutes. Add 3 cups granulated sugar and continue cooking 5–7 minutes longer or until the juice has become thick like jam. Remove from fire and cool.

Now roll out ⅓ of the pastry and cut it in 1-inch strips. Brush the edge of the dish with water and place the strips over and around the edge. This is to anchor the top crust to the dish. Fill the dish with the cold apricots. Roll out the rest of the pastry and cut it into a circle—10 inches in diameter. Wet the edge around the dish, then roll the circle of pastry up onto your rolling pin and unroll over the top so that it falls in place. Press the edges together all around, then crimp prettily. Make several deep gashes in the center of the pastry and brush with cold water. Place in preheated hot 450° F. oven and bake until crust is a golden brown or for about 15–20 minutes.

Peach Pie
(for 6–8)

Make recipe for plain pastry (page 58). Chill for ½ hour or longer. In the meantime, pour boiling water over 12 large, juicy, ripe peaches and allow them to stand for 1 minute or 2, then plunge them into cold water, and remove the skins. They should slip off easily, leaving the peach un-marred. Slice thin and sprinkle them as you go along with 1½ cups granulated sugar. Crack open 6 of the pits, being careful not to bang them too hard, then remove the kernels. Remove the skins and add the white kernels to the peaches and place on moderate fire and cook for 15 min-

utes, watching carefully so that they do not stick. Remove from fire and cool.

Roll out ½ pastry and line a 10-inch Pyrex pie plate allowing the pastry to lap over 1 inch. Now fill the pastry with the cold peaches. Then roll out the rest of the pastry and cut about 15 big strips about ½ inch wide, long enough to go across the center of the pie. Now wet the edge of the pie and start laying 7 of the strips across one way and then weave the rest of the strips in and out the other way to form a lattice. This sounds complicated but is very simple if you don't try to hurry it. Cut off the strips when they are too long, and roll the overhanging under crust up and over the strips to secure them. Then crimp the edges as usual. Paint the strips and edge lightly with a pastry brush dipped in milk, then sprinkle a very little granulated sugar along each strip to make them sugary and crispy when baked.

Place in preheated 450° F. hot oven and bake about 20 minutes or until the crust is a golden brown. Serve lukewarm with 1 cup heavy cream, whipped and flavored with about 1 teaspoon almond extract.

Sour Cherry Latticed Pie
(for 6–8)

Make full recipe for plain pie pastry (page 58). Chill for ½ hour or longer. Roll out ½ of it and line a 10-inch Pyrex pie plate. Trim the edge, leaving ½ inch overlapping the edge.

Drain juice from 4 15½-ounce cans of tart red cherries. Add 1 tablespoon flour to ⅔ cups granulated sugar and mix well. Place ½ the cherries in the pan, sprinkle with ½ the sugar, add rest of cherries and top with remaining sugar. Dot with 1 tablespoon butter and pour just enough of the juice to come to the level of the cherries. Roll out the rest of the paste and cut in ½-inch strips. Moisten edge of pie and lay the strips crosswise over the pie, making a lattice. Roll edge of crust up over the strips at the edge and crimp prettily. Place in 450° F. oven and bake for 12 minutes, reduce heat to 375° F. and continue baking until the crust is nice and brown or for about 25 minutes longer.

Apple Pie Made with Applesauce
(for 6–8)

First make recipe for plain pastry (page 58). Chill for ½ hour or longer while you make 4 cups of good slow-cooked applesauce. Wash, peel, quarter, and core 12 large early, spicy, green apples and cook them slowly in 2 cups water until tender or for about 15 minutes. Remove from fire and rub through a fine sieve. Add 1½ cups granulated sugar and cook it about 5 minutes longer. Cool until ready to bake the pie.

Light your oven and set the control at 450° F. Roll out ½ the pastry, and line a 10-inch Pyrex pie plate with the pastry. Fill with the cooled applesauce, and cover with the remainder of the pastry. Roll the over-lapping pastry under the edge of the bottom crust to make a firm border. Crimp the edge prettily and cut a 1-inch cross in center of pie and make several more smaller gashes around this to provide a good outlet for the steam, and place the pie in a hot 450° F. oven and bake until the crust begins to brown lightly, or for about 20 minutes. Then reduce heat to 375° F. and continue baking until done and lightly browned all over or for about 25 minutes longer. Remove from oven and cool. When ready to serve, take a sharp pointed knife and cut carefully around the upper crust inside the crimped edge, and with the help of a spatula and a pan-cake turner, lift off the crust. Fold into the applesauce, without disturbing the lower crust, 1 cup heavy cream, beaten until very stiff. Replace the top crust as it was in the beginning and serve at once.

Green Apple Custard Pie
(for 6–8)

Wash and peel and core 8 small green apples. Add ½ cup water and bring to a boil and cook until soft, or for about 10 minutes. Rub through a fine sieve and add ½ cup granulated sugar. Place back on fire and bring to a boil just long enough to melt the sugar. Flavor with 1 tablespoon lemon juice, the grated rind of 2 lemons, and 1 teaspoon lemon extract.

Make ½ the recipe for plain pastry (page 58). Chill for ½ hour or so, then roll it out and line a 10-inch Pyrex pie plate. Crimp the edges prettily.

Beat 4 eggs well and add 4 tablespoons milk and 2 tablespoons melted butter, then stir in 2 cups applesauce. Place in the pastry-lined pie plate and place in preheated 375° F. oven and bake for about 10 minutes or until crust begins to brown lightly, then reduce heat to 325° F. and continue baking 35 minutes longer. Beat the whites of 3 eggs until stiff and beat in 9 tablespoons granulated sugar. Flavor with vanilla. Remove pie from oven and quickly spread the meringue over the apple custard so that it is all covered, and put back in the oven and continue baking until the meringue is a pale brown, or for about 15 minutes. Remove from fire and serve lukewarm with or without cream.

Cranberry Raisin Pie
(for 6–8)

Make full recipe for plain pastry (page 58). Chill for an hour or so. In the meantime, wash 3 cups cranberries and cut them in half. Wash 1 cup raisins and dry them well. Mix together 1½ cups granulated sugar, 1 tablespoon flour, 1 teaspoon cinnamon, and ½ teaspoon nutmeg.

Roll out ½ the pastry and line a large 10-inch pie plate with it. Mix the raisins and cranberries together and place in pastry-lined pan. Sprinkle over all the sugar and spices and dot with 1 tablespoon butter. Roll out the rest of the pastry to a circle large enough to cover the pie and hang over a bit. Roll it up on your rolling pin. Moisten the edges of the bottom crust, and unroll the top crust over the pie. Roll the overlapping crust under and crimp prettily. Make several gashes in the top crust. Place in preheated 425° F. oven and bake 30–40 minutes.

Cranberry Pie
(for 6–8)

Make full recipe for plain pastry (page 58). Wash and pick over carefully 4 cups cranberries. Now cut them in half one by one. Now take ½ of the pastry, roll it out and line a 10-inch pie tin with it. Fill the shell with the cranberries and 1 tightly packed cup light brown sugar. Trickle over all 2 generous tablespoons molasses. Cover with top crust, having first moistened the rim of the under crust with water. Trim and crimp the edge. Now make 1½-inch crosslike incision in the center of the pie and roll back the four flaps, forming a fairly large square hole in the center. Prick the rest of the surface of the pie all over with a fork.

Place in 425° F. oven for about 10 minutes, then reduce the heat to 325° F. Continue cooking slowly for about an hour longer. Every so often during the cooking process, replenish the liquid in the pie, as it goes down, by pouring into the hole in the center a little hot thick syrup made by boiling together a minute or two, 2 tablespoons molasses, ½ cup light brown sugar (tightly packed) and ¼ cup water. The pie when done should be moist and syrupy inside and the bottom crust should be almost caramelized on the bottom. Serve warm accompanied by rat-trap cheese.

Blueberry Tart
(for 6–8)

Make the full recipe for plain pastry (page 58). Roll out ½ of it at a time and line 2 9-inch Pyrex pie plates. Turn the edges under and crimp prettily. Prick the bottom and sides with a fork and place in preheated 450° F. oven and bake until a light golden brown or for about 15 minutes. Remove from oven and cool.

In the meantime, pick over and wash and drain well, 2½ quarts superior blueberries. Put 6 cups berries in a large enamel pan and stir into them 3 cups granulated sugar. Add 2 teaspoons powdered cinnamon and place on low flame and stir constantly until they form their own juice and are boiling in it. Continue cooking for 10 to 15 minutes or until nice and thick. Remove from fire and cool. When ready to serve the pie, place 2 cups plain blueberries in each one and glaze with the cooked blueberries, dividing it equally. Serve at once accompanied by a big bowl of sour cream or whipped heavy cream and a bowl of confectioners' sugar in which you have kept a vanilla bean.

Plum Tart
(for 6–8)

Sift together 2 cups pastry flour with ¼ teaspoon cinnamon, add a pinch of salt. Sift it once more into a bowl and make a well in it. In a separate little bowl beat together 1 egg and ½ cup sugar until light and creamy. Grate the rind of 1 lemon and stir it into the egg. Pour the egg mixture into the hole in the flour and add 6 tablespoons butter. Now gradually work the whole into a smooth paste using a fork at first and ending with your fingers. Form into a ball and roll out on lightly floured board, making it into an oblong strip about 10 inches by 5 inches and about ¼ inch thick. Transfer onto a well-buttered cookie sheet and crimp the edges so as to form a rim at least half an inch high. Now prick the entire surface with a fork. Bake in preheated hot 450° F. oven until a pale golden brown, or for about 15 minutes.

Now pit 14 large ripe red plums. Make a very thick syrup by boiling together 1 cup sugar moistened with ¼ cup water for 5 minutes. Add the plums and cook until they are barely tender, then strain them out spreading them out on a platter. Add another ½ cup sugar to the plum syrup and continue cooking until very thick, or for about ½ hour. Remove from fire and cool. It should become a moderately thick jelly when cold. When ready to serve the tart, place it on an oblong platter and cover the surface with the plums. Now spread the jelly evenly over all and serve at once, accompanied or not, with sweet cream, or sour cream.

Deep Dish Gooseberry Tart
(for 6–8)

With scissors cut off the ends of 2 quarts gooseberries. Wash them, and place in deep baking dish (2-quart size) in alternate layers, with 2 cups granulated sugar. Bake in hot 500° F. oven for about ½ hour, stirring occasionally, then reduce heat to 350° F. and continue cooking 45 minutes longer, likewise stirring occasionally. Remove from oven and drain off the juice. Add another ½ cup sugar to the syrup and boil down 10 minutes. Pour back over the gooseberries and allow the whole to cool completely.

When ready to finish baking the tart, make a cookie dough in the following manner. Cream ¼ pound butter with 1 cup granulated sugar. Beat 1 whole egg and add it to the butter and sugar, and beat well. Add gradually 3 cups cake flour sifted with a pinch of salt and 2½ teaspoons baking powder, adding also about ⅛ cup milk. The dough should be very stiff. Roll out on heavily floured board to approximate size of dish and, quickly and skillfully, roll up the dough onto the rolling pin, and unroll over the dish and let the dough fall on top of the gooseberries. Trim off what overlaps, and roll up the scraps and cut 6 diamonds and lay in the center, forming a design. Poke your finger down into the center. Roll up the rest of the scraps, and roll around your finger and insert the rose you have made into the hole, managing, however, still to leave a hole. This is so that the steam can escape. Crimp the edges with floured fingers. Place immediately into preheated 400° F. oven and bake until lightly browned or for about 10 minutes. Reduce heat to 300° F. and continue baking about 20 minutes longer, or until an inserted tooth pick or cake tester comes out clean. Serve hot with sour cream, or sweet cream if you prefer. It may be made ahead of time and warmed in 450° F. oven for a few minutes.

Huckleberry Pie
(for 6–8)

Pick over and wash and drain carefully 1 quart huckleberries. Place them in an enamel pan and add 1 cup granulated sugar. Place on low flame and bring gently to boiling point, shaking the pan frequently so that the berries don't stick. Cook for about 3 minutes, remove from fire and cool.

Make recipe for plain pastry (page 58). Chill for ½ hour, roll out ½ of it and line a large 10-inch Pyrex pie pan with it, allowing a little of the pastry to lap over the edge. Fill with ½ of the cooked huckleberries, sprinkle with a very little all-purpose flour (about 1 tablespoonful). Cover with remainder of the berries, and dot with 1 tablespoon butter. Cover with the other ½ of the pastry rolled out, large enough to cover the top and also lap over the edge about ½ inch. Roll top crust under the overlapping bottom crust and crimp prettily all around. Make several

*gashes in the top crust. Place in preheated hot 450° F. to 475° F. oven and
bake until the crust begins to brown lightly, or for about 10 minutes,
then reduce heat to 375° F. and continue baking for about ½ hour longer,
or until the crust is a golden brown. Serve lukewarm with plenty of heavy
cream.*

Blackberry Pie
(for 6–8)

*Make exactly as Huckleberry Pie above, substituting blackberries for the
huckleberries.*

Lime Chiffon Pie
(for 6–8)

*Soak the grated rind of 1 green lime in ⅔ cup strained lime juice for 1
hour. In the meantime, make a graham cracker crust by rolling fine 16
graham crackers. Next cream until very soft, ¼ pound sweet butter. Add
to the crumbs 1 teaspoon flour, ½ cup granulated sugar, and 1 teaspoon
cinnamon. Mix well and add gradually to the creamed butter. Butter a
round 10-inch Pyrex pie plate and press the crumb mixture evenly over
the bottom and sides to form a crust. Place in refrigerator to chill for 1
hour. Soak 1 envelope and 1 extra teaspoon of Knox gelatin in ¼ cup
cold water. Beat the yolks of 5 eggs, beat into them gradually 1 cup granulated sugar, and add the lime juice strained through a fine sieve to remove the green rind, then place in top part of an enamel double boiler
over hot water and cook, stirring constantly until thickened (about 5
minutes). Remove from fire, add the soaked gelatin and stir until melted.
Cool until it begins to stiffen (about ½ hour). Beat the whites of 5 eggs
until stiff and beat in ½ cup granulated sugar. Fold the egg whites in the
yolks and gelatin mixture until all of the whites have disappeared. Then
pour into the pie shell and return to the refrigerator until ready to serve.*

Two Lemon Meringue Pies
(for 6–8)

Sift together 2½ cups pastry flour with 1 teaspoon salt. Work into it with finger tips 6 tablespoons vegetable shortening and 6 tablespoons butter. When mealy in consistency, moisten with not more than 6 tablespoons ice water. Form into 2 balls, wrap in waxed paper and chill until ready to use. Roll out 1 ball at a time on lightly floured cloth, using as light a pressure as possible. Place rolling pin on pastry and roll up onto pin and unroll onto a 9-inch pie plate, so as to completely cover the pan. Let it settle down into the pan, then trim off the excess pastry with floured scissors, leaving, however, about ½ inch hanging over the edge. Roll this under and crimp edges, using floured fingers. Repeat the process and line the second pie plate. Prick the entire surface of each with a fork, to prevent puffing, and bake for 15 to 20 minutes in preheated 450°–500° F. oven, or until done and lightly browned.

In the meantime, make the filling. Mix together in top part of large enamel double boiler, 14 level tablespoons cornstarch with 3 cups granulated sugar. Add gradually, stirring constantly, 3 cups boiling water. Cook over direct heat, stirring all the while, until thick and boiling. Then, still stirring, continue cooking over boiling water for 10 minutes longer. Beat the yolks of 6 eggs slightly, then add them gradually to the cornstarch. When well mixed, add 6 tablespoons butter and stir until melted. Then add 8 tablespoons strained lemon juice and 2 tablespoons of grated lemon rind. Remove pan from double boiler and cool. Pour into the baked pie shells.

Now make the meringue. Beat the whites of 6 eggs, to which you have added 1½ teaspoons cream of tartar, until stiff enough to hold a peak, then gradually beat in 12 tablespoons granulated sugar, flavor with 2 teaspoons vanilla, and continue beating a second or two. Pile lightly on the filling of the two pies, being sure the meringue touches the crusts all around (this to prevent its shrinking away from the edge while browning) and being sure that all the filling is covered too. Bake until a golden brown, in a 350° F. oven for about 10 to 15 minutes. Serve cold.

Squash or Pumpkin Pie
(for 6–8)

Make full recipe for plain pastry (page 58). After pastry is made chill in refrigerator ½ hour or longer. Roll out and line 2 9-inch Pyrex pie plates, crimping around edge prettily.

Open 2 14½-ounce cans of squash or pumpkin, or use 3 cups home-cooked squash or pumpkin put through a sieve. Place it in a large bowl, add 1 cup light brown sugar, 1 cup white granulated sugar, 1 scant teaspoon salt, 2 tablespoons New Orleans molasses, ½ teaspoon powdered cloves, 3 level teaspoons ground cinnamon and 3 level teaspoons ground ginger. Mix well. Beat 4 whole eggs slightly and stir them into the squash or pumpkin mixture. Last of all add 1 cup thick cream and 1 cup milk scalded together. Mix well. Fill the two crusts.

Place in a hot, preheated 450° to 500° F. oven for 10 minutes, or until crust is slightly brown, then reduce heat to 350° F. and continue cooking slowly about 30 minutes longer, or until set. Watch carefully and turn the flame lower if the custard is cooking too fast, which would cause it to become watery. Remove from oven and cool slightly before serving.

Galette with Blazing Mincemeat
(for 6–8)

Sift some pastry flour and measure out 2 cups of it. Sift it again with ½ teaspoon salt, 1 teaspoon sugar, and ½ teaspoon baking powder. Work into this with the finger tips, ⅜ pound sweet butter or 1½ bars. Moisten with ⅓ cup cream, beaten slightly with the yolk of 1 egg. Mix with a large fork until it may be formed into a ball. Flatten the ball a bit, then wrap it in waxed paper and place in refrigerator for several hours. When ready to bake, set your oven at 500° F., light it, and then proceed to roll out the dough on a lightly floured board, forming a perfect circle ½ inch thick. Place carefully on lightly buttered tins. Then with a knife score the surface of the cake, forming a pattern of diamonds all over. Now beat together 1 whole egg and 1 tablespoon of cold water, using a fork, and beat just long enough to mix well. Then paint the surface of the galette with the egg. Be sure your oven is hot, put the galette into the oven and bake 15 minutes, or until lightly browned all over, then decrease the heat to 400° F. and cook about 25 minutes longer. Watch carefully, don't let it burn. Serve hot. If you must cook it ahead of time, reheat before serving, and just before serving, sprinkle it lightly with confectioners' sugar; accompany it with a bowl of mincemeat, which you have cooked for 1 hour over boiling water in a double boiler. Pour over the mincemeat at table 2 or 3 tablespoons kirsch, which has been heated separately over a low flame in the kitchen and sent to table in a little pitcher. Light the kirsch and let it burn out while you cut the galette in pie-shaped pieces, to be eaten with the hot mincemeat.

Banbury Tarts
(for 6–8)

First make the full recipe for plain pastry (page 58). Wrap it in waxed paper and chill in refrigerator while you make the filling for the tarts.

Chop fine in a wooden chopping bowl, 1 cup shelled English walnuts and add 1 cup white seedless raisins likewise chopped fairly fine. Place the two together in a bowl and add the grated rind and strained juice of 1 large lemon. Stir in 1 cup granulated sugar and moisten with 1 tablespoon boiling water in which you have melted 1 tablespoon butter. Beat 1 whole egg lightly and stir it into the rest and flavor with 1 teaspoon vanilla. Sprinkle the whole with 2 tablespoons cracker crumbs and mix once more.

Now butter 2 large cookie sheets lightly. Roll out the pastry until ⅛ inch thick, then cut it carefully into 4-inch squares. Separate one from the other slightly and place a scant tablespoon of the filling on each. Dip your fingers in cold water and moisten the edges of each square. Then fold them over to form triangles and press the edges firmly together. Last of all dip a fork in flour and crimp the cut edges of each. Lay them on the cookie sheets and prick each one 3 times with a fork. Place in refrigerator for 15 minutes to chill.

Light your oven and set it at 450° to 475° F. Gather up all the leftover scraps of pastry and use it to make more tarts until all has been used.

*In all, this quantity should make 12 full-sized tarts and a few baby ones
for private sampling when done.*

*When chilled paint each one with a little milk and place in preheated
hot oven and bake for 20–25 minutes until lightly browned. Remove from
oven and serve while still warm if possible. If not, reheat them slightly.
Just before serving, sprinkle lightly with confectioners' sugar in which
you have kept a vanilla bean.*

Butterscotch Black Walnut Pies
(for 6–8)

*Make the full recipe for plain pastry (page 58). Chill for ½ hour or so.
When ready to make the pies, light your oven and set it at 375° F. Roll
out ½ the pastry at a time and line 2 9-inch Pyrex pie plates, trimming
and crimping the edges as usual.*

*Break 4 whole eggs into a bowl. Melt 3 tablespoons butter. Open 2
4-ounce cans of broken black walnut meats. Look them over and be sure
there are no bits of shells. Beat the eggs well with a rotary beater, add 1⅓
cups white Karo syrup, and 1⅓ cups light brown sugar (well packed)
and the 3 tablespoons melted butter, and beat well. Sift over it 3 tablespoons all-purpose flour, add 1 teaspoon vanilla and beat with rotary
beater until all the flour has been mixed in. Add the black walnuts and
pour into the 2 pastry-lined pie plates. Place in moderate 375° F. oven and
bake for 30 minutes or until lightly browned, then reduce heat to 300° F.
and continue baking until done, or for about 20–25 minutes longer. To
test, insert the blade of a knife in the center of one of the pies and if it
comes out clean, the pies are done. Serve lukewarm with cream.*

Chess Pie
(for 6–8)

*Make a paste by sifting together 1⅓ cups pastry flour with 3 tablespoons
granulated sugar. Work into this ¼ pound sweet butter. Moisten with
1 tablespoon vinegar or a drop or two more if necessary. Form into a flat
ball, and wrap in waxed paper and chill for 1 hour in refrigerator.*

Roll out and line a 9-inch pie plate and crimp the edges prettily.

Cream ⅛ pound sweet butter with ½ cup granulated sugar and 1½ teaspoons pastry flour. Now add 4 egg yolks beaten until very light and into which you have beaten ½ cup granulated sugar. Stir in gradually ½ cup milk, and add 1 tablespoon vinegar and 2 teaspoons vanilla. Pour this immediately into the pie dish and place in preheated, slow 300° F. oven and bake for 1 hour or until an inserted knife comes out clean.

Shoo-Fly Pie
(for 6–8)

Make a paste by sifting together 1⅓ cups pastry flour with 3 tablespoons granulated sugar. Work into this ¼ pound sweet butter. Moisten with 1 tablespoon vinegar or a drop or two more if necessary. Form into a flat ball and wrap in waxed paper and chill for 1 hour in refrigerator.

Roll out and line a 9-inch pie plate and crimp the edges prettily. Place in refrigerator temporarily.

Now make a crumb mixture by sifting ¾ cup pastry flour with ½ cup light brown sugar, ¼ teaspoon nutmeg, ¼ teaspoon ginger, ¼ teaspoon clove, ¾ teaspoon cinnamon and ¼ teaspoon salt. Work into this with the finger tips 2 tablespoons butter.

Now beat 1 egg yolk well with small beater and add ¾ cup good molasses, then add ¾ cup boiling water in which you have dissolved 1½ teaspoons baking soda.

Now sprinkle the bottom of your pie with about ⅓ of the crumb mixture, then cover with ½ of the molasses mixture, add another ⅓ of the crumbs, then the rest of the molasses and top it off with the last ⅓ of the crumbs. Place in preheated 450° F. oven for 8 minutes or until the pastry begins to brown lightly around the edge, then decrease heat to 350° F. and bake until an inserted knife comes out clean or for about 12 minutes longer or 20 minutes in all. Serve while still warm with heavy cream.

Sweet Potato Pie
(for 6–8)

Make ½ recipe for plain pastry (page 58). Chill for an hour or so in the refrigerator. In the meantime, peel and cut into quarters 3 large sweet potatoes. Cover with cold water and boil until tender or for about 15 minutes. Drain well, then put through the potato ricer or a fine sieve. You should have 1¼ cups. Add while hot ½ cup butter and mix well. Beat 3 whole eggs well and add gradually 1 cup granulated sugar. Add this to the potato and stir until well mixed, then add 1 cup cream. Last of all, stir in ½ cup good sherry, and the grated rind of 1 lemon—and a pinch of nutmeg.

Roll out the chilled pastry and line a 10-inch Pyrex pie plate. Roll the edges under and crimp prettily. Pour in the well-stirred potato mixture and place in preheated 450° F. oven and bake for about 10 minutes or until the crust begins to brown lightly, then reduce the heat to 325° F. and continue cooking until it tests done when a thin knife blade is inserted in the center and comes out clean, or for about 50 minutes longer. Watch carefully and reduce heat even further if the mixture gives any sign of boiling in the center. Remove from oven and cool. Serve accompanied by a bowl of powdered sugar and cinnamon mixed together in the proportion of 2 of sugar to 1 of cinnamon.

Cheese Custard Pie
(for 6–8)

Make ½ the recipe for plain pastry (page 58). Chill for ½ hour or longer. In the meantime, prepare the following filling: Crumble enough dry cake crumbs to make 3 cups. Cream ¼ pound butter with ½ cup granulated sugar until light and fluffy, then beat in 2 well-beaten egg yolks, and stir in ¼ cup dry sherry wine and the same of good brandy.

In a separate bowl, place 1 cup cottage cheese, and add to it 1 cup heavy cream. Beat with rotary beater until well mixed, then add the grated rind of 1 large lemon, 1 teaspoon grated nutmeg, and 1 teaspoon powdered cinnamon. Beat well and add to the butter and sugar mixture. Beat and stir in the 3 cups cake crumbs. In a separate bowl beat the whites of 4 eggs until very stiff, then fold them into the other ingredients. Roll out the chilled pastry and line a 10-inch Pyrex pie plate. Roll edges under and crimp prettily and fill with the custard cheese mixture. Place in preheated 300° F. slow oven and bake gently for 1 hour and 15 minutes or until it tests done in center and has browned lightly all over. Cool and serve, with or without slightly beaten heavy cream.

Chocolate Pies
(for 6–8)

First make the pastry. Sift together 2½ cups pastry flour and 1 teaspoon salt. Work into this with the finger tips, 6 tablespoons butter and 6 tablespoons vegetable shortening. Moisten with 3–6 tablespoons ice water, form into 2 balls, wrap in wax paper and chill ½ hour. Roll out on lightly floured board, 1 ball at a time. Line 2 8-inch glass Pyrex plates with the pastry. Prick the bottom of each with a fork. Roll the edges under and crimp prettily. Place in preheated 425° F. oven and bake for about 15 minutes or until a light golden brown. Remove from oven and cool while you make the following chocolate filling.

Place 4 ounces (4 squares) unsweetened chocolate in top part of an enamel double boiler and melt over boiling water, stirring constantly. Add 2 cups granulated sugar, 6 tablespoons flour, 3 cups scalding hot milk, and the well beaten yolks of 6 eggs. Cook over boiling water, stirring constantly for about 10 minutes or until well thickened. Stir in 4 tablespoons butter and flavor with 2 teaspoons vanilla. Pour into the 2 pie shells. Cover with a meringue made of the 6 egg whites. Add 1½ teaspoons cream of tartar to the whites, and beat until stiff enough to hold a peak, then gradually beat in 12 tablespoons granulated sugar. Flavor with 2 teaspoons vanilla, and continue beating a second or two. Pile lightly on the 2 pies, being sure the meringue touches the crust all around and covers all of the filling. Place in preheated 350° F. oven and bake until a golden brown or for about 10–15 minutes. Serve cold.

Banana Cream Pie
(for 6–8)

Make ½ the recipe for plain pastry (page 58). Chill for ½ hour or longer. In the meantime, make the following cream filling:

Scald 2½ cups milk. Mix 3½ level tablespoons cornstarch with ¾ cup granulated sugar and add ½ cup cold milk, then add it to the hot milk gradually. Cook 20 minutes over boiling water, stirring frequently. Beat

the yolks of 6 eggs well and add them slowly to the hot cornstarch, stir-
ring vigorously. Continue cooking until very thick (about 7 minutes).
Remove from fire and cool, stirring occasionally. Flavor when cold with
1 tablespoon vanilla.

Roll out the pastry and line a 10-inch Pyrex pie plate. Roll the edges
under and crimp prettily. Prick with a fork and place in preheated 425°
to 450° F. oven and bake until a delicate brown or for 15–20 minutes. Re-
move from oven and cool.

When cold, cover bottom of crust with ⅓ of the custard and cover with
a layer of ripe bananas cut thin. Cover the bananas with another ⅓ of the
custard, and again a layer of bananas and top with remainder of custard.
Now beat the whites of 6 eggs until frothy, then add 1½ teaspoons cream
of tartar and beat until stiff, then beat in ¾ cup granulated sugar adding
it gradually. Flavor with 1 teaspoon vanilla and spread over the custard
so that the custard is covered all over. Place in preheated 350° to 400° F.
moderate oven and bake until a beautiful golden brown or for about 15
minutes.

Coconut Cream Pie
(for 6–8)

Make half the recipe for plain pastry (page 58). Roll out and line a
10-inch Pyrex pie plate, rolling the edges under and crimping it prettily.
Prick the bottom of it with a fork and place in preheated 425°–450° F.
oven and bake for about 15 minutes or until a light golden brown. Re-
move from oven and cool. In the meantime, make the following coco-
nut cream filling:

Scald 2½ cups milk. Mix 3½ level tablespoons cornstarch with ¾ cup
granulated sugar and add ½ cup cold milk, then add the hot milk gradu-
ally. Cook 20 minutes over hot water in a double boiler, stirring fre-
quently. Beat the yolks of 6 eggs well, and add them slowly to the hot
cornstarch, stirring vigorously. Continue cooking over hot water until
very thick or for about 7 minutes. Remove from fire and cool, stirring
occasionally. Flavor when cold with 1 tablespoon vanilla and stir in 1 cup
canned moist coconut. Pour into pie shell and spread smooth. Cover with
the following meringue:

Beat the whites of 6 eggs with 1½ teaspoons cream of tartar, and add

¾ cup granulated sugar gradually. Flavor with 1 teaspoon vanilla and fold in ¼ cup canned moist coconut cut with scissors into shorter shreds. Spread lightly over the custard, being sure that the meringue touches the crust all the way around to avoid having the meringue shrink away from the edge while baking. Sprinkle the top with another ¼ cup coconut, likewise cut with scissors. Place the pie in a 350° F. oven for about 10–15 minutes or until a beautiful golden brown. Watch carefully so that it does not burn. Serve this pie when just barely cooled or lukewarm to have it at its best.

FOUR

Begged, Borrowed, Maybe Stolen

Every housekeeper should have a cook book of her own making, not a scientific expert exhaustive cook book, but a sort of eating-your-way-through-life compilation of recipes which have been begged and borrowed and maybe stolen. My own tome of this kind is large and originally was all blank pages, but now it is well filled. It has for frontispiece a picture post card of the Castle of Lucullus, that Roman noble and politician who has been labeled by history and the French dictionary as *"le type des fins gourmets."* My book is a mixed bag of memories and recipes, and those of the latter which I offer here are for the most part easy to make and not expensive.

To entertain in the grand manner is no longer possible for most of us, but here is a tidbit to serve as first course which will dress up a plain luncheon or dinner. The recipe was given to me by Adelaide Heilner of Spring Lake, New Jersey, in whose home "Seawood" I have often eaten it with gusto.

Canapé Seawood: From slices of fresh soft white bread cut out two-inch rounds with a cookie cutter, two for each canapé required. Cut half as many rounds from thin slices of firm tomatoes. Salt and pepper the tomato slices and let drain while coating the rounds of bread all over with highly seasoned mayonnaise. Put a slice of tomato between each two slices of bread, the result being sticky sandwiches, and if not sticky enough add more mayonnaise to the outside. Have ready two or three cold hard-boiled eggs, shelled, whites and yolks separated and each put through a strainer to reduce to fine bits. Roll the sticky sandwiches all over in either the egg white or the egg yolks, making the same number of each color. On top of each canapé put a stamped-out star of thin tomato or green pepper, or a slice of stuffed olive. At table, place white and yellow sandwiches alternately. This is a quickie to make and a delicious light morsel to eat.

Soup should logically follow the canapé and the easiest I know is an onion soup which I saw made and afterward ate at La Providence, the famous inn at Jouy near Chartres. It was a chilly, gray fall day and I was nearly frozen by the ride from Paris and hungry enough to eat anything and like it. It was too raw to sit in the courtyard among the last autumn flowers but Mme. Delaunay welcomed me into the warm crowded kitchen and sat me down at the big table where the family had its meals.

Now the chef—Madame's son-in-law—sprang into action. Bang went a long-handled frying pan on top of the range; bang went a saucepan of milk beside it. Into the frying pan he put a lump of butter and into that he sliced very thin a couple of medium-sized onions. While the onions fried slowly and aromatically into soft brown richness, the milk was growing hot, and to it he added salt and ground pepper. He made a slice of crusty toast, put the onions in a bowl, laid the toast upon them, poured the scalding milk over all and added a liberal dusting of Parmesan cheese. It was all done so quickly that I scarcely had time to inquire for the health of Madame and pat the fox terrier by my side before the dish was on the table in front of me. The chef explained that if he had had chicken or beef consommé at hand he would have used these instead of the milk; personally I like the milk soup better and it is the easiest and quickest sustaining hot dish I know. Anyone can make it and everyone will devour it by the gallon. You need one large onion and a pint of milk for each person to be served. Don't let the onions fry too fast—they must be soft, just cooked through and a lovely golden brown in color.

And now for some dishes that are purely American. As a true Marylander let me tell you about a recipe for Maryland Crab Cakes—almost too good to be real—as made by a house so near a tidewater river that you can walk down to the dock and catch the crabs yourself and remain in hailing distance of the front porch. The crabs being caught, they must be boiled and the meat picked. Then into each pint of crab meat mix the slightly beaten yolk of one egg, one level teaspoon of salt, one-half teaspoon pepper, one-half teaspoon dry mustard, one tablespoon cream or mayonnaise and two teaspoons Worcestershire, or, if you don't like the flavor of Worcestershire, use very dry sherry or rye whisky instead. If the mixture seems dry, just add a little bit more cream or mayonnaise.

When well mixed shape into flat cakes, dip in flour, then into beaten egg and sauté in hot fat, butter by preference, but whatever it is be sure it is fresh and sweet. This amount of mix will only make four or five cakes, barely enough for two hungry people. Canned crab meat may be used if fresh is unavailable and will require the same amount of ingredients. These crab cakes are blander in flavor than deviled crabs, but if your taste calls for a higher seasoning simply increase the pepper and mustard and add a dash of cayenne.

A very sophisticated and unusual dish is Mushroom Fritter, which is not a true fritter, but large fine mushrooms dipped into batter and fried in deep fat. My friend who serves these has a wonderful but temperamental man cook and he is very proud of his skill and kind about giving his recipes. The batter for the mushrooms is made of one cup of milk, one-half cup flour, one-half teaspoon salt, pinch of dry mustard, two eggs, whipped well together with egg beater. (I think he put in a bit of grated nutmeg, too.) You need one pound large mushrooms, stems cut off but not peeled. Wash if brown and wipe excess water off. Dip mushrooms in batter, covering thoroughly, drop into pan of hot fat and remove when golden brown and *tender*. Place on brown paper to absorb grease. Serve on hot platter with tartar sauce to which has been added some grated horse-radish. This dish actually requires no sauce and makes a fine main course for luncheon, or can be served at dinner in place of a starchy vegetable. It needs a skilled cook as well as very fresh fine mushrooms and I wouldn't advise a beginner to try it.

Something much simpler and homelier are Sausages in Blankets which a country friend of mine sometimes gives her guests on cold days. They are her own idea and were designed to make a meager supply of sausages go a long way. First fry your sausages and pour off the fat, leaving the brown residue in the pan; keep both sausages and residue hot. Now make plain pancakes either of white or buckwheat flour, using a good mix and following the recipe on the box. Roll each sausage in a pancake and put on a hot platter in a neat row. Add a little boiling water, a dash of salt if needed and plenty of pepper to that brown crust in the frying pan, let it boil up and stir and scrape with a spoon into a rough pan gravy, dark and full of flavor. Pour over the pancake rolls and run to the table with it. It's easy and hearty for a winter brunch. Economical, too.

This recipe naturally leads me to thoughts of other pancakes which are always a great helper-outer in emergencies. One of the favorite desserts of my childhood was a pancake into which had been stirred before cooking a quantity of small sweet blackberries. This was accompanied by a thin transparent sauce flavored with wine and lemon. In some parts of New England, big pancakes are buttered and heaped into a celestial sort of layer cake with melting ripe blueberries and granulated maple sugar between the layers. More sugar is lavished on the top and I am told that there are some people who gild this flower of culinary art by pouring cream over it, though I can't believe it needs it.

My vivacious old friend Maria Magruder Wolfe, who, going abroad at eighty, opened the liner's Gala Ball by dancing with the Captain, gave me this recipe for Date Cupcakes which has been used many times in my kitchen and never fails no matter who makes them. To one cup of cut-up dates (or raisins or figs) add one teaspoon baking soda and pour on one cup of hot water. Mix and let cool. Mix one-half cup shortening with one scant cup of sugar and one and one-half cups of flour, two eggs slightly beaten and a pinch of salt. Then add the fruit, soda and water mix and beat just enough to blend well. Bake in greased muffin pans in a moderate—but not slow—oven. These cakes do not dry out quickly because of the fruit. You can skimp on sugar or use granulated maple sugar if you can get it—which you probably can't.

The best, bar none, amateur man cook I know is Karl G. Pfeiffer, Ph.D., a Professor of Literature at New York University, also a writer of learned articles (not about cooking) in many national magazines. When Dr. Pfeiffer goes into the kitchen and takes charge he cooks better and more quickly than most professionals. Should he ever invite you to dinner, don't walk but *run, race, fly!* By special request he has given me for this book two of his best numbers—but what am I saying?—*all* of his numbers are his best. Here is his Baked Tomatoes, Sweet and Hot. "Choose firm ripe tomatoes, one per person, and peel by dunking them into boiling water. Set them close together in a pan, stem-side up. In another saucepan put brown sugar, one half to three quarters of a cup—add about one-fourth cup water and a dozen or so dried red peppers, the small hot kind, bring to a boil and pour over the tomatoes. Bake slowly for three quarters of an hour, basting frequently. Be sure to remove from oven before they break. If sauce seems too thin, pour off carefully, boil down and return to tomatoes. About twenty minutes before serving time add a quantity of diced green pepper. The sauce should be thick, but it takes skill to have it that way."

And here is Karl Pfeiffer's recipe for *Potage Chantilly,* also in his own words: "I got this recipe from a dining car chef, the last place you expect to get good food. It seems to me a natural yet I have never been served it elsewhere. It is an excellent soup when made the most expensive way but a mediocre one if you skimp or make with any but good ripe tomatoes. Make a rich chicken stock. Get rid of most, but not quite all of the fat. Into this stock put a quantity of firm ripe peeled fresh tomatoes—about three good-sized ones to about a quart of stock. Simmer for half an hour or so, add about a cup of cream, heavy cream if you don't mind getting fat. Put the whole through a blender if you have one. If you haven't, mix thoroughly and strain. Season. Made properly this is a wonderful soup. Otherwise it is no better than what people think it is when it comes to table—cream of tomato!" And there, my friends, you have a Doctor of Philosophy on Tomato Soup!

This is a very mixed bag of recipes, but take it on the word of one who isn't a good cook but is certainly an appreciative eater—they are all worth trying.

Adelaide Heilner's Canapé Seawood
(for 6–8)

First, hard boil 4 large eggs, boiling them gently for 15 minutes. Plunge into cold water and remove the shells.

From slices of fresh, soft, white bread sliced thin, cut out 32 rounds, 2 inches in diameter. Slice about 6 small ripe but firm tomatoes in not too thick slices. Using the same-sized cutter as for the bread, cut the centers out of each slice of tomato. Spread these out on a large plate. Sprinkle them with salt and coarsely ground black pepper and let them drain a bit.

Now spread all of the rounds of bread generously with mayonnaise.

Lay a slice of tomato on half of them and use the rest of the rounds to cover, making thereby 16 tomato sandwiches.

Now, remove the yolks from the whites of the hard-boiled eggs. Rub the whites through a coarse sieve, using a wooden spoon. Then over a separate bowl, rub the yolks through the same sieve.

Place the powdered yolks and the whites in separate piles on 2 pieces of waxed paper. Have ready 8 small plates.

Now spread the top of all the tomato sandwiches with more mayonnaise, and sprinkle over half of them, half of the yolks, and over the other half, half of the whites. Now transfer a yellow and a white sandwich to each little plate, placing them egg side down. The next process is to coat the top of each with another layer of mayonnaise and a sprinkle of white and a sprinkle of yolk, completing the sandwiches. These are slightly sticky but delicious and I have found this the best way to accomplish making them. As a final pretty touch, garnish with tiny green stars cut from green peppers. Make these as soon before serving as possible, but if they must be made ahead of time, cover them with waxed paper or chef's foil, and keep in refrigerator until ready to serve, as the yolks exposed to the air for too long will darken, which would be a calamity.

Aimée Evans' Mozzarella in Carroza
(for 6–8)

Have ready 8 small individual shallow casseroles, rubbed lightly with olive oil. Remove crusts from 10 slices of coarsish whole or cracked wheat bread, then cut each in 4 pieces, making 4 squares. Spread some paper toweling on a tray, and light your oven and set it at 450° F.

Slice ½ pound Mozzarella cheese in ¼-inch slices (the kind kept in cold water in Italian stores or, if unobtainable, substitute the pear-shaped kind). Cut each slice in two, making squares of cheese the same size as the squares of toast. You should have 40 squares of bread and 32 squares of cheese.

Heat 5 tablespoons good olive oil in a small 6-inch frying pan. When smoking hot, drop 3 or 4 squares of bread into the oil and turn over almost immediately with a fork, to brown lightly on both sides. Drain on paper toweling and repeat the process until all the bread is browned.

When cool, spread both sides of the croutons ever so lightly with an-chovy paste. Alternate 5 croutons with 4 squares of cheese, forming 8 elongated sandwiches securing them together with toothpicks at both ends. Place in the oiled casseroles until ready to bake. In the meantime, melt ¼ pound sweet butter and stir it into 3 scant tablespoons anchovy paste.

When ready to serve and when the guests are assembling at table, place the casseroles into the preheated hot 450° F. oven and bake for about 5 minutes or until the cheese begins to run out. Pour a little of the hot melted butter and anchovy sauce over each and send to table immediately as the cheese congeals in seconds and the Carroza should be eaten im-mediately.

Karl Pfeiffer's Potage Chantilly
(for 6–8)

Wash a 4- or 5-pound fowl cut up as for fricassee, put it to soak with ½ pound of ham for an hour in 3 quarts cold water. Put on the fire and bring slowly to a boil. Skim and add 2 large carrots, 2 leeks or 1 large onion, 2 stalks of celery, some parsley and very little salt and pepper to taste. Simmer gently for 3 hours. Strain, cool and remove some of the fat. Reduce the broth by boiling until you have 5 cups of it left. Peel 4 large juicy red, ripe, garden tomatoes and remove as many seeds as pos-sible. Add them to the broth and simmer for about ½ hour. Remove from fire and cool partially.

Place ½ the mixture in your electric blender and add ½ cup heavy cream. Beat until well blended. Pour into top part of enamel double boiler. Repeat the process using the rest of the soup and another ½ cup heavy cream. Add to the first lot and you should have about 7 cups of pale pink tomato soup. Season to taste with additional salt and pepper and place when cool in refrigerator until ready to heat for serving. To heat, place the pan over boiling water and heat until scalding hot. Serve at once.

Note: *If by any chance you happen to have 2 fine carcasses of roast chicken left over some time, they may be used as a very good sub-stitute for the chicken broth given above. Proceed as follows: Place all the bones in a large pan. Cover with 3 quarts cold water.*

Add 5 or 6 big stalks celery, 3 carrots peeled and quartered, 1 large Bermuda onion peeled and quartered, a sprig of parsley and salt and pepper to taste. Place on low flame and bring gently to a boil. Stand by and skim carefully, then simmer gently for about 2 hours, or until reduced to about 5 cups. Remove from fire, strain and cool, and use to make the above Potage Chantilly.

La Providence Milk Onion Soup
(for 6–8)

Cut 16 slices French bread. Peel 12 large onions, quarter them and slice very thin. Put 3 quarts milk in a large pan ready to be heated. Prepare 1½ cups grated Parmesan cheese. Place ¼ pound butter in a large frying pan. Melt it and add the sliced onions. Cook over low flame, stirring constantly with wooden spoon until the onions are transparent and a pale golden brown or for about 10–12 minutes. Heat the milk until scalding hot, stirring it so that it won't form a scum. Toast the bread, lightly on both sides. Place the toast in a bread basket. Put 1 teaspoon salt and ½ teaspoon pepper in a soup tureen with a small lump of butter and pour into it the scalding hot milk. Place the onions in a serving dish and send to table. Place 2 slices of toast in each deep soup plate and top each piece of toast with a spoonful of onions, and fill the plate with hot milk. Pass the grated cheese to be sprinkled over the top by each person as his taste requires.

Gazpacho—Stolen
(for 6–8)

Prepare 4 big tablespoons mixed chopped fresh herbs such as parsley, chives, basil, dill, marjoram, savory, etc. Add 2 small cloves garlic either chopped fine or extract their juice using a little garlic juice extractor sold especially for the purpose.

Peel 6 large ripe juicy tomatoes, dipping them in boiling water for a second or two to facilitate the removal of the skins. Cut them crosswise in half and remove as many seeds as possible, then chop them roughly and add them to the herbs. Also wash, stem, and quarter 2 big sweet green or red peppers, and chop them fine and add to the other ingredients. Now, using a potato masher, crush the whole together and add gradually the juice of 2 lemons and 1 cup olive oil, until the mixture is a paste. Now stir in 4 cans concentrated consommé thinned with 2 cups water, or substitute 6 cups homemade clear chicken broth. Season to taste with salt and coarsely ground black pepper. Add 2 cups cucumber, peeled, seeded, and chopped fine, and 1 Bermuda onion, peeled and chopped fine, and 2 tablespoons of the hearts of celery chopped fine likewise. Chill 4 hours before serving, accompanied by homemade toasted bread crumbs, rolled not too fine; these to be sprinkled on at table, or serve with this soup a big bowl of sour cream.

Note: *Unless you can procure really good garden tomatoes, substitute a 2-pound 3-ounce can of Italian pear-shaped tomatoes flavored with basil and omit the 2 cups water.*

Mary Elizabeth Taylor's Amalfi Lasagne à la Mrs. Pistone
(for 6–8)

First make the sauce. Chop fine 1 medium-sized onion and cook it until lightly browned in 3 tablespoons good olive oil, in a large heavy aluminum frying pan. Add 1 pound of top round of beef ground as for hamburgers. Brown the meat lightly, distributing it over the bottom of the pan. Turn it over with a pancake turner. Don't cook it too hard nor too fast. When it is just beginning to brown lightly, add a large can (2 pound 3 ounces) Italian-style pear-shaped tomatoes seasoned with basil. Also add 1 6-ounce can Italian tomato paste. Stir well, then add 2 whole peeled cloves of garlic, a pinch of thyme, 1 teaspoon oregano, 1 teaspoon chopped parsley, 1 bay leaf, 1 teaspoon coarsely ground black pepper, and salt to taste (about 1 generous teaspoon). Cover and simmer gently, stirring frequently, for 2 hours. Fish out the garlic and discard it.

In a separate small frying pan, cook slowly for ½ hour about ½ pound Italian sausage, pricking it all over with a fork, so that the fat will cook out of it. Do not use the hot kind of sausage known as pepperoni, as the flavor is too strong. Remove from fire and when cool enough to handle, split it lengthwise and scrape out the sausage meat, discarding the skin. Crumble the sausage into little pieces.

Place a great big pot containing 6 quarts water on the fire to boil. Have ready besides the sauce and the sausage, 1 pound ricotta (Italian cheese of the cottage-cheese type), ½ pound Italian Mozzarella cheese cut in thin slices, and about 1 cup of freshly grated imported Parmesan. And if you can get it, a few fresh basil leaves. Rub a large rectangular baking dish, approximately 12 by 8 by 2½ inches deep with olive oil. Add 2 tablespoons olive oil to the boiling water and season to taste with salt. When boiling hard, add piece by piece without breaking, ¾ of a 1-pound package lasagne (preferably Ronzoni lasagne). These are an extra wide broad-ribbed Italian paste resembling noodles. Cook for 25 minutes separating the noodles one from the other with a big wooden spoon—if they show signs of sticking together. Remove from fire when done and drain immediately, pouring an extra quart hot water over them to rinse them well. When well drained, and cool enough to handle, but still warm, cover the bottom of the baking dish with 5 strips of the lasagne laid lengthwise. On this lay 6 slices of the Mozzarella cheese and interspace with about ¼ of the ricotta cheese. Next sprinkle ¼ of the sausage over the cheese and spread ¼ of the sauce over all, and sprinkle with 3 tablespoons grated Parmesan cheese. Lay 1 or 2 leaves fresh basil on the sauce, if you were able to get some, otherwise just skip it. Repeat the layer-laying process 4 times ending up with a coating of the sauce, sprinkled generously with Parmesan cheese. Trickle a little olive oil over the surface, or dot with butter and place in preheated 400° F. oven and bake about ½ hour or until bubbling hot and nicely browned. Remove from oven and allow the dish to stand for about 5 minutes before serving as this brings out the flavor and the consistency is improved. Garnish with chopped parsley and serve on hot plates, accompanied by a dry full-bodied red wine and a green salad dressed with French dressing and chopped parsley and tarragon.

Marte's Heavenly Squash
(for 6–8)

Peel 8 large tender yellow squash. Cut lengthwise in quarters and remove seeds. Cut in thin slivers, sprinkle with salt and let stand for 1 hour. A *lot of juice will form. Drain this off, then place squash in a clean tea cloth and gently squeeze, to extract even more juice. Prepare ⅔ cup coarsely grated onion. Cook the onion in ¼ pound butter until a light golden brown, then sprinkle with 2 scant teaspoons good paprika, stir well, then add the squash and another 4 tablespoons butter and cook for a minute or two, stirring lightly. Then season to taste with salt and a little pepper, and sprinkle with 2 tablespoons finely chopped fresh dill and 2 generous teaspoons vinegar. (Pickled dill or finely powdered dried dill may be substituted for the fresh.) Simmer for about 15 minutes or until squash tastes done, being careful to stir occasionally lightly with a fork. Just before serving, add about 1 cup sour cream thinned with just a little sweet cream, and cook about 3 minutes longer or until heated through. Serve at once accompanied or not with fluffy mashed potatoes, or warmed French bread.*

Drexel's Mushroom Fritters
(for 6–8)

For this recipe it is essential that the mushrooms be perfect, fresh and white, and of fairly equal size, about the size of a walnut. Allow at least 3 or 4 to a person. Wash, stem, and dry each one separately on a cloth. Sprinkle the heart of each with a little salt and coarsely ground black pepper.

Now make the following batter. Separate the yolks from the whites of 2 eggs. Beat the yolks with a small beater and add ½ teaspoon salt, a pinch dry mustard and a pinch nutmeg, then stir in ⅓ cup milk. Stir in gradually 1 cup pastry flour to make a smooth batter. Then add another ⅓ cup milk. Beat the whites of the 2 eggs until stiff and fold them into the egg mixture.

Have ready a deep French frying pan with 3 pounds melted vegetable shortening. Heat to 360°–375° F. Dip each mushroom into the batter and with a fork drop into the hot fat, cooking not more than 4 or 5 at a time. Cook them until brown on bottom and roll over with fork, and cook until brown on other side or for about 2–3 minutes in all. Place on paper towel to drain, in warm place, until all have been fried and serve at once, on hot platter, with tartar sauce.

As a variation the mushrooms may be marinated for ½ hour in a tart French dressing made of tarragon vinegar, salt, pepper and seasoned with fresh chopped tarragon.

Karl Pfeiffer's Tomatoes Sweet and Hot
(for 6–8)

Dip 12 large, ripe, juicy tomatoes into boiling water and peel. Place them stem side up in a large baking dish and bake for 1 hour in 475° to 500° F. At this point drain off into a little pan all the juice and add to the juice ½ cup water, ¾ cup light brown sugar, 12 hot red pepper pods, and boil for 10 minutes. Strain this over the tomatoes and bake again for 25 to 30 minutes. At this point, sprinkle with salt and pepper and 1 fresh green pepper (seeds removed) chopped fine. Reduce heat of oven to 400° F. and continue baking the tomatoes 30 to 40 minutes longer. Watch the tomatoes carefully during the whole cooking process and do not allow them to burn. The result should be of a delectable caramelized tomato jam consistency, but is served as a vegetable with or without meat as an accompaniment.

Mlle. Blanchard's Lenten Tomatoes and Rice
(for 6–8)

For this you will need a quart good chicken broth, preferably homemade. Proceed as for Potage Chantilly (page 82), but it is unnecessary to boil the chicken broth down as long as for that recipe. Once the chicken is done, drain off 4 cups of the broth, and leave the rest on the chicken to prevent its drying out. Right now we are concentrating on tomatoes and rice.

Wash 10 large juicy ripe tomatoes and cut off the stem end, cutting down into the tomatoes to form sizable hollows. Place upside down on plate to drain while you prepare 3 generous tablespoons chopped parsley. Peel 2 large cloves garlic. Wash 1⅓ cups long grain rice in cold water and place it in a saucepan. Cover the rice with 1 quart cold water. Place on fire and bring to a lively boil, then remove from fire and drain well. Now place the drained tomatoes cut side up in a large oval baking dish large enough to hold them all firmly together. Sprinkle the center of each with salt and coarsely ground black pepper, then fill the centers with the par-boiled rice, filling them level full. Sprinkle over them the 2 cloves garlic chopped fine or better still put through a garlic press. Now pour over all 1 quart good strong chicken broth, being sure that the rice is well mois-tened. Next, with scissors, cut 6-8 strips of good lean bacon into small pieces and sprinkle them evenly over all, being sure the rice is covered with bacon. Last of all sprinkle lightly with a little salt and pepper and 2 tablespoons previously prepared chopped parsley, keeping out 1 table-spoon for garnishing just before serving.

Cover the dish with chef's foil or with a cover to fit the dish and place in preheated, very hot 500° to 550° F. oven to come to the boiling point, then reduce the heat to 450° F. and continue baking moderately fast until the rice is tender or for about 1 hour. At this point, remove the cover and continue baking until the rice and bacon begin to brown nicely and the broth has been mostly absorbed, or for about 20 minutes longer. Sprinkle with green chopped parsley before serving.

Hard-Boiled Eggs with Grandmother Schaffner's Boiled Dressing
(for 6–8)

Prepare 3 tablespoons finely chopped onion and 6 tablespoons finely cut celery.

Hard boil 10 eggs in the usual manner. Plunge them in cold water to cool rapidly. Remove shells, and place in a pretty serving dish. Cover with the following dressing:

Put the yolks of 3 eggs in a little enamel pan. In a separate little enamel pan, heat 3 tablespoons vinegar until steaming hot but not boiling. Beat the yolks slightly and stir in the hot vinegar slowly. Place pan over very low flame and stir vigorously and constantly while cooking, until thick or for about 1 minute. Remove from fire. In a separate bowl place 2 table-spoons butter. Cream it with 1½ teaspoons granulated sugar, ¼ teaspoon salt and ½ teaspoon coarsely ground black pepper. Add the prepared chopped onion and celery and mix well. Now stir into this gradually the *egg and vinegar mixture. Mix the whole together with a spoon and let it cool.*

Now beat until stiff, ½ cup heavy cream, and fold it into the cooled mixture and last of all, fold in ½ cup mayonnaise. Pour over the hard-boiled eggs and chill until ready to serve, at which time garnish with chopped parsley.

Minny Cover's Crab Cakes
(for 6–8)

Make a heavy cream sauce by melting 3 tablespoons butter and adding to it 3 tablespoons flour. Cook a minute or two, stirring constantly, then add gradually 1 cup milk, to make a smooth thick sauce. Season to taste with salt and a dash of cayenne. Pick over 2 cups (1 pound) cooked crab meat. Season to taste with very little salt, a little pepper, and ¼ teaspoon dry mustard, then add the sauce and stir well. Cool and chill for several hours.

When ready to cook, form into 12 flat cakes about ½-inch thick. Roll both sides and edges in bread crumbs. Melt ¼ pound butter in big iron frying pan and when sizzling hot add the cakes. Cook about 3 minutes on either side until a rich golden brown. Serve immediately on hot platter garnished with parsley and accompanied by tartar sauce to which has been added a little grated horse-radish.

Cheese Popovers—Stolen
(for 6–8)

Grate American cheese until you have ⅛ cup. Butter copiously 18 little junior popover tins. Beat 1 egg well. Add ½ cup milk, and stir in ½ cup sifted all-purpose flour and ⅛ teaspoon salt. Beat with rotary beater well. Then add ⅛ cup grated cheese and beat again with rotary beater. Fill the tins half full with the mixture. Place in cold oven, light the oven and set it at 400° F. and bake for about 25 minutes or until a golden brown. Remove from oven and run a knife carefully around the edge and lift out of pans and serve immediately.

Tartines of Roquefort—Stolen
(for 6–8)

Cream 6 ounces good imported Roquefort cheese with 6 tablespoons sweet butter. Slice a loaf of 1 day old whole wheat bread as thin as possible, making 24 slices. Trim off the crusts with a sharp knife. Spread 18 of them with the Roquefort mix. Pile these 3 deep making 6 triple-decker sandwiches. Top with the remaining 6 slices plain bread. Place on a flat tin on waxed paper. Cover with waxed paper, and cover with another tin. Place in refrigerator to chill, weighting it down with anything suitable such as 2 pounds butter or a heavy plate the idea being to press the bread well together.

When ready to serve, cut each sandwich in 3 strips, using a very sharp knife so that the edges will be nice and sharp and neat. Serve as soon as possible after cutting. Makes 18 tartines.

Hot Cheese Tartines—Stolen
(for 6–8)

Trim crusts from 6 slices white bread. Cut each slice in 4, making 24 squares. Melt 3 tablespoons butter and dip both sides of each square lightly into the butter. Place on cookie sheet, ready to be toasted.

Cream 2 packages Kraft's Philadelphia cream cheese with 2 tablespoons heavy cream and stir in 2 tablespoons red wine vinegar. Open a small 4-ounce can pimentos and cut 1 of them very fine into tiny pieces. Wash 1 small green pepper, remove seeds and stems and cut into tiny slivers and then again crosswise to make tiny squares. Add both the pimentos and green pepper to the cream cheese, and season to taste with a little salt and coarsely ground black pepper.

Shortly before you will be ready to serve the tartines, light the oven and set it at 450° F. When hot, place the cookie sheet of buttered bread into the oven and bake until lightly browned or for about 5 minutes. Remove from oven and cool slightly, then spread the croutons with the cream cheese mixture, piling it on thick. Place pan in preheated 450° F. oven and bake until lightly browned or for about 5 minutes. Serve immediately.

Julia Hunt's Marguerites
(for 6–8)

Place 24 saltine crackers on a cookie sheet. Chop ½ cup shelled English walnuts, in a wooden chopping bowl, until fine. Place 1 cup granulated sugar in a little saucepan. Moisten with ½ cup cold water. Bring to a boil, skim carefully, and boil until it forms a hard ball when a little is dropped into cold water or for about 7 minutes. Remove from fire. Add ⅟₁₆ teaspoon cream of tartar to 2 egg whites and beat until stiff. Then add the hot syrup gradually to the whites, beating constantly with a rotary beater. Unless you have an electric beater it will be helpful to have someone pour the syrup for you, while you beat. When nice and stiff, fold in 1 teaspoon vanilla and 1 teaspoon almond extract and the chopped nuts. Place a heaping teaspoonful on each cracker, using all the icing. Place in preheated 350°–375° F. moderate oven and bake until a delicate brown or for about 7 minutes. Serve soon after baking.

Pecan Macaroons—Stolen
(for 6–8)

Measure out 1 cup light brown sugar (well packed). Put ½ pound fresh, shelled, unsalted pecan meats through a nut grater, add a pinch of salt to the brown sugar and the powdered nuts. Moisten with the unbeaten white of 1 large egg and 1 teaspoon vanilla or almond extract. Stir well with wooden spoon. Form into small balls, and place on 2 well-buttered cookie sheets not too close together. Press into each one a small pecan meat. Place in preheated moderate 350°–375° F. oven and bake for about 10–12 minutes. Remove from pan with help of a spatula while still warm. Makes about 3 dozen.

Mrs. Wolfe's Date Cupcakes
(for 6–8)

Light your oven and set it at 350° F. Pit and cut into medium-sized pieces enough dates to make a full cup. Pour over them 1 cup boiling water in which you have dissolved 1 level teaspoon baking soda. Allow this to cool while you cream together ½ cup butter with a scant cup granulated sugar. Beat 2 eggs slightly and beat them into the butter and sugar. Sift in gradually 1½ cups unsifted all-purpose flour to which you have added 1 big pinch of salt. Butter 16 muffin tins well. When the dates and water have cooled, add them to the batter and mix well. The mixture will seem thin but it is correct. Fill your muffin tins with the mixture, place in preheated 350° F. oven and bake for about 30 minutes or until they test done.

Katherine Emmet's Orange Cake
(for 6–8)

Cream ½ cup butter with 1 cup granulated sugar and stir in ¼ cup boiling water. Add 2 unbroken yolks of eggs and beat well. Add slowly 1½ cups unsifted pastry flour sifted twice with 2 teaspoons baking powder and 1 pinch of salt, alternating it with 3 tablespoons cold water. Flavor with 1 teaspoon vanilla. Fold in the stiffly beaten whites, and place in 2 well-buttered and -floured 9-inch cake tins. Bake for 20 minutes in preheated 375° F. oven or until it tests done. Turn out on cake racks to cool.

Grate the rind of 1 California orange, and add it immediately to 1 pound confectioners' XXXX sugar, then add gradually the strained juice of ½ lemon and ½ orange, stopping when it is the right consistency to spread. It should be quite stiff.

Whip ½ cup cream and before it gets quite stiff, fold in 3 tablespoons of the sugar mixture. Place in refrigerator to chill, for ½ hour, then beat it well with the egg beater. Place 1 layer on a large cake plate and pile the cream on it. Spread the other layer with the sugar frosting. Lift it carefully onto the cream-topped one and serve immediately.

Election Cake—Stolen

Prepare, the night before making the cake, a yeast sponge in the following manner: Have ready 1 tablespoon soft butter. Add 1 tablespoon granulated sugar, ½ teaspoon salt, and stir in 1 cup warm water, and mix until butter is melted. Add 1 yeast cake and stir until completely dissolved. Add 2½ cups unsifted all-purpose flour and beat it with a wooden spoon until smooth and free from lumps. Cover and allow it to rise overnight.

The next morning butter copiously 2 large bread pans. Put 1 cup butter in a large bowl and stir until creamy and then stir in 2 cups light brown sugar. When well mixed add 4 whole eggs well beaten. Add 1 tablespoon grated lemon rind, 1 tablespoon strained lemon juice, and 2 cups seedless raisins.

Place in a sifter 1½ cups sifted all-purpose flour and add ½ teaspoon powdered clove, 1 teaspoon nutmeg, 1½ teaspoons baking soda and ½ teaspoon salt.

Now mix your yeast sponge into the brown sugar batter and stir well. Last of all sift in gradually the spiced flour. Beat thoroughly. Divide it equally into the 2 well-buttered bread pans. The pans should not be more than ½ full. Cover and place in a room temperature of 70° F. and allow it to rise 1 hour. Pour over each 2 tablespoons Bourbon whisky. Place in preheated 375° F. oven and bake about 45 minutes or until it tests done in the center with a cake tester. Turn out carefully onto cake racks and frost the tops only, while hot, with a thin coating of confectioners' icing made in the following manner:

Sift 1½ cups confectioners' sugar into a bowl, and add about 2–3 tablespoons hot milk, in which you have melted 1 teaspoon butter. Flavor with 1 teaspoon or more of Bourbon whisky and spread on cake.

Gingerbread—Stolen
(for 6–8)

First butter a shallow cake tin 11 by 7 by 1½ inches deep, and line it neatly with white paper, and butter the paper. Prepare ½ cup chopped English walnuts and ½ cup seeded, or seedless black raisins. Place 2 level table-spoons soft lard in a big bowl and add to it ⅔ cup molasses and ⅔ cup granulated sugar. Over this pour ⅔ cup boiling water in which you have dissolved 1 level teaspoon baking soda. Mix well and allow the mixture to cool. Light your oven and set it at 350° to 375° F. for a moderate temperature.

When the molasses mixture has cooled, add to it the nuts and the raisins and 1 teaspoon powdered cinnamon, 1 teaspoon ginger and ¼ teaspoon cloves. Mix and add 1 well-beaten egg, then stir in 1½ cups all-purpose flour, sifted once. Mix well and pour into the paper-lined tin. Place in preheated oven and bake until it tests done with an inserted cake tester or for about 40–45 minutes.

Turn out onto cake rack and remove paper carefully and invert it onto a flat serving platter and serve at once with plenty of slightly beaten heavy cream.

Mary Palmer's Apricot Turnovers
(for 6–8)

The night before the party, make the following pastry: Cream together until nice and soft and well mixed, ¾ cup sweet butter and 4½ ounces (1½ packages) of Kraft's Philadelphia cream cheese. Sift some pastry flour and measure out 2 cups of it. Add a big pinch of salt and sift it gradually into the cheese and butter mixture, using a fork. When all the flour has been added and the paste clings together, place it on a piece of heavy waxed paper and wrap it up, pressing on the paste to make it into a flat package. Place in refrigerator overnight.

Have ready some dried apricots which have been thoroughly washed in cold water, one by one, then soaked in cold water to cover for 2 hours. Place on moderate flame and cook for about 10 minutes or until tender, then add *1* cup granulated sugar and cook another 5 minutes. Strain off the syrup but keep it. Spread the apricots out on a flat platter to cool.

When ready to bake the turnovers, roll the paste out very thin and cut in 3-inch squares. Place *1* apricot half on each with *1* scant teaspoon of apricot jam and cover with a second apricot. Wet two edges of the square and fold the paste over to form a triangle, and with floured fork press the two edges together. Prick with fork in two places and place on lightly buttered tin. Place in preheated hot 400°–450° F. oven and bake about 15 minutes or until lightly browned. The jam will run out a bit but don't worry about it. When they are done, remove immediately from the tin with a pancake turner and place on a serving plate. In a minute or two, sprinkle them all copiously with confectioners' sugar in which you have kept a vanilla bean to give it the vanilla taste. This makes about 24 turnovers.

Blueberry Pancake Pies—Stolen
(for 6–8)

First grate on the coarse side of your grater, 12 ounces of maple sugar which usually comes in 3-ounce cakes.

Have ready 4 cups superior blueberries, washed, picked over and drained. Place in enamel pan and sprinkle over them scant cup granulated sugar. Place on low flame and bring gently to the boiling point, shaking the pan frequently so that the berries don't stick. Cook just long enough to make the sugar come to a syrup, or for about 3 minutes. The berries should remain almost whole. Keep warm, while you make the following batter:

Sift together 1½ cups flour, 1 teaspoon salt, 3 level teaspoons baking powder, 1 tablespoon granulated sugar and 1½ tablespoons cornmeal. Beat 3 eggs well with 1½ cups milk. Add slowly to the flour mixture and beat until smooth. Stir in 4½ tablespoons melted butter.

For 6–8 people it will be best to make two servings—or two pies. To do this, cook 3 large pancakes, using 4 serving spoons of batter for each, on a hot griddle, very lightly buttered. Turn these over just once. Keep them warm until the 3 are made.

Heat the blueberries slightly. Place *1* pancake on a hot round serving platter, dot with butter, cover with ¼ of the berries, sprinkle copiously *with grated maple sugar, cover with another pancake, more butter and another ¼ of the blueberries, more sugar and top with the third pancake. Sprinkle top with more maple sugar and send to table to be cut in 6–8 pieces and eaten immediately with plenty of heavy cream. In the meantime, repeat the process and make the second pie and serve.*

Amanda Kerr's Pancakes with Blackberries and Wine and Lemon Sauce
(for 6–8)

Pick over carefully 3 pints ripe blackberries. Wash and drain. Add 2 tablespoons cold water, place on low flame and cook, stirring constantly until the blackberries are soft. Sweeten to taste with about 1½ cups granulated sugar, bring to a boil and cook about 10 minutes, or until the syrup has thickened. Keep warm over boiling water until ready to use. Make recipe for wine and lemon sauce as below and keep this warm.

Prepare twice the recipe for plain pancakes (page 123). Make 6 extra-large 8-inch pancakes, keeping them warm in the oven until all are made. When ready to serve the pancakes, make 2 separate 3-layer cakes with stewed blackberries between. Sprinkle top pancake with confectioners' sugar in which you have kept a vanilla bean and serve at once, accompanied by the wine and lemon sauce in a separate bowl. Cut in pie-shaped pieces at table and serve.

Wine and Lemon Sauce
(for 6–8)

Grate the rind of 3 big lemons and add to it ⅓ cup strained lemon juice. Place ¾ cup granulated sugar in the top part of an enamel double boiler and stir into it 1½ tablespoons cornstarch. Moisten with 1½ cups good dry white wine. Place on low flame and bring to a boil stirring constantly until thickened. Place over boiling water, cover and cook 15 minutes. Remove from fire and add the prepared grated lemon rind and lemon juice, and 4 tablespoons butter. Stir until the butter has melted. Reheat over boiling water before serving.

Berta Mueller's Lemon Pudding
(for 6–8)

Butter a 2-quart round Pyrex baking dish. Light your oven and set it at 350° F. Grate the rind of 1 lemon and pour over it immediately 5 tablespoons strained lemon juice. Cream 2 tablespoons butter with 1 cup granulated sugar. Separate the yolks from the whites of 3 eggs. Beat the yolks of 3 eggs and add them to the butter and sugar. Stir in the lemon juice and rind and 1½ cups milk. Place 4 tablespoons flour in a sifter with pinch of salt and stir it into the mixture. Last of all beat the whites of the 3 eggs until stiff and fold them into the mixture. Pour into the well-buttered baking dish, set the dish in a shallow pan of hot water and place in preheated 350° F. oven and bake for about 45 minutes, until a beautiful golden brown. Serve at once with or without cream and confectioners' sugar. Double the recipe and bake in 2 dishes for a party of 8.

Won Kim's Apricot Pudding
(for 6–8)

Strain off the juice from 1 pint-sized can of apricots (the pitted, unpeeled, halved variety) but save the juice.

Melt 1½ tablespoons butter in a little pan and add ½ cup granulated sugar. Mix and place on low flame and simmer for 10 minutes. Spread out evenly over the bottom of an oblong Pyrex baking dish, 10 by 6½ by 2 inches deep (1½-quart size). Now light your oven and set it at 375° F. Cream together ½ cup butter and ½ cup granulated sugar. Beat 1 small egg well and beat it into the butter and sugar. Measure ½ cup buttermilk and stir into it ¼ teaspoon baking soda. Sift together 1 cup all-purpose flour with 1½ teaspoons baking powder and add it alternately with the buttermilk to the first mixture, beating it just enough to make a smooth batter.

Spread this evenly over the apricots and place in preheated, moderate 375° F. oven and bake for 30–35 minutes or until it tests done in the center, when an inserted cake tester comes out clean.

Serve at once accompanied by a bowl of stiffly beaten heavy cream into which you have stirred 2 tablespoons apricot brandy and ¼ cup of the apricot juice.

Amanda Kerr's Blackberry Mush
(for 6–8)

Wash 2 quarts ripe blackberries and drain well. Place in enamel pan and sprinkle with 1⅓ cups granulated sugar. Moisten with 2 cups cold water. Place on fire and bring to a boil, and skim carefully. Simmer for 5 minutes. Remove from fire and pour off 1 cup juice. Cool this juice partially, then pour it gradually onto 4 scant tablespoons cornstarch, and stir until smooth and free from lumps. Now pour it gradually into the blackberries, and place back on fire to cook, stirring constantly, until well thickened or for about 1½ minutes. Remove from fire and pour into mold, cool and chill. Run knife around the edge, and turn out onto serving dish. Serve with cream.

Julia Hunt's Sweet Rice Cream
(for 6–8)

First, blanch ¾ cup almonds by pouring boiling water over them and allowing them to stand for 2–3 minutes, then, after pinching off the skins wash and dry them on a cloth. Spread out on a plate and let them dry for an hour or so, then reduce them to a fine powder in a nut grater.

Now wash thoroughly, 1 cup rice and place in top part of large enamel double boiler. Add 1½ quarts whole milk, cover and cook over boiling water, stirring occasionally, for 20 minutes. Then add ½ cup granulated sugar, ¼ teaspoon salt and the powdered almonds. Cover and continue cooking, stirring occasionally until the rice tastes done, or for about 25–35 minutes longer. It will be still quite soupy but will thicken up when cold. Flavor after it has cooled with ½ teaspoon each of good lemon and vanilla extract and orange-flower water.

You will have a luscious creamy mixture which may be eaten as a sort of ethereal rice pudding or used to dress up any plain stewed fruit. If you can't obtain orange-flower water, use ½ teaspoon grated orange rind, but orange-flower water is better.

Dr. Francis Trudeau's Favorite Orange Marmalade Soufflés
(for 6–8)

The only trouble with this dessert is that for 6 or 8 people you have to have 2 large enamel double boilers, 2-quart size, preferably ones with the top parts having rounded bottoms. Butter the insides of the tops well with butter and sprinkle with granulated sugar so that they are both well buttered and sugared. Beat the whites of 8 eggs until stiff, then beat in gradually 8 tablespoons granulated sugar. When very stiff, fold in a little vanilla and 1 cup orange marmalade. Place in tops, dividing the mixture equally. Place both over boiling water. Cover tightly with their lids and cook ½ hour. At this time, the meringue should have risen to the top of the pans. Remove the lids and place the tops directly over moderate flames and allow them to stay there for about 1 minute. This is to brown the soufflés lightly, so that when they are turned out onto hot platters they will be a beautiful golden color and have a slightly crusty outer surface. To turn them out, run a sharp knife around the edge of each to separate it from the pan. Turn out immediately on hot round platters. Serve with sauce made of yolks of 2 eggs beaten with ½ cup granulated sugar, seasoned well with brandy, and just before serving, fold in 1 cup heavy cream whipped until stiff.

Emmy Reynolds's Lemon Mousse
(for 6–8)

Grate the rind of 2 lemons and add to it immediately their strained juice. Stir in 1½ cups granulated sugar, then stir in 2 cups milk. Now beat with a rotary beater, until not quite stiff, 2 cups extra heavy cream. Fold it into the first mixture and place in large freezing tray in your electric refrigerator, having first spilt just a little water under the tray—to help the freezing along a bit. Turn the control to coldest and allow the mousse to remain undisturbed until partially frozen, or for about 1½ hours, then scrape down the sides and mix well with a spoon and allow it to freeze until solid. This will take about 6 hours.

If you prefer, the mixture may be frozen in the usual manner in a hand freezer with salt and ice; or if you are the proud possessor of an electric freezer tray for your refrigerator, by all means use it as it freezes more smoothly and quickly and should be ready to serve in 2 hours.

Oriental Sauce—Stolen
(for 6–8)

Stem and wash 1 quart ripe strawberries. Slice and sweeten them to taste with about ½ cup powdered sugar. Grate the rind of 1 large orange and sprinkle over the strawberries. Squeeze a few drops of lime juice over all and stir in lightly a small glass of currant jelly beaten soft with a fork. Now beat 1 cup cream until stiff and fold it into the other ingredients, and send to table to be served with vanilla ice cream.

Maryland Jellied Mixed Pickles

You can use this recipe for jellied chowchow, mustard or other pickles which are chopped small, and it makes them much more easy and attractive to serve. Soak 1 envelope plain gelatin in ½ cup cold water. Drain off the juice from a pint-sized bottle of chowchow or mustard pickle, heat this juice and add enough boiling water to make 1 cup in all. Add the gelatin and stir until dissolved, then add the drained pickle, stir well, pour into mold, cool and chill until set. Slice and serve, or use as garnish around cold meat.

FIVE

La Quiche Lorraine

This is a story of Paris in the summer of 1938, the story of a wedding luncheon, with a context of true love and happiness and good feeling and good living. It is a story without social consciousness, with no implication of world affairs, and no moral to point. Of it I may say, as Virgil did of far more important matters: "All of this I saw, part of this I was."

I was one of two American godmothers to a little French girl, and in 1938 we went to Paris to attend our godchild's wedding. There were many small festivities and this luncheon was one of the pleasantest. It was given by the groom's parents just after the civil ceremony at the *mairie*. The apartment was directly across the street from that corner of the *Jardin des Plantes* where grows the historic cedar brought by Buffon from Syria and the great tree might—may still I hope—be seen from the front windows. The family lived on the second floor and there was an elevator, but when the godmothers looked at it they felt it might be better to walk upstairs. So they did and were warmly welcomed.

The apartment might have made a picture in the genre of Renoir or Alfred Stevens. The salon, dining room and hall had a high wainscot painted white, and the walls above this wainscot were papered in mingled light gray and white, giving space and unity to the three rooms which opened together with wide doors. The salon had a figured rug, chairs upholstered in rose velvet and one in tapestry, some small tables and a couple of small hassocks. There was also an upright piano, its back hung with folds of purplish silk, which stood meekly at one side. The pictures were mostly family photographs, one of the groom's twin brother now absent in Senegal, and others of his brother's wife and two sons. There was one of the groom, aged sixteen, on a vacation bicycle, very much *le sport*.

When we were all in the salon we added up to twelve: the groom's parents, Mama tall, dark and vivacious, Papa with an oddly Irish face and figure; a sardonic Monsieur H. with a stunning blonde wife who was a hypochondriac rejoicing in her symptoms; the bride's widowed mother and her brother Uncle L., a silent, gentle soul; a couple of middle-aged, handsome and merry cousins; the bride and groom; and the American godmothers. Mild *apéritifs* were poured, Byrrh, vermouth and port. There was no hurrying over these but the godmothers felt a certain backstage anxiety and bother—it seemed that the special waiter hired for the occasion hadn't turned up and Mama was having the sort of qualms American hostesses know in such difficulties.

When the *apéritifs* were disposed of everyone went into the dining room. The table was covered with heavy white damask. There was a large oval centerpiece of tiny sweet white roses and on the big, light fruit-wood sideboard there was another bowl of roses, blush pink with strong red-tinged foliage. The china was clear white with bright red and blue borders in a modern design, very smart. There were small glass bars at each place to rest knife and fork when plates were changed, fresh silver was not brought with each course. Because of the special waiter's defection, the luncheon was served by an elderly maid, a typical *bonne à tout faire,* in light gray calico blouse, and black skirt, big apron, sleeves rolled up, very slow, very unprofessional but giving a nice homey touch.

At each place there was a folded card with silver edges and within, in a fine slanting hand, the menu was written. Here it is exactly as it appeared:

LA LANGOUSTE À LA PARISIENNE

LA QUICHE LORRAINE

LE POULET DE BRESSE

LES HARICOTS VERTS

LES POMMES DE TERRE

COEUR DE LAITUE

LA TERRINE DE FOIES GRAS DU PERIGORD

LES FROMAGES

LA GLACE SIMONNE

FRAISES DES BOIS AU VIN DE CHAMPAGNE

LES FRIANDISES

VINS

VOUVRAY BOURGOGNE
BLANQUETTE DE LIMOUX
CAFÉ   CHAMPAGNE   LIQUEURS
2 JUILLET, 1938

The call bell hung from the centerlight above the table and the hostess had to make a very long arm to reach it, but the first course came on without any ringing. It was an enormous *langouste,* boiled and chilled and cut in cross slices and served with mayonnaise. Never was there a fresher, sweeter giant crustacean, nor a more perfect sauce!

The next course, the *Quiche Lorraine,* was the dish that intrigued the godmothers for they had never met it before. It was a round, thick, unsweetened custard pie with bits of ham scattered through it and more than a hint of cheese, baked in a rich puff-paste crust. It was a rich and melting concoction and the French-speaking godmother asked at once for the recipe—this was too noble a dish not to be copied.

After the superb *Quiche* came the *Poulet de Bresse,* roasted with butter —and possibly some of its own fat—crisp, crackling brown without and as tender within as a smile of affection. The vegetables were not served with the chicken but as a separate course, the string beans just cooked through, the potatoes mashed into a creamy fluff.

Perigord is the native city of the groom's Papa, and the *Terrine de foies gras* which accompanied the Hearts of Lettuce Salad had been specially chosen by him. It was super by all standards. Of cheese there was an ample tray, and one godmother took a bit of an excellent Coulommiers and was greatly pleased with her choice.

After this came the vanilla ice cream and the wild strawberries in champagne to dip over it, and there were quantities of sweet little dry cakes and others of a more fancy bonbonish variety, all of them wonderful.

The year of the wines was not given but obviously both the Vouvray Bourgogne and the Blanquette de Limoux were at the height of their flavor. The champagne served with the dessert was dry and full of life, properly iced. It was a Perrier-Jouet of an exceptional year.

The whole luncheon was leisurely and gay. There were family jokes and much laughter and chatter. The young couple sat at the head of the table side by side and looked so ecstatically happy that they made everyone share their bliss. When the champagne was served they each took a glass and went round the table, formally greeting and clinking glasses with each guest and embracing their closest relatives. The two godmothers were embraced and felt properly *en famille*.

There were some rolled wafers among the cakes, wafers about the length and thickness of a lead pencil, and one of these was carefully measured and its center nicked. Then the groom put one end between his lips and the bride put the other end between *her* lips and they ate up the wafer as fast as they could, the idea being that the one who reached the center first would rule the household. The result was apparently fifty-fifty—plus a quick kiss.

The maid came in with two champagne corks for the wedded pair to keep and it was explained that the corks from wedding wine were kept and strung on cords, for "good luck." There was then a session of everybody autographing everybody's menu card for souvenirs. *"Très amicalement"* and *"Très sincèrement"* and *"Avec mes hommages"* and *"Avec mon meilleur souvenir"* were all on one godmother's card, and the bride and groom wrote *"Souvenir de notre mariage civil avec nos plus affectueuses pensées bien reconnaissantes"* and signed their names.

At long last the whole company got back in the salon for black coffee in little shell-pink cups, and there was a great variety of liqueurs, but of these the godmothers took none for by this time they were feeling terribly overstuffed and stodgy. Presently they went back into a very bright pink bedroom to put on their hats. It was difficult to imagine the hard-boiled Papa of the groom sleeping in that roseate room with its pink curtains and pink bedcover and pink beruffled pillows and the long-legged pink doll resting against them. It was a very, very pink room. The godmothers wondered (silently) if Papa wore pink pyjamas.

There is a brief epilogue to this story. When the war came on the bridegroom joined France's army, was made a prisoner in the great blitzing break-through of June 1940 and was at last released. Today he and his wife are together, they have two fine young sons and they are facing the future with typical French courage and high hopes. Their happiness together is as great as it was on the day here described. May it long continue.

Note: To the recipes for the principal dishes of the wedding luncheon, June Platt has added a small group of fine, very French recipes.

La Quiche Lorraine
(for 6–8)

First make a paste in the following manner: Sift 1½ cups pastry flour with ½ teaspoon salt. Work into it with finger tips, 1 bar salt butter (¼ pound). Moisten with just enough ice water to make it hold together (about 4 tablespoons). Make a smooth ball of it, wrap in waxed paper, and place in refrigerator for ½ hour or so, before rolling it out thin on a lightly floured board. Line a large 10-inch Pyrex piepan with it, trim the edges, roll them under and crimp prettily. Prick the surface with a fork and place in refrigerator, while you prepare the following ingredients. (But first set your oven at 450° F. and light it.)

Grate Swiss cheese until you have 1 cup. Fry or grill about 1½ dozen strips bacon until crisp, but don't overcook it. Break or cut into small pieces. Break 4 whole eggs into a bowl and add to them 2 cups thick or thin cream, 1 pinch nutmeg, 1 pinch sugar, ¾ teaspoon salt, 1 big pinch cayenne, and plenty of freshly ground black pepper. Beat with rotary beater just long enough to mix thoroughly. Now rub a little soft butter over the surface of the pastry and sprinkle the bacon over the bottom, sprinkle the cheese over the bacon, and pour the egg mixture over all. Place in preheated hot 400° F. oven and bake 10–15 minutes, then reduce the temperature to 325° F. and continue cooking until an inserted knife comes out clean, showing the custard has set (about 25–30 minutes). If not a light golden brown on top, place under a hot grill for a second before serving piping hot. Cut in pie-shaped pieces.

Cold Boiled Lobsters in their Shells
with Mayonnaise
(for 6–8)

Buy 8 live lobsters weighing about 1¼ pounds each. Fill a large preserving kettle with water, add a few mixed whole pickling spices, and a little salt and bring to an active boil. Drop the lobsters head first into the boiling water, covering the kettle immediately. Boil 20–25 minutes, counting from the time they actually come to a boil again. When done, remove from boiling water using 2 wooden spoons or tongs, and plunge into cold water for a second or two. Turn them tummy side down on a drain board pulling their tails out straight and allow to become completely cold, before placing in refrigerator to chill. When ready to serve, place tummy side up on a chopping board and using a sharp knife, cut down through the shell and meat from head to tail. Remove from each the sac near the head (sometimes called the lady) and the black intestinal vein which you will see or find running from head to tail. Do not remove the liver or green part, because it is edible, but make it look as tidy as possible. A little pile of capers may be placed where the lady was removed, and the platter on which the lobsters are placed for serving should be garnished with quartered lemons and crisp watercress. It is well to crack the claws before putting the lobsters on the serving platter but it is also a good idea to provide nutcrackers at the table for further cracking if necessary. Serve accompanied by a big bowl of homemade mayonnaise and another bowl of capers.

Mayonnaise
(for 6–8)

Place the yolks of 2 eggs in a bowl, adding to them 1 teaspoon salt, a little white pepper, 1 pinch cayenne, and ½ teaspoon dry mustard. Stir well, with a small wooden spoon, then add 1 tablespoon lemon juice or vinegar, as the case may be; then add, gradually, drop by drop, at first, stirring constantly, 1⅓ cups olive oil. Whenever it gets too thick, add a few drops of additional vinegar or lemon. At the very last, add, gradually, 1 tablespoon boiling water. This improves the consistency and helps to keep it from separating. Thick cream may be added, or not, to thin to the right consistency, depending on what it is to be served with.

Roast Chicken
(for 6–8)

Clean inside and out, 2 fine roasting chickens, weighing about 4 to 4½ pounds each. Singe, wash and dry well, and sprinkle them inside with salt and pepper. Place in each cavity ⅛ pound butter. Place side by side in a roasting pan, dot with ¼ pound butter, place in preheated, very hot 500° F. oven to brown quickly, basting frequently. When breasts are browned, salt and pepper the birds lightly, turn the birds breast down and brown on the other side before reducing the heat to 400° F. and continue roasting, basting frequently, turning them over occasionally until well done, allowing about 25 minutes to the pound in all, or for about 2 hours. About 10 minutes before the chickens should be done, remove them carefully to the top part of your roasting pan, and pour over them a little of the fat, and place back in the oven, while you make the gravy.

If you wish a clear gravy, add to the pan in which the chicken was cooked, 1 cup water, or better still chicken broth, made from the necks by boiling them in 2 cups water with 1 carrot sliced fine, a little celery and 1 onion, until reduced to 1 cup. Place the roasting pan on low flame and stir until all the brown residue in the pan has been incorporated, and simmer until a syrupy consistency. Pour into a small saucepan, and when the fat comes to the surface, ladle off most of it, and baste the chicken with it. When ready to serve the chickens, place on a hot platter and place in each cavity a tidy bunch of parsley. Heat the gravy and send it to the table with the chicken.

If you wish a cream gravy, proceed as follows. Ten minutes before the chickens should be done, transfer them to the top part of your roasting pan, ladle over them some of the fat from the roasting pan, and place back in the oven. Add 1 cup cream to the roasting pan, and place over a low flame, and stir constantly until the brown residue has been incorporated, then transfer to a little saucepan. Keep warm over hot water until ready to serve. Place chickens on hot platter, garnish each cavity with a bunch of parsley and send to the table with the cream gravy in a pitcher or gravy boat.

If you decide to have the clear gravy, try serving the chicken with a lettuce or watercress salad, dressed with French dressing, instead of with a vegetable. The clear gravy mingled with the salad is particularly delicious.

Willa Roberts Plank's Friandises of Chocolate
(for 6–8)

Melt over hot water in the top part of an enamel double boiler, 1½ ounces unsweetened chocolate (1½ squares) and 6 tablespoons butter. Add ¾ cup granulated sugar and ¼ teaspoon salt and cook gently until well blended. Then add 3 ounces good almond paste (about ⅓ cup tightly packed) and stir over boiling water until well mixed and all is blended together. Remove from fire and stir in 1 unbeaten egg and 1 teaspoon almond extract.

Butter an oblong cake tin, 11 by 7 inches, and spread the mixture evenly over the bottom. Place in preheated 300° F. oven and bake for about 15 minutes. Remove from oven and cool slightly then cut in squares so as to make 15 cookies. Loosen around the edge with a spatula but do not remove from pan until almost cold. Slip the spatula under them carefully one by one and remove from pan.

These may also be made in round cookies by first chilling the mixture in refrigerator for an hour or so, then forming them in balls the size of big marbles. Place on buttered cookie sheets not too close together; place in 300° F. oven and bake about 20 minutes. Remove from pan when slightly cooled.

Coquilles Saint Jacques
(for 6–8)

Wash 1½ pounds fresh bay scallops and dry them on a towel. Place them in an enamel pan and pour over them ½ cup cold water and the same of dry white wine. Bring gently to boiling point, remove from the fire, drain off but save the juice. Chop fine 1 small onion, and add to the scallop broth and reduce to only ¼ cup juice. Drain and save. Wash, peel and slice fine ½ pound fresh mushrooms, discarding tough part of stems. Place the mushrooms in a small enamel pan, and pour over them ½ cup dry white wine, and ½ cup cold water and add 2 tablespoons butter. Bring to a gentle boil and cook until almost no juice is left.

Now remove from each scallop the small tough piece which can be readily felt as you finger them. This is the part where the scallop was attached to the scallop shell, and the scallops are more tender when this has been removed.

Now make a cream sauce in the usual way, using 3 tablespoons butter, 3 tablespoons flour and 1 cup milk. When smooth and thick, remove from the fire and stir in 3 tablespoons heavy cream. Add the reduced scallop water and the mushrooms and their juice. Season lightly to taste with salt and pepper and cayenne.

Now butter 8 scallop shells and place in each about 10 scallops. Pour over these the sauce, dividing it equally.

Now melt 3 tablespoons butter in a small frying pan and stir into it about 1 scant cup bread crumbs. Cook for a minute or two over low flame, stirring constantly until they barely begin to brown, at which time remove from the fire and sprinkle lightly over all the shells, using all the crumbs. Place in refrigerator until ready to heat for serving at which time place in preheated, very hot 500° F. oven and bake until hot through, but be careful not to cook too long as this would toughen the scallops. If not a golden brown, place for a second or two under a preheated hot grill. Serve at once, garnished with a little finely chopped parsley.

Lobster à l'Armoricaine
(for 6–8)

For this you will need certain equipment; namely, a sturdy chopping board, a sharp cleaver, a mallet, 2 large heavy iron frying pans with covers and a large enamel fish boiler, and courage on somebody's part to execute the poor lobsters, of which you will need from 6–8, weighing 1 pound or a little more each.

Prepare 1 heaping teaspoon chopped tarragon, 2 tablespoons chopped parsley, 2 large cloves garlic, peeled and crushed, or chopped fine. Also prepare 2 medium-sized onions peeled and chopped fine and 1 tablespoon shallots likewise peeled and chopped. Have ready 2 large iron frying pans, into each of which you have poured 6 tablespoons olive oil. Measure out 4 tablespoons good brandy, and place it in a small aluminum pan. Also measure out 1 cup good dry white wine. Open a 6-ounce can tomato paste, and a 2-pound 4-ounce can Italian peeled plum tomatoes. Drain off all the juice from the canned tomatoes. Also have ready 6 tablespoons butter and the strained juice of ¼ lemon. You are now ready to proceed with the splitting of the lobsters, which must be done while they are alive, and once this is accomplished they must be cooked immediately. They will be easier to manage, if they have been placed for several hours in your refrigerator before killing them.

Lay them tummy side up on the heavy chopping board, one at a time, and chop them, with the cleaver, in two lengthwise from head to tail. This supposedly kills them mercifully. I can't imagine it, but, anyway, it must be done. Now, as quickly as possible, pull out all the green part and the stomach, a small hard sack found near the head, and the intestinal vein that runs through the middle of the tail meat. If you find any coral, save it carefully. Allow cold water to wash away all the rest of the unattractive part and chop the lobsters in two, crosswise, leaving the tails intact. Also chop off the 2 claws and give them a sharp blow crosswise with the cleaver to facilitate the removal of the meat when it is eaten at table.

When all the lobsters have been cleaved and cut, place them on a towel to drain, while you heat the olive oil in the 2 pans until smoking hot. Distribute the lobster, bodies and claws, in the 2 pans and cook rapidly, turning them over and over with a fork or spoon, until the shells have turned a lovely bright red. At this point, transfer all the lobster into one of the pans, and add to the hot oil in the empty pan 6 tablespoons butter. Add the prepared chopped onion and cook, stirring constantly until a golden brown, then add the crushed garlic and chopped shallots, and cook for 1 minute or 2 longer, then add the drained tomatoes and the tomato paste and 1 tablespoon chopped parsley, and the teaspoon chopped tarragon, salt to taste and plenty of coarsely ground black pepper and about ¼ teaspoon cayenne. Bring to a boil, then pour it into the fish boiler.

On this bed, place all the lobster, not including however the oil left *in the first pan. Pour over the lobster, 1 cup dry white wine, and last of all place the pan containing the brandy onto a low flame, and heat slightly, then place the pan in a safe place and light the brandy. Be careful not to burn yourself in the process. Allow the alcohol to burn itself out, then pour the brandy over the lobster. Cover and simmer gently for about 25–30 minutes, stirring occasionally with a long wooden spoon.*

In the meantime, if you have found any coral, add it to 2 or 3 tablespoons butter and put it through a fine sieve. When the lobster is done, stir in the coral butter, or the equivalent amount of plain butter.

Tie 2 large napkins, knotted together, around the fish boiler, sprinkle the lobster with the second tablespoon of parsley and serve at once in soup plates, accompanied by good, crisp French, Italian, or Portuguese white bread. A truly delicious dish, and well worth the trouble of making it.

Brandade of Salt Codfish
(for 6–8)

Soak 2 pounds salt codfish in plenty of cold water for 12 hours, changing the water frequently. Drain and put it on to cook in enough fresh cold water to cover well and bring it, ever so gently, to a bare simmer; reduce the heat even more, cover, and continue to simmer for about 1 hour. In the meantime, peel and boil, until cooked, 2 good-sized old potatoes. When the fish is done, drain it well and pick it over carefully, removing bones and any discolored pieces there may be. Now cut a fresh piece of garlic in 2 pieces and rub well over the inside of a large, heavy enamel pan. Drain the potatoes and put them through the potato ricer into this pan and add the fish, broken into little pieces. Now, with a wooden potato masher or spoon, work the two together vigorously until well mixed, then add gradually, drop by drop, beating all the while, 1 cup lukewarm olive oil. An electric beater may be used instead of the masher. Place the pan on a very low flame and beat it constantly while it heats, then work into it another ¼ cup olive oil, and about 1¼ cups heavy cream, into which you have grated the rind of 1 lemon, and which you have heated to scalding point. Season to taste with salt and plenty of coarsely ground black pepper, and, when hot and very light and fluffy, pile it in a mound on a hot platter and sprinkle over it ¼ cup chopped green pitted olives, heated in a little olive oil, but well drained, and garnish the edge with whole pitted olives, also heated in the same manner.

Beignets Soufflés
(for 6–8)

Have ready 5 pounds vegetable shortening in a large deep iron or heavy aluminum pan suitable for deep fat frying.

Place ½ cup cold water in small, 1-quart-size enamel pan. Add 4 tablespoons butter cut in small pieces and 1 teaspoon granulated sugar and 1 pinch of salt. Sift onto a piece of waxed paper, ½ cup all-purpose flour. Put the pan on a low flame and allow it to come slowly to a lively boil. Remove from fire entirely and add quickly all of the sifted flour at once, and beat vigorously with wooden spoon until well mixed and smooth, then place back on low flame and stir vigorously until the batter all clings to the spoon, leaving the sides of the pan clean. Remove from fire and add 1 unbeaten whole egg and stir vigorously until well mixed then add a second egg and continue beating until very smooth. Add 1 teaspoon good strong vanilla and the grated rind 1 whole lemon.

Heat the fat until it registers 360° F. with the fat thermometer, or until a tiny lump of the batter dropped into the fat comes immediately to the surface. Remove the pan to the side of the stove, and with a teaspoon and the help of your index finger, drop 5 or 6 little balls of batter into the fat, then place the pan back on a low flame and allow the beignets to cook, until they have blown up to 3 or 4 times their original size, increasing the heat very gradually during the process. They should roll themselves over occasionally, but may be helped with a prod from a sieve spoon. They should be nice and brown in from 6–8 minutes. Remove from fat with sieve spoon and drain on paper towel and continue cooking the rest of the batter until all are done. This should make 1½ dozen beignets the size of extra large eggs. Sprinkle with confectioners' sugar in which you have kept a vanilla bean and serve at once for dessert.

Madame Le Douzen's Café de France Crêpes Bretonne, with Hazelnut Butter

(for 6–8)

Scald 1½ cups milk, remove from fire and add 2 tablespoons butter. Stir until butter has melted. Cool, while you measure out 1 cup (well shaken down) unsifted flour. Place in a bowl and make a well in the center. Break 3 whole eggs into the well and using a wooden spoon gradually incorporate the flour into the eggs until all the flour has been used, and the batter is smooth and thick. Now gradually add the cooled milk and keep stirring until smooth and free from lumps. If it should have lumps, put it through a sieve. Then stir in 2 tablespoons sugar, 2 teaspoons orange-flower water, if obtainable, otherwise substitute vanilla. Also add 2 teaspoons white rum and last of all the grated rind 1 lemon and ½ orange. Allow to stand at least 15 minutes while you prepare the hazelnut butter with which these crêpes will be spread before serving.

Place 4 dozen shelled hazelnuts in a little pan in a 500° F. oven to toast lightly or for about 5 minutes, at which time the skins should rub off easily when rolled in a cloth. Place the nuts in a nut grater and reduce to a powder. Cream ¼ pound butter with 1 cup confectioners' sugar. Add 2 generous teaspoons grated lemon rind and 4 tablespoons good brandy. Stir in the powdered nuts and the juice 1 lemon.

When ready to make the crêpes, heat a heavy aluminum 10-inch frying pan and when hot rub lightly with a piece of paper toweling or little cloth dipped into a mixture of 3 tablespoons lard and ½ an unbeaten egg yolk. When sizzling hot lift the pan slightly from the fire, and pour into the center of it about ¼ cup of the thin batter and instantly tilt the pan in all directions so as to coat the entire bottom with a very thin coating of the batter. Place back on fire and cook quickly until well browned on bottom side or for about 1 minute, then slip a spatula or pancake turner under the crêpe and flop it over onto the other side and cook slightly less than the first side. Have ready some soft butter. Flop the pancake over onto a hot plate and butter the light side with a very little butter and fold the crêpe in four. Place in warm (not hot) oven while you repeat the process until all the crêpes have been baked and folded. This should give you *16* crêpes. *Now working quickly, unfold them one at a time and spread lightly with the hazelnut butter and fold back again into their original folds. Place on hot serving platter and serve immediately.*

Note: *These same* crêpes *may be used for* Crêpes Suzette.

SIX

As Good As Bread

The best bread I ever ate was in Spain at the inn of Rivadeo on my way from Oviedo to Corunna. Rivadeo is an unpromising-looking town but it was the best place to stop for lunch; the inn was unpromising-looking too, from the outside—an old shabby house with no yard or greenery, not even a balcony to give it grace. The street was bare and shabby and bleak even in the golden September sunshine. When my Spanish chauffeur, Alejandro—specialist in missing by the thousandth of an inch the Galician dogs which all seem to sleep by preference in the road—left me there I felt sure my uncertain Spanish would never be understood and that the food would be bad. I wished I had stayed in the car and lunched on chocolate and fruit.

I was utterly mistaken. The house was roomy and cool, there were excellent pieces of old furniture about and two competent, well-dressed *señoras* not only understood what I said but smilingly led me to a wide, low-ceiled, completely sophisticated dining room where I was served a gorgeous meal.

For *hors d'oeuvre* there were the freshest of sardines fried crisp and dry in oil; then a delicious mess of tripe and marrow bones, tomatoes and chick-peas; then a small juicy steak; then a salad; lastly cheese and high-flavored little yellow peaches and pale juicy grapes.

But the bread! Big longish rolls, pure, firm white crumb in an all-over quarter-inch crust, a crust that broke easily but did not flake, a crust that melted on the tongue! The waiter had a long fork with a red handle equipped with a tricky apparatus that pushed the roll off the tines untouched by his hand; he was proud of the fork and worked it with a flourish so that I would be sure to notice and appreciate it. I don't know how those rolls were made but they were the essence of wheat, they tasted of wheat, smelled of wheat and their crust was the color of ripe wheat. They were celestial.

As I ate I knew why the Spaniards say *"Bueno como el pan"*—as good as bread—for a superlative compliment. Kind buxom ladies of Rivadeo, I hope and pray you did not have to eat the mean little grayish hard loaves that were Spain's wartime ration, or the heavy dark slices your Government ordered for so many years after the war. I have tried both of these items and I know what you would have thought of them.

My greatest adventure with bread began the summer I was seventeen. I had come home from college for vacation and my mother said, "This summer you are to make all the bread for the family." I must have looked daunted for she added, "All the light bread." This meant all the loaf bread and rolls that have yeast as leaven and excused me from the quick-mixed muffins, waffles and beaten biscuit which every Southern table offers so lavishly. It was a sufficient chore but not overwhelming.

So I learned to make bread. The mixing pan was heavy tin and used for nothing else. The flour was sifted into a light mound; pure white lard, salt and a pinch of sugar were rubbed in by hand until they disappeared; sometimes two or three hot boiled Irish potatoes were rubbed in too. Then the yeast was poured from its special jar, an orchid-tinted semi-liquid yeast made at home with grated raw potatoes. It had a faint earthy smell. Tepid water was added to make a smooth dough. This was left in the pan, covered with a thick white cloth and set away for the first raising. Perhaps I should say "the first rising" but I can't do it, it simply does not sound right. This was raised not risen bread in our vocabulary.

When the dough was up to the top of the pan it was dumped onto a floured breadboard and the heavy work of kneading began. Back and forth, back and forth with a dexterous quick gathering movement, it had to be worked for what always seemed to me a terrifically long time. At last the moment came when it felt right. I cannot describe this feeling but everyone who has made bread knows it. The dough communicates its state exactly to the human hand.

Then the baking pans were brought from the kitchen cupboard, wiped and set ready. They were so tempered by use they required no greasing. If plain rolls were on the program I began with them. It took fingers automatic in calculation to pull off exactly the same amount of dough each time, shape it and set it in the pan, three across the end, five along the side, not too close, not too spaced. For the round pan I placed the outside row first, working in to the center. It took me a long time to learn the required symmetry of a pan of rolls.

The loaves also required balance and there had to be just enough dough in them so that the finished loaf would not run over the pan rim yet not sink so far below as to make a poor, flat slice. When all the rolls and loaves were in the pans their tops were lightly greased with ham or bacon fat and they were again set away, covered, for the second raising. As they reached the proper height the fire was made hot and steady, the oven tested, again by hand. We had a cranky oven that baked too hot at the back so when the bread was half done the pans must be turned and rearranged. I usually got a couple of blisters or a singed wrist doing this. Once I dropped a pan of half-done rolls on the floor.

At last came the great moment when the finished bread could be taken from the oven. My mother came out to look. Sometimes she was pleased. Sometimes she told me just where along the line I had missed the right turn, the right timing. She always knew.

It is related in the book of Genesis, third chapter, nineteenth verse that the Lord said unto Adam: "In the sweat of thy face shalt thou eat bread." Sometimes on breathless July mornings when our wood-fire range was going full blast I thought that the Lord might well have addressed his remark to Eve and all the Eves of this world thereafter and said, "In the sweat of thy face shalt thou *make* bread," for it was a hot, hard business. Only the wonderful homely sweet smell of baking bread and the satisfaction of seeing the decorous brown loaves turned out right and light on the thick snowy cloth reserved for their cooling were consolation for all effort. Just to see and smell them was as much satisfaction as to eat them, though I may be forgiven, I hope, for reporting that they tasted very well indeed and always—well, nearly always—were right in texture with no hard lumpy spots or big holes.

There is a peculiar fine pride in being able to make good raised bread. It goes far beyond whipping up a cake, or baking a ham or turning out a mold of fresh creamy cottage cheese, or even the thrill of a row of jellies that have set properly and glow with clear deep fruit color.

For bread is elemental. It is essential. It has a basic value in life. Thackeray's rich wise old Jew who picked from the muddy gutter a little lost coin saying "A penny is two men's bread" had the right phrase and the right idea. When we say of a man "He earns his bread," we make an exact and vivid picture of honest industry. And do you recall *The Baker's Wife,* that movie of the French village shaken to its foundation when the baker would bake no more because his wife had run away with another man—an incident lifted from one of the lesser books of Jean Giono and played so movingly and yet so drolly by the great Raimu? There was deep truth in it. A community without bread is painfully disorganized.

We would be amazed if we knew the number of the varieties of bread developed in America and Europe. We know some of them. We know the plain Italian loaf so absolutely right with *antipasto;* and we know some of the Italian specials, the bread sticks, the *panforte,* the *panetones;* we know the flat hard discs of Scandinavian bread and the delicious Swedish *Limpa;* there is a braided Finnish coffeecake at least four feet in circumference made especially for birthdays and festivals that is superduper, good to the last crumb for it makes a perfect zwieback when sliced and dried; we know the French *brioche* and *croissant* and *galette* as well as the three-foot *flûtes* that stick out of every Gallic market basket, bought by the yard and eaten by the yard; we know the Mexican *tortilla* —we buy them canned when far from their native heath; we know the Dutch rusk and *kerenten brodje,* a currant-studded bun to eat with coffee; we know the Spanish *Suizos* and *buñuelos,* and *ensaimadas,* the latter soft and spongy, faintly dusted with sugar; we know the heavy Russian black bread; and the Scottish scone, which is, I imagine, the great grandmammy of our own baking-powder biscuit; we have at least heard tell of the flaps of soft unleavened bread eaten by the peoples of Iraq and thereabouts. But very few of us know all the breads of all the countries, uncountable, the odd shapes, the subtle flavors, the cunning additions of raisins and currants and citron and poppy seed and sesame and caraway and chopped nuts and spices and salt crystals and sugar. Bread pale green with spinach, bread pale yellow with carrots, zestful orange bread, bread with cornmeal, bread with bran, bread with soya, protein bread, old-fashioned milk-rising bread—these and many others are sold only a few blocks from my New York home; bread for every taste, or every occasion, the backbone of the anatomy of food.

The coarse dark breads loosely called peasant breads have had a great renaissance in the last decade. Some of them have become high style. But how they have changed! Where once they were eaten for health with chatter about the body's need for roughage, as if we were cows, they are now eaten for pure deliciousness. Little circles of a fine rye bread with aromatic seed scattered through appear buttered or spread with fish paste at elegant cocktail parties. Boston brown bread, thick, sweetish and beraisined, is canned to assuage the nostalgic hunger of Boston's children far from home. There is an almost forgotten bread something on the order of the famous Boston brown that used to be made occasionally in my grandmother's kitchen and I wish I might taste it again. It was called Togus Loaf, a combination of whole wheat and corn meal, touched with molasses, steamed in a kettle like a pudding; excellent when eaten hot with lashings of sweet butter but rather dull when cold. The name sounds just the way it tasted, old-fashioned, solid, stick-to-the-ribs; true country bread for winter meals. It would be fine for ski or skating suppers.

America has a pleasing legion of quick breads made usually with baking powder, or soda combined with sour milk, and muffins, biscuit, waffles, pancakes, popovers, coffeecakes, crullers, of infinite variety. Of these quick breads there are three which seem to me unique—spoon bread, Sally Lunn and beat biscuit. If you want to avoid the colloquialism you can call these last beaten biscuit, but on the Eastern Shore of Maryland where the best are made, we say beat and let it go at that. They are described in detail in the first chapter of this book.

Every Eastern Shore kitchen used to have a biscuit block, a foot-thick slice of a big hard wood log, mounted on three stout legs. On this the dough made of flour, lard, salt and cold water was laid and beat with a heavy hammer or the back of an ax for forty-five minutes. Then small pieces were broken off, molded and kneaded by hand, pricked with a silver fork, baked in a hot oven. Believe me a cook must be expert if her biscuits look right, and she must be favored by the gods of cookery if they taste right. The very simplicity of a beat biscuit is why they are so difficult to make. They are temperamental, too—sometimes they will turn out beautifully, at other times with apparently the same care and work they won't be right at all.

My own recipe for spoon bread is very old and very simple. One quart of milk, two cups white corn meal, four eggs, one tablespoon sugar, salt to taste, butter the size of an egg. Beat eggs well, whites and yolks together. Add sugar, butter, salt and meal. Heat milk scalding hot and pour in, beating hard for at least five minutes. Bake in a slow oven. This spoon bread has a ravishing custard on top and a quivering smooth corn bread below. It is a natural to serve with bacon, ham or sausage or any pork dish and is surprisingly good with roast beef instead of potatoes or Yorkshire pudding.

As for Sally Lunn, I have eaten in England what they call by this name but it has no relationship to the Sally Lunn made by Miss Sallie Fisher, one of the many notable housekeepers of the Eastern Shore. Her recipe was sent me by her niece. Here it is:

"One egg, two tablespoons sugar, one-eighth cup butter and lard mixed, one-half cup clabber well beaten, one-half teaspoon soda dissolved in one teaspoon boiling water, scant one-half teaspoon cream of tartar sifted into one and one-half cups flour or enough flour to make a stiff batter. Cream sugar, shortening and egg thoroughly, add clabber, stir in flour and beat all vigorously before putting in soda. Add one-half teaspoon salt. Bake in a round shallow pan, serve very hot." Please don't ask me where you are going to be able to find clabber, but try sour milk as a substitute.

American muffin variations are endless and as harmonious as Bach's fugues. It always amazes me when I am offered a dry and tasteless muffin, because they are so easy to make. At my home in Maryland we used to have a hot muffin bread, made with a simple batter, into which was incorporated a generous amount of mashed boiled sweet potatoes or sometimes mashed white potatoes. It was baked thick in layer-cake tins, split while steaming hot and buttered with a wasteful hand.

And I must say one word about blueberry muffins, favorite of the greedy from ocean to ocean. They are delicious with roast beef, but they ought to be so full of berries that they fall apart in a rich unmanageable purple juiciness. I once had a Korean cook who made muffins with red raspberries instead of blueberries and they were almost too luscious to eat. They were subtle!

What? You're on a slimming diet and not eating bread of any kind?

You're missing at least half the joy of a good meal. Remember, man lives but once, his pleasures few and frail. Best take the loaf and let the waistline fail, nor heed the warning of the mounting scale.

Basic Baking Powder Biscuits
(for 6–8)

Sift together 3 cups flour, 6 teaspoons baking powder, and ¾ teaspoon salt. Work in with the finger tips 6 tablespoons lard or butter. Add gradually about 1⅛ cups milk, just enough to form a soft dough. Toss out on lightly floured board, knead lightly just a second or two, then pat or roll it out to ½-inch thickness, cut out with small biscuit cutter, place on hot tin, and put immediately in a very hot oven, preheated to about 450° F., and bake for about 12 minutes. Place in breadbasket lined with a pretty tea napkin and serve at once. This makes about 20 biscuits.

Baking Powder Drop Biscuits
(for 6–8)

Make the same as basic baking powder biscuits, adding, however, to the flour, 3 tablespoons granulated sugar, and use a little more milk. Drop by tablespoonfuls onto well-buttered tins. Bake in the same manner, about 12 minutes in preheated 475° F. oven.

Scotch Scones
(for 6–8)

Wash 1 cup dried currants well, and dry on tea cloth. Mix and sift together 4 cups pastry flour with 8 teaspoons baking powder, 1½ teaspoons salt and ⅓ cup granulated sugar. Work into this with finger tips, 8 tablespoons or ¼ pound sweet butter. Add the dried currants and mix to a dough with about 1⅓ cups cold milk. Divide into 12 parts and pat out on floured board, into 4 inch circles about ½-inch thick. Have ready 2 large iron frying pans placed on low flame with asbestos mats under them. Butter them well with 2 tablespoons butter in each and when hot, place 6 scones in each and brown slowly on one side, and until well risen, then with a pancake turner, turn them over and bake the other side until they test done through with a cake tester. Remove from fire and cool slightly. Have ready 2 cookie sheets and when ready to toast and serve the scones, split them in half as you would English muffins and place under pre-heated hot grill until toasted a pale golden brown. Serve at once with plenty of butter.

Basic Egg Muffins
(for 6–8)

Beat 2 eggs very light. Add 1 cup milk, beat again until well mixed. Sift together twice 2 cups all-purpose flour with 4 teaspoons baking powder, 2 tablespoons sugar, 1 teaspoon salt, then add it all at once to the liquid mixture. Stir until all the flour has been incorporated, then beat with spoon just long enough to remove any lumps there may be. Now add 4 generous tablespoons warm melted butter. Stir and fill 16 well-buttered muffin tins, and bake quickly in a hot oven (475° F.) about 10–12 minutes or until a golden brown. Serve immediately.

Blueberry Muffins
(for 6–8)

First pick over and wash 1 full cup choice blueberries. Drain and place on paper towel and pat dry with another towel. Light your oven and set it at 400° F. Butter copiously 2 muffin tins of 8 muffins each.

Cream 5 tablespoons butter with ½ cup granulated sugar until light and fluffy, then add 1 whole unbeaten egg and beat until smooth. Sift some flour and measure out 1½ cups. Sift it again with 1½ teaspoons baking powder and ¼ teaspoon salt. Add it to the egg and butter and sugar mixture, alternating it with ½ cup milk. Beat just long enough to mix well, then fold in the cup of blueberries which you have floured lightly. Place in the 16 muffin pans and bake for about 25 minutes in the preheated, moderately hot oven. Run a small palette knife around the edge of each and loosen from pans.

Serve at once.

Raspberry Muffins
(for 6–8)

Look over some juicy, ripe raspberries, and measure out 1 cup of them. Butter copiously 12 muffin tins. Light your oven and set it at 425° F. Melt some butter and measure out ¼ cup. Sift some flour and measure out 2 cups. Place in sifter with ¼ cup granulated sugar, 4 teaspoons baking powder, and ½ teaspoon salt. Sift it 3 times. Beat 1 whole egg well and beat in ¾ cup milk. Add this gradually to the dry ingredients and stir in the ¼ cup melted butter. Fold in the cup of raspberries and fill the buttered muffin tins. Place in preheated 425° F. oven and bake 20–25 minutes or until a lovely golden brown. Run a small knife around the edge of each and lift carefully from pans. Place on hot plate, sprinkle lightly with confectioners' sugar and serve while still very hot, with plenty of butter.

Pancakes
(for 6–8)

Sift together 1 cup flour, 1 teaspoon salt, 2 level teaspoons baking powder, 1 heaping teaspoon granulated sugar, and 1 tablespoon corn meal. Beat 2 eggs well with 1 cup milk. Add slowly to the flour mixture, and beat until smooth. Stir in 3 tablespoons melted butter. Fry on hot griddle.

Popovers
(for 6–8)

First light your oven and set it at 450° F. Butter copiously 2 iron popover pans. Sift together 2 cups all-purpose flour with ½ teaspoon salt. Sift it again into a big bowl. Measure out into another bowl 2 cups milk. Make a well in the center of the flour and break into it 4 whole eggs. Place the popover pans into the oven to heat while you mix the batter. Add the milk to the bowl containing the eggs and flour and, using a rotary beater, beat just long enough to make a smooth batter free from lumps. Pour the batter into a pitcher. Remove the popover pans from the oven. Pour the batter into the pans, distributing it equally into the 2 pans, working as quickly as you can. The pans should be only partially filled. Place immediately into the preheated oven and bake for 20 minutes at 450° F., then reduce the heat to 350° F. and bake about 25 to 30 minutes longer. Loosen the popovers from the pans by running a small spatula around the edges and serve at once.

Arline's Rich Waffles
(for 6–8)

Separate the yolks from the whites of 3 eggs. Beat the yolks until very light and beat in 1 cup heavy cream. Sift in 1 cup pastry flour in which you have sifted 4 level teaspoons baking powder and ¼ teaspoon salt. Beat with rotary beater just long enough to make a smooth batter. Beat the whites until stiff but not dry and fold them carefully into the batter. Place in refrigerator to chill for ½ hour. Cook 4 tablespoons at a time in preheated hot waffle iron, without stirring the batter again. When the iron stops steaming the waffle should be done. Remove at once and serve with creamed butter (to facilitate spreading) and powdered cinnamon mixed with confectioners' sugar, or with hot maple syrup.

Basic Corn Meal Muffins
(for 6–8)

Light your oven and set it at 425° F. Butter 12 muffin tins. Sift together 1 cup white water-ground corn meal, 1 cup all-purpose flour, ½ teaspoon salt, 4 teaspoons baking powder, and 3 tablespoons granulated sugar. In a separate bowl, beat 2 whole eggs and add 1 cup milk. Add this gradually to the dry ingredients. Beat just long enough to make a smooth batter and stir in 3 tablespoons melted butter. Fill the 12 muffin tins ¾ full and *place in the preheated oven and bake about 25 minutes or until a light golden brown, and serve at once.*

Corn Meal Batter Cakes
(for 6–8)

Sift together 1½ cups white corn meal, ¾ cup all-purpose flour and ¾ teaspoon salt. In a separate bowl beat 3 eggs well, then add to them 2¼ cups buttermilk and beat well together, then make a smooth batter by pouring the liquid into the dry ingredients, mixing it all with a spoon. Now dissolve 1½ teaspoons baking soda in another ¾ cup buttermilk, and add it to the first mixture. Stir in at the end 4½ tablespoons melted butter. Cook 5 or 6 at a time on a hot griddle rubbed over with a piece of bacon. Be sure the griddle is not smoking hot, but very hot. Use a pancake turner to turn the cakes over at the moment when the top surface is covered with little holes. Cook about 2 minutes on the first side and about 1 minute on the other side. Serve at once with sweet butter, creamed or melted, and soft maple sugar or maple cream, or try them with heavy cream and a sprinkle of cinnamon mixed with powdered sugar. Makes about 4 dozen 3-inch pancakes.

Johnny Cakes
(for 6–8)

Put 2 cups Rhode Island white corn meal in a pan in the oven to heat through, but do not allow it to scorch. Remove from oven, and stir in 1 scant teaspoon salt. Add, gradually stirring with a big wooden spoon, enough boiling water to make a stiff paste, or about 2 cups. Then add 1 cup milk and beat hard. It should be smooth and free from lumps, but not at all liquid. It should be the right consistency to be dropped by heaping tablespoonfuls, not poured, onto a hot iron griddle, well greased with beef drippings, bacon fat, or butter. Cook slowly, 15 minutes on each side. The cakes should be about 3 inches in diameter and ¾ inch thick. Serve butter and apply jelly with these for breakfast, or omit the jelly and serve with broiled lobster and butter.

Corn Sticks
(for 6–8)

Butter well, 3 corn-stick iron molds (7 sticks to each mold) and place in 450° F. oven to heat.

Sift together 3 cups white corn meal, 3 teaspoons baking powder, 1½ generous tablespoons granulated sugar and 1½ teaspoons salt. Beat 3 eggs, and stir into them 3 cups buttermilk and 5 tablespoons melted butter. Dissolve 1½ teaspoons baking soda in 2 tablespoons cold water. Add the dry ingredients to the egg mixture and beat with a spoon just long enough to make a smooth batter. Stir in the dissolved soda and mix well and fill the hot cornstick molds. Place in preheated oven and bake until brown or for 15–20 minutes. Serve at once.

Spoon Bread
(for 6–8)

Butter a large 2-quart-sized Pyrex baking dish. Beat 4 eggs well, add 1 tablespoon sugar, ¾ teaspoon salt and ⅛ pound butter, melted. Place 2 cups white corn meal in a bowl and stir in the egg mixture. Scald 1 quart milk and add it gradually to make a smooth thick batter. Beat well for 5 minutes, pour into the baking dish, place in preheated slow, 325°–350° F. oven and bake for 1 hour or until a golden brown. Serve at once.

Custard Corn Bread
(for 6–8)

Sift together 1½ cups white water-ground corn meal, ½ cup all-purpose flour, 4 tablespoons granulated sugar, 1 teaspoon salt, and 2 teaspoons baking powder. Stir into this 2 well-beaten eggs, then add 2 cups cold milk. Beat well with egg beater. Melt 4 tablespoons (⅛ pound) butter in large baking dish—approximately 10 by 6 by 2 inches deep—and pour in the mixture. Place in preheated, medium 350° to 400° F. oven and, be-

fore closing the door, pour 1 cup milk over the batter. Do not stir it in. Bake 30 to 35 minutes. The bread is firm below and custardy on top.

Indian Meal Bannocks
(for 6–8)

Sift together 2 cups water-ground white corn meal, 2 cups all-purpose flour, 1 teaspoon salt, 1 teaspoon powdered ginger, and 1 teaspoon baking soda. Add 4 teaspoons molasses to 1 cup buttermilk and add it gradually to the flour mixture, using a big wooden spoon. Mix well and place in well-buttered round layer-cake tin and bake for 1 hour in preheated, moderate 350° F. oven.

Fried Corn Meal Mush

Add 1 teaspoon salt to 6 cups water in top of large double boiler. Bring to an active boil and add gradually, stirring constantly, 1 cup yellow corn meal. Cook until thick and then place over boiling water, cover and cook for ½ hour longer. Pour into a buttered bread pan, and when cold place in refrigerator until ready to fry. Slice and roll in flour and fry in bacon fat or butter until brown on both sides and serve with butter and syrup.

Togus Loaf
(for 6–8)

Sift together 1 cup whole wheat flour, 2 cups water-ground white corn meal, ½ teaspoon salt, 1 generous tablespoon granulated sugar, and 2 scant teaspoons soda. Mix together ½ cup molasses and 1⅓ cups buttermilk. Add this to the flour mixture and mix well with wooden spoon. Put it into a well-buttered 2-quart-sized pudding mold, and steam at least 4 hours. Five is better. To steam, be sure the cover of mold is tightly clamped on. Place mold in deep pan and pour boiling water around it, keeping the water well below the level of the rim of the mold. Place on fire, bringing to a boil, cover the pan and keep the water boiling all the time, adding more hot water as the water boils down. When done, remove the mold from the boiling water, unclamp the rim, remove cover and turn the bread out carefully onto a hot plate and serve at once.

Boston Brown Bread
(for 6–8)

Butter the top part of a large 2-quart-sized double boiler. Place together in a flour sifter, 1 cup all-purpose flour, 1 cup white corn meal, and 1 cup entire wheat flour, and ¾ tablespoon soda and the same of salt. Sift into a large bowl, and add ¾ cup molasses and 2 cups buttermilk. Add 1 cup seedless raisins, and place in the buttered top of the double boiler. Cover and place over enough boiling water in bottom part of double boiler to come well above the bottom of the part containing the batter. Steam slowly for 2 hours, replenishing the boiling water as needed. Turn out onto a buttered tin and place in preheated, slow 300° F. oven for 15 minutes to dry out a bit.

Large Brioche
(for 6–8)

Sift 1 cup all-purpose flour into a bowl and add to it 1 yeast cake well dissolved in ¾ cup lukewarm scalded milk. Mix and beat it with a wooden spoon until very well mixed and smooth. Place in medium-sized buttered bowl, cover with a cloth, and place in warm place to rise 3 times its size or for about 3 hours. This mixture is called the sponge.

In the meantime, sift 3 cups flour into a large bowl and make a well in the center of the mound. Drop into the well 1 teaspoon salt and 1 tablespoon granulated sugar. Pour 2 teaspoons cold water onto the sugar and stir with small spoon to melt the sugar. Melt 2 bars (1 cup) butter. Pour this into the well and, with a wooden spoon, stir, gradually working the flour into the butter and melted sugar. When it gets to the point where the process becomes difficult, complete the mixing with your hand, and add gradually 1 unbeaten egg at a time until you have used 3 eggs and the whole is worked smooth and free from lumps. At this point add the sponge and knead it into the egg dough until thoroughly mixed. Place a large napkin in a large bowl and sprinkle it lightly with flour. Transfer the dough to this nest, forming it into a neat ball, smooth on top. Fold the four corners of the napkin over the dough to cover it lightly and completely. Put it in a cool place to rise until 3 times its bulk, or for from 5–6 hours.

Lift it from the bowl onto a lightly floured pastry board and knead it lightly. Turn the cloth over in the bowl, flour it lightly again and replace the dough as before in a neat ball, smooth side up and let it rise for the third time, until triple its bulk or for about 2–3 hours longer.

You are now ready to shape the Brioche. *Butter an earthenware baking dish with slanting sides, approximately 2-quart-sized. Lift the dough from its floured cloth and place once more on a floured pastry board and knead lightly. Cut off about ⅙ of the dough and form it into a ball, then shape it into a point at one end or until it looks like a top. Shape the rest of the dough into a smooth ball, and place it in the buttered baking dish, smooth side up. Now, using a wooden spoon, poke the center, making a hole, and paint the hole with a little cold water and quickly insert the pointed end of the small piece in the hole, making a top knot on the dough. Cover lightly with a cloth and allow to rise for the fourth time until triple its bulk or for about 2 hours longer.*

In the meantime, light your oven and set it at 400° F. When the dough has risen, paint the dough with a whole beaten egg. Place the baking dish carefully into the preheated oven and allow the Brioche *to bake until lightly browned, or for about half an hour, then reduce the heat to 350° F. and continue baking until it tests done in the center with a cake tester, or for about 40 minutes longer. Turn out immediately onto a cake rack and cool. This may be sliced and served cold, or it may be sliced and toasted and served hot with butter and jam or jelly or honey, with tea or coffee.*

Portuguese Sweet Bread
(for 6–8)

Sift 4 cups unsifted all-purpose flour with 1 scant tablespoon salt into a big bowl. Have ready in the sifter another 4 cups flour. Scald 1 cup milk, remove from fire and add 2 cups sugar and ¼ pound butter. Stir until the butter and sugar have dissolved. Dissolve 1½ fresh yeast cakes in ½ cup lukewarm water. Warm 7 eggs by placing them in a pan of lukewarm water. Break the eggs into a bowl and beat well. When the milk has cooled to lukewarm, start mixing the batter by adding the milk, eggs, and the yeast all at once to the flour in the bowl and beat with a big spoon until well mixed, and add the grated rind of 3 lemons and 1 tablespoon lemon extract. Now add the rest of the flour little by little, kneading it in with your hand. Continue kneading right in the bowl for 10 minutes. Cover with a clean cloth and place in warm spot to rise, for at least 5 hours.

Grease copiously with sweet butter, or with vegetable shortening, 3 round 9-inch layer-cake pans, or better still 3 8-by-3-inch spring form pans.

When the dough has risen for 5 hours, divide it into 3 equal parts and form it into 3 round balls and place them in the buttered pans. Cover and let rise again for 4 hours. Take a sharp knife and make a gash quickly across the top of each one. Brush with beaten egg. Place in preheated 300° F. oven and bake slowly for about 1 hour or until an inserted cake tester comes out clean. Watch carefully and if the loaves seem to be browning too quickly, reduce the heat for the last 10 minutes to 275° F. Remove from oven when done, and if you have used spring form cake pans, release the springs and remove the outer rims. Slip a spatula under the loaves and loosen them from the bottoms of the pans. Place the loaves on cake racks to cool. If you have baked them in layer-cake pans, run a small spatula around the edge and then slip a larger spatula underneath carefully and loosen the bread from the bottom.

If you like, the sweet bread may be made with fruit and nuts kneaded in at the moment you are shaping the loaves for their second rising. For this you will need 1 cup almonds, blanched and cut in thin slices, 1 cup white seedless raisins washed and thoroughly dried, and ¼ cup candied angelica or citron, cut in thin slivers. Knead them well into the dough before shaping the loaves for their second rising of 4 hours. Make a gash as described above, paint with egg and bake in the same manner as for the plain sweet bread. Plain or with fruit, this bread is delicious cut in slices ½-inch thick and toasted lightly on both sides, then copiously buttered with sweet butter.

Louise's Portuguese Bread

Put 8 cups all-purpose flour into a big bowl. Place in a pan 3 cups water, 1 tablespoon salt, 2 tablespoons granulated sugar and ¼ cup vegetable shortening. Bring to boiling point and cool until lukewarm. Dissolve 1 yeast cake in ¼ cup lukewarm water.

Add about 1 cup of the lukewarm water and the dissolved yeast cake to the flour, pouring it in at one side of the bowl, all in one spot. Then work it into the flour with the hand, and add the rest of the water gradually until it has all been used and the flour has all been incorporated.

Now poke the hand down into the dough and continue mixing until quite smooth. Continue mixing, using a punching technique, until the dough no longer sticks to the hands, or for about 10 minutes. Every so often lift the dough and fold it over. When done sprinkle very lightly with flour, and make the sign of the cross on it with the side of the hand.

Cover the bowl with clean cloth. Place in warm place until it has doubled in bulk or for about 1¼ hours.

Grease 3 round layer-cake tins, wet your hands with cold water, and place ⅓ dough in each one shaping it into a round ball smooth on top. Cover and let rise in warm spot for about 1 hour.

When ready to bake take a sharp knife and cut into the dough slightly to make a gash. Place in preheated oven 450° F., decreasing it to 350° F. when slightly browned. Bake 1 hour. Turn out on to cake rack to cool.

Aimée Evans's Orange Bread

Sift together 2 cupfuls all-purpose flour, ⅓ cupful sugar, 1 teaspoon salt and 4 level teaspoons baking powder.

With the finger tips work in 3 tablespoons butter and 2 tablespoons lard. Then add ½ cupful black walnuts broken into small pieces, and ⅔ cup fresh orange peel cut into small shreds.

To 1 cupful milk add 1 well-beaten egg, and the yolk of another. Stir milk mixture into dry mixture and beat well. Turn into a well-greased bread pan, let rise for 20 minutes and then bake in a moderate 375° F.

oven 45 to 50 minutes, or until a nice brown crust has formed. Is best used as toast or for sandwiches when 24 hours old.

The distinctive flavor is the combination of black walnuts and fresh orange peel. The peel should be cut with a very sharp knife so as not to include any of the white portion.

Nut Bread—Two Loaves

Grease 2 small bread tins, 8½ by 4½ by 2½ inches deep with plenty of vegetable shortening. Chop moderately fine 1 cup English walnuts. With scissors, cut 1 cup plump seedless black raisins in halves. Sift together 2 cups whole wheat flour, 2 cups all-purpose white flour, ½ cup granulated sugar, 1 teaspoon salt, and 1 teaspoon baking soda. Stir in ½ cup good molasses and 2 cups buttermilk. Mix with big spoon and at the last stir in the cup of chopped walnuts and the cup of raisins. Place ½ dough in each of the 2 greased pans, and place in preheated, slow 350° F. oven and bake until it tests done with an inserted cake tester, or for about 1 hour. Turn our immediately onto a cake rack and cool before slicing. This bread slices beautifully and is delicious lightly buttered with whipped butter for tea.

Oatmeal Bread

Put 2 cups water in top of double boiler, and bring to a boil; add gradually, stirring all the while, 1 cup oatmeal. Place pan over boiling water, cover and steam for 1 hour. Remove from fire and cool. Soften 1 yeast cake in ½ cup water and, when the oatmeal is lukewarm, add the yeast to it; also add ½ cup molasses, 1½ teaspoons salt, and 1 tablespoon melted butter. Mix all well together, then add gradually 4½ to 5 cups all-purpose flour, beat with hand until well mixed, then cover with cloth and set away to rise in warm place. When light and well risen, toss onto a floured board and knead well, or, if you prefer, beat it right in the bowl with your hand. Place in 2 small or 1 large well-buttered bread pans, cover, and let rise again to double its bulk, then bake in a moderate oven (400° F.) for about ¾ hour. Remove from tin as soon as baked and place on cake rack to cool. This bread is particularly good sliced paper thin and buttered with creamy whipped butter. It slices beautifully.

Irish Bread
(for 6–8)

Using scissors or a sharp knife, cut ¾ cup seedless raisins in half. Place them in a big bowl. Sift together, 2 cups whole wheat (graham) flour, ½ cup white bread flour, 1½ teaspoons baking powder, ½ teaspoon soda, 2 teaspoons caraway seeds and ½ teaspoon salt.

Sift this once more over the cut raisins, then stir in gradually 1 cup buttermilk. When well mixed, place on lightly floured board and knead for about 1 minute or until just smooth. Form into a round loaf, slightly flattened, and place in a well-buttered round baking tin. With a knife cut the dough lightly twice, making a cross on the top. Place in pre-heated 350° F. oven and bake until an inserted cake tester or toothpick comes out clean, or for about 45 minutes. Turn up the heat to 500° F. and cook about 5 minutes longer or until it has browned lightly. Remove from the oven. Place on a rack to cool. Do not cut until completely cold.

Sweet Potato Bread-Cake
(for 6–8)

Peel 3 medium-sized sweet potatoes and cut into ½-inch slices. Cover with cold water and boil until tender or for about 20 minutes. Drain, add 1 tablespoon butter and mash well. This should give you 1 full cup. Cream 2 tablespoons butter, with ½ cup granulated sugar. Add 2 eggs well beaten and mix well, then stir in the mashed potato.

Sift some all-purpose flour and measure out 2 cups. Place in sifter with 1 scant teaspoon salt and 3 teaspoons baking powder. Sift this into the egg mixture alternately with ¾ cup milk. Beat until smooth, then fill 12 well-buttered muffin tins, or if you prefer, 1 10-inch layer-cake pan, and place in preheated 375° F. oven to bake for 20–25 minutes, or until nicely browned and until they test done with the cake tester. Remove from pan and sprinkle with confectioners' sugar in which you have kept a vanilla bean and serve at once.

Sally Lunn
(for 6–8)

Cream together until very soft 2 tablespoons lard and the same amount of butter. Stir in gradually 4 tablespoons granulated sugar. Beat 2 whole eggs in a separate bowl and beat them into the butter and sugar. Add 1 generous cup buttermilk and beat well. Place 3 cups all-purpose flour in the sifter and add to it 1 teaspoon salt and 1 teaspoon cream of tartar. Sift this into the butter, egg, and buttermilk, and beat with spoon until smooth. It should be quite stiff, but if it is too stiff to beat, add a very little more buttermilk. At the last moment dissolve 1 teaspoon soda in 1 tablespoon boiling water and stir it into the dough. Butter a round 9-inch shallow pan and spread the dough out evenly in it. Place in preheated 450° F. oven and bake for about 30–35 minutes. Serve at once. Cut in pie-shaped pieces.

Allentown Potato Doughnuts
(for 6–8)

Cream together 3 tablespoons butter and ¾ cup granulated sugar. Beat 3 eggs and blend them into the sugar and butter. Add 1 cup dry, unsalted mashed potatoes (freshly mashed with no milk nor seasoning). Stir well, then add 2⅔ cups sifted all-purpose flour sifted again with 4 teaspoons baking powder, 1 teaspoon salt, 1 teaspoon mace, and ¼ teaspoon nutmeg, alternating it with ¼ cup milk.

Chill the dough 2 hours to make it easier to handle. Place ⅓ of it on a well-floured board, round the dough and roll out to ⅓ inch thickness. Cut with floured doughnut cutter.

Have ready a deep fat frying pan in which you have melted 3 pounds vegetable shortening. Heat to 350° F. to 375° F. or smoking hot, then with floured hands or spatula lift the doughnuts and drop them into the hot fat. When 5 or 6 have been dropped in, cook until brown on bottom side, turn over using a sieved spoon and when nice and brown on that side, or in about 3 minutes cooking in all, lift from the fat with a 2-pronged fork through the hole (do not prick the doughnut) and place on paper toweling to drain.

Roll out another ⅓ of the dough and repeat the process so on and so forth until all the dough has been used. Gather up all the centers and scraps and do likewise and cut and cook these in the same way. The recipe should make in all about 4 dozen medium-sized doughnuts.

When the doughnuts have cooled they may be sugared by placing them in a paper bag with confectioners' sugar and shaking them around a few at a time. Do this just before serving them. Some people prefer to shake them in powdered sugar mixed with a little cinnamon.

Raised Doughnuts
(for 6–8)

These take about 6 hours in all to make so plan your time accordingly. First scald 1 cup milk. Remove from fire, and cool until lukewarm. In the meantime dissolve ¾ yeast cake in ½ cup lukewarm water. Add to the yeast water ¼ cup all-purpose flour and mix to a smooth batter. Add the cooled milk. Stir in 1 teaspoon sugar and 1⅓ cups flour. Beat until smooth. Place in big bowl, cover with a clean cloth, place in warm spot to rise for 2 hours. Now beat 3 eggs well and beat into them ¾ cup granulated sugar and at least 1 teaspoon freshly grated nutmeg (I like more), and ¾ teaspoon salt, and ⅛ cup melted butter. Stir this into the batter and mix thoroughly. Then add about 2 cups more flour or enough to make the batter so thick that you can no longer stir it with a spoon. Cover and set aside to rise for the second time for about 1¾ hours.

Then roll out about ⅓ of the dough at a time on a well-floured board, to about ¼ inch thickness, and cut out with a doughnut cutter. Discard the centers and scraps temporarily and place the circles on a piece of waxed paper. They may be a little difficult to handle, but they will be that much better for not being too stiff with flour. When all the dough has been rolled and cut, gather all the scraps and centers and roll them out together and cut in the same manner, keeping these separate from *the others. They will be very good, but not quite as superlative as the first ones because of the second handling. Cover them all with a cloth and let them rise once more for about 1½ hours. Have ready a deep fat frying pan in which you have melted over a low flame 3 pounds fresh vegetable shortening. Also spread out on a table plenty of paper toweling on which the doughnuts drain after they are fried.*

When ready to fry the doughnuts, place the pan containing the melted vegetable shortening on a moderate flame and heat until it is just beginning to smoke or to 360°–370° F. by the fat thermometer. Now carefully pick up the raised doughnuts one at a time and drop them raised side down into the fat, not attempting to fry more than 4 or 5 at a time. Cook 2–3 minutes turning them over with a long fork when half done. Remove from fat when they are a lovely golden brown and place immediately on the paper toweling to drain. Repeat the process until all have been fried. This amount will make about 3½ dozen doughnuts.

When they are cold, place a few at a time in a paper bag containing confectioners' sugar in which you have kept a fresh vanilla bean and shake to coat them well with sugar. They may also be eaten without sugar. Some people like to dunk them into molasses and eat them. Others like to dip them in liquid honey as they eat them, and of course they are heavenly eaten with café au lait, sugar coated or not.

Milk Toast
(for 6–8)

Place 1½ quarts rich milk in top part of double boiler over boiling water and place on flame to heat, stirring it frequently to avoid a scum forming. In the meantime, place 8 slices bread on a large cookie sheet and place under grill to toast lightly on both sides. Place in oven while you make 8 slices more. Put these in a pretty basket, sprinkle lightly with salt, and send to table accompanied by the milk in a big pitcher and a smaller pitcher of cream and a plate of butter cut in squares. Place 2 pieces toast in each soup plate, and top with 1 or 2 squares butter. Allow each person to help himself to hot milk and a dash of cream and more salt if so desired.

French Toast
(for 6–8)

Beat 3 eggs slightly with 2 cups milk, and season with ¼ teaspoon salt. Dip 8 slices white bread both sides into the mixture. Have ready 2 large heavy frying pans. Place ⅛ pound butter in each and heat until butter has melted. Tip the pans so that they are coated all over with sizzling hot butter. Lay the 8 slices bread in the 2 pans and brown slowly and evenly both sides. Place on hot serving platter and serve at once, to be eaten with butter and a sprinkle of cinnamon and confectioners' sugar mixed together.

Melba Toast
(for 6–8)

Buy a loaf of unsliced, white American bread. Allow it to get at least a day old. Slice it as thin as possible. Spread out on cookie sheet, place in slow 300° F. oven and bake for about 20 minutes or until a light brown. Serve hot.

SEVEN

Vegetables
Needn't
Be Dull

There comes a time in the life of every traveler in far-off lands when he looks dourly at all the tempting native dishes, pushes away the sweets and the sauces and thinks, The first thing I eat when I get home will be a great big plain baked potato.

Well, maybe he does and maybe he doesn't, because when he is home again he may have forgotten all about the baked potatoes and that is a pity for truly there is nothing in the culinary world which is much better than a baked potato when it is the right kind of potato and has had the right kind of baking. It should, of course, first be washed and brushed to that state of cleanliness which is next to godliness. Then its outside should be lightly rubbed in grease of some kind, maybe butter, maybe oil or vegetable shortening, maybe a wipe with the interior of a bacon rind. The oven shouldn't be too hot, and it should be baked through and through until every bit of it inside is a sweet mealy dry goodness. After that, while it is still burning hot, it should be gently broken open and a generous dollop of butter and some salt and pepper applied. Or, salt alone, if you're off fats. Or, if you're still eating fats but don't care much for butter, add a great big spoonful of cream, or cream mixed with cream cheese. In any case, it is fine eating, and the outside of it is apt to be the tastiest of all.

Now it is a very much heard complaint that "vegetables are dull." Too often this is true. The limp string bean, the bullet-hard pea, the pasty carrots, the watery turnip, the tasteless beets, the overcooked sweet corn, the tomato apparently stuffed with dog biscuit, the spinach that seems flavored with beetles, the coarse strong broccoli—I could go on and on and you would recognize them all. Such vegetables are worse than dull, they are horrible, and every cook who butchers good food material in this way should be made to eat nothing else, no matter what happens to them. When I hear mothers saying "I can't get little Jane and little Tommy to eat their vegetables," I wonder what sort of mess the poor child is being offered.

All vegetables can be cooked so they will be tasty, even vegetable marrow, though there are many who will dispute this last statement with violence. Some vegetables naturally have more flavor than others, and these are good by themselves; but the odd or the lacking in flavor only need to be blended, sauced, jazzed up to be palatable even to the critics. When I was a child I hated stewed tomatoes stiffened with breadcrumbs and liberally sugared which was the way my father preferred them and therefore the way we most often had them. But when I found that I might eat tomatoes Provençal, or plain fried tomatoes, or tomatoes pushed about in the frying pan with rich cream, or tomatoes gently baked in chicken stock with rice—well, my idea of tomatoes changed at once. And spinach cooked in cream is so wonderful that eating it anyone might forget all he has suffered from the watery, sandy, dead-flavored spinach too often served. Fresh sweet corn that has leaped from the field to the boiling pot to the table is no more like tired old corn that has been hours coming to market, and hours more coming to the cook who has boiled it mercilessly, than cheese is to chalk. And think of sweet corn pudding, and sweet corn fritters judiciously prepared if you can't get field-fresh corn and therefore must forego the sublime sensation of gnawing it off the cob!

Some people shudder at the mere mention of a parsnip, but if they could have them parboiled, sliced and lightly sautéed in bacon fat they might change their ideas. And for those who look stonily at the humble carrot I would recommend them boiled whole, skinned, the boiling liquid reduced somewhat, butter and a touch of garlic added and poured over the skinned yellow lengths, and all as hot as Hades and licking good. As for red cabbage cooked with apples, or plain young green cabbage quickly boiled, drained and chopped, seasoned with salt, pepper and a little grated nutmeg, and given a few last minutes of cooking with a good piece of butter and half a cup of meat stock—well—these are excellent to anyone however ordinarily scornful of cabbage.

If we are going to eat vegetables—and most of us are—we ought to see what can be done to bring out the best in them, because vegetables in this respect are much like human beings, we must seek their best if we wish to enjoy them.

Boiled Artichokes with Sauce Hollandaise
(for 6–8)

Wash 8 fine artichokes. Cut off split or discolored outer leaves, cut off the stem ½ inch below base of leaves. With scissors cut off the sharp pointed end of each leaf. Have ready a big pot containing plenty of boiling water seasoned with 1 tablespoon salt, the juice of 1 lemon and 2 tablespoons olive oil. Drop the artichokes into the boiling water and cook, uncovered for 25–40 minutes, depending on size of artichokes. To test, pull off 1 leaf and if it comes off easily, it is done. Drain well, and serve hot with Sauce Hollandaise as follows.

Sauce Hollandaise
(for 6–8)

Squeeze and strain the juice of ½ lemon. Put 4 tablespoons vinegar in top part of enamel double boiler with a big pinch of salt and about ⅛ teaspoon white pepper (coarsely ground black pepper may be substituted but it will show). Reduce the vinegar by simmering until only 2 teaspoons are left. Add 2 tablespoons cold water and the yolks of 4 eggs, being sure not to include any of the whites. Beat well with wire whisk or rotary beater, and add ⅛ pound butter cut in little pieces. Place the pan directly on a very, very low heat (or to be safer still, place over boiling water in bottom part of double boiler, on low flame, being sure that the bottom part of the top pan does not actually touch the boiling water) and beat constantly with wire whisk until the mixture has thickened. At this point, remove the pan from the fire entirely, and add little by little (beating constantly with wire whisk) ½ *pound butter. When all the butter has been added, stir in the lemon juice and season to taste with salt, pepper and cayenne. Serve in warm, not hot, bowl.*

Asparagus Old-Time Style
(for 6–8)

Wash thoroughly enough tender young green asparagus to make 4 cups when cut in ¼-inch slices, using the tender part. Place the cut asparagus in the top part of an enamel double boiler with 1 scant teaspoon salt.

In another pan, place 4 eggs and cover with cold water. Place on fire and boil gently for 10–12 minutes.

In the meantime, pour 3 cups boiling water on the asparagus and cook until just tender or for about 15 minutes. Drain well, but save the asparagus water. Keep the asparagus warm by placing the pan over hot water.

When the eggs are done, plunge into cold water and remove the shells, then allow them to stand in warm water until ready to use.

Cut 8 slices bread in ¼-inch slices, and toast them lightly both sides, and place them on a hot platter and keep warm.

Now make a sauce by melting 4 tablespoons butter in an enamel pan. Add 4 level tablespoons all-purpose flour and cook together, stirring constantly for a minute or two, then add gradually the asparagus water of which there should be 1⅓ cups. Stir until smooth and cook for a minute or two. Add about ½ cup heavy cream, a pinch of mace, and a little coarsely ground black pepper. Keep warm.

Now butter the toast lightly and distribute the asparagus in mounds on each one. Working quickly, slice the 4 eggs and place them on top of the asparagus and cover with the sauce, nice and hot. Serve at once.

Boiled Lima Beans
(for 6–8)

Shell 6 pounds tender baby lima beans, wash carefully, place in a large enamel saucepan, add 1 teaspoon salt and a pinch of baking soda and cover with rapidly boiling water. Cook until tender or for about 30–35 minutes. Remove from fire, drain well, add 6 tablespoons or more butter, sprinkle with coarse ground black pepper, put over low flame and shake until butter has melted. Place in hot serving dish and serve at once.

Sautéed Raw Beets
(for 6–8)

Wash 12 medium-sized beets. Peel and shred them, using any device you may have as a vegetable shredder. Place 1½ bars (⅜ pound) butter cut in little pieces in the bottom of a heavy enamel pan. Add the shredded beets and a little salt and coarsely ground black pepper. Place on a low flame and stir with fork until butter has melted. Cover tightly and cook for about 15–20 minutes, stirring frequently. Squeeze a few drops of lemon juice over them, sprinkle with parsley and serve very hot.

Glorified Red Cabbage
(for 6–8)

Remove outer leaves from 2 fine red cabbages weighing about 2½ pounds each. Cut in quarters, remove all of the core, and place temporarily in large pan of cold water containing the juice of 1 lemon. This is to keep the cabbage from discoloring. Take the quarters one at a time and cut in moderately fine slices, then chop crosswise. Place in collander as you proceed until all of the cabbage has been chopped. You should have about 4 pounds of it.

Now in a great big pan, melt 1½ bars or ¾ cup butter. Peel and chop fine 2 large Bermuda onions, and peel, core and chop fine 2 large juicy apples. Place the onions in the pan with the butter and cook slowly for 5 minutes, stirring constantly so that they brown lightly, add the apples and continue cooking for 5 minutes, stirring likewise. Then add all of the cabbage and 1½ cups cold water, cover the pan and cook for 1 hour, stirring frequently as it burns easily. Watch carefully and if necessary add a tablespoon cold water from time to time, but don't let it be wet at all. When done, add ⅓ cup cider vinegar and ⅓ cup granulated sugar and salt and pepper to taste and cook 5 minutes longer. Serve at once.

Carrottes à la Nonne
(for 6–8)

Peel about 12 fine carrots, wash and cut them crosswise in thin slices. You should have at least 4 generous cups of them. Slice fine 2 large peeled onions. Place 6 tablespoons butter in a large enamel pan and add the sliced onions and the carrots. Sprinkle with 1 teaspoon granulated sugar and ½ teaspoon salt. Place pan on low flame and cook uncovered for about 45 minutes, shaking the pan frequently to avoid having the carrots stick to the bottom of the pan. At this point, sprinkle the carrots with 1 level tablespoon flour and stir carefully so as not to break up the carrots. Then add ½ cup milk and 1 can consommé (1¼ cups), 1 pinch nutmeg and about ½ teaspoon coarsely ground black pepper. Continue cooking for about ½ hour longer, or until the carrots are quite tender and the juice has reduced considerably. Sprinkle with 1 tablespoon finely chopped parsley and serve at once.

Boiled Cauliflower
(for 6–8)

Remove the outer leaves from a fine large head of cauliflower. Soak head down in cold water, with a little salt for ½ hour. Place in enamel pan large enough to hold it comfortably and pour over it boiling water enough to cover. Add 1 teaspoon salt and a piece of lemon rind and cook until just barely tender or for about 20–25 minutes. Drain well, and place right side up in a hot serving dish, accompanied by Green Hollandaise Sauce.

Green Hollandaise Sauce
(for 6–8)

Make the full recipe for Sauce Hollandaise on page 140. Have ready 12 cold asparagus tips cooked with a little soda and salt to keep them green. Drain them well on a cloth, then rub them through a fine sieve. Add the *purée of asparagus to the Hollandaise, and stir well and serve on Boiled Cauliflower (see page 143).*

Braised Celery
(for 6–8)

Remove imperfect outer branches from 12 bunches of celery and cut off the leaves, making the bunches all the same length. Wash very carefully, pulling the branches apart slightly and letting the cold water run through the hearts to remove all sand. Remove as many strings as possible by scraping with a knife. Parboil in boiling salted water. Drain, place side by side in oblong Pyrex baking dish. Dot well with butter. Squeeze a little lemon juice over all and sprinkle lightly with a little salt and pepper. Pour over celery 1½ cups chicken broth, in which you have dissolved 1 teaspoon meat extract. Bake in moderate oven for about 1 hour, basting occasionally, or until it is tender clear through and just beginning to brown. Sprinkle copiously with chopped parsley and serve at once right in the dish in which it was baked.

Baked Corn
(for 6–8)

Butter copiously a large 2-quart-sized rectangular Pyrex baking dish, approximately 7 by 12 by 1½ inches deep. Husk 24 large ears fresh-picked corn. With a sharp knife score each row of kernels, then scrape well with the dull side of a knife to extract all the pulp. You should have about 8 full cups of it. Season to taste with about 1½ teaspoons salt and a little coarsely ground black pepper and 2 generous teaspoons granulated sugar. Cut ½ pound butter into little pieces and mix it into the corn. Place in buttered dish and bake in preheated 350° to 375° F. oven for about 40–50 minutes or until sides and top are a crusty golden brown. Remove from oven and serve at once.

Delicate Corn Fritters
(for 6–8)

Husk 12 ears tender sweet corn, and remove all the silk. Run a sharp knife down the center of each row of kernels and scrape out the milky part or use a corn scraper, sold for that purpose. Beat 4 egg yolks well, and beat into them 2 teaspoons all-purpose flour, and 2 teaspoons granulated sugar, and ½ teaspoon salt and a very little coarsely ground black pepper. Add the scraped corn and mix well, and stir in 4 tablespoons melted butter. Beat the whites of the 4 eggs until stiff, and fold them carefully into the corn mixture. Drop by tablespoonfuls onto a hot, lightly buttered griddle or iron frying pan and bake until brown on one side, then turn them over with a spatula or pancake turner and bake until brown on the other side. Serve a few at a time on a hot platter. These are very delicate and should be eaten immediately and it is almost essential to have someone stay in the kitchen to bake them, if they are to come to the table in a state of perfection.

Onion Pie
(for 6–8)

Make ½ recipe for plain pastry on page 58. Chill for ½ hour or longer. Peel 5 large onions and slice them crosswise in thin circles, then cut once more making half circles. Place them in an enamel pan and cover with boiling water. Cook for 6 minutes, then remove from fire, drain in a sieve and plunge them immediately into cold water. Drain again thoroughly, then pat dry on clean tea cloth.

Cut 5 slices bacon in little squares. Place in little pan, cover with cold water, place on low flame and bring slowly to a boil. Simmer for 5 minutes, drain in a sieve and plunge into cold water. Drain and pat dry on a tea cloth. Prepare 2 tablespoons finely chopped parsley. About an hour before you will be ready to serve the pie, roll out the crust and line a 10-inch Pyrex pie plate, roll the edges under and crimp prettily. Melt 3 tablespoons butter in a frying pan and add the bacon. Cook for a minute, then add the onion and cook very slowly, without browning, for 15 minutes, stirring frequently. Remove from fire, add the 2 tablespoons chopped parsley, cool slightly while you beat 4 large whole eggs with a rotary beater but for not too long. Beat in 1½ cups milk, add the onion and bacon and what little butter there is, and season to taste with salt (about 1 teaspoon) and ¼ teaspoon coarsely ground black pepper. Pour into the prepared pie shell, place in preheated 450° F. hot oven and bake for about 10 minutes or until the pastry begins to brown lightly, then reduce heat to 325° F. and continue baking until set like custard, or for about 20–25 minutes longer or until a golden brown on top. Serve at once.

Mashed Parsnips
(for 6–8)

Buy 3 pounds small young parsnips. Wash and peel, and cut in thick slices. Cover with boiling salted water, and boil until tender or for about 30 minutes. Drain well, add ⅛ pound butter and mash with wire potato masher. Season with additional salt if necessary and a little coarsely ground black pepper. Serve at once.

Parsnip Stew
(for 6–8)

Peel 8 or 10 large fresh parsnips and slice them lengthwise in ¼-inch slices. Have ready 12 slices lean bacon or salt pork cut in ¼-inch-thick strips. Place a layer of parsnips side by side in a large, deep, rectangular pan and cover with 6 slices of the bacon, then sprinkle lightly with salt and pepper and cover with another layer of parsnips and a second layer of bacon and a little more salt and coarsely ground black pepper. Pour over all enough hot water to cover. Place in preheated, moderate 350° F. oven and bake slowly for 3 hours. By this time the parsnips should have absorbed most of the liquid and the top will be a golden brown.

Green Peas with Mint
(for 6–8)

Shell 6–8 pounds fresh young green peas as soon before cooking as possible. Place them in an enamel pan and add 2–3 sprigs mint. Pour just enough boiling water over them to cover, and cook until tender, or for about 20 minutes. Drain off what little water remains, add 6 or more tablespoons butter, and season lightly with salt and coarsely ground black pepper. Hold the pan above but not on the flame and shake the pan, to melt the butter. Place in hot serving dish and serve at once.

Note: If the peas are old, add a pinch of soda when you cover them with boiling water.

Petits Pois à la Française
(for 6–8)

Shell 5 pounds tender fresh green peas. Wash 1 small head Boston lettuce, pulling the leaves apart. Insert in the center 1 small bunch parsley. Peel 1 cupful small white onions or shallots, leaving them whole. Place the peas in a 2-quart-sized enamel pan and add the lettuce cut in two lengthwise, each half tied with thin string to keep it in shape. Also add the onions or shallots, and 2 lumps sugar broken in half, and 4 tablespoons soft butter. Pour over it 1/3 cup cold water. Now cover with a deep soup plate or bowl, one that fits securely down into the pan. Place in this bowl a few cakes of ice. Place the pan on a lively flame and bring quickly to a boil, then reduce the heat slightly and cook for about 35 minutes or longer if the peas are not very young; replacing the melted ice in the dish 2 or 3 times during the process, with more ice. Shake the pan occasionally to be sure the peas don't stick and be careful not to allow them to boil completely dry. Just before serving add another 4 tablespoons butter and season lightly with salt and coarsely ground black pepper.

Note: Remove the strings from the lettuce, of course, before serving.

Baked White Potatoes

(for 6–8)

Select 8 perfect medium large white potatoes, weighing about ½ pound each. Scrub them meticulously, wipe dry, and rub each one with about ½ teaspoon butter. Place in shallow pan in preheated 450° F. hot oven and bake for about 1 hour. To test if they are done, protect your hand with a cloth and press the potato. If it feels soft, it is done. Serve at once, with plenty of butter, or sour cream or sweet cream.

Potatoes Boiled and Baked in their Jackets

(for 6–8)

Wash 8 medium-sized old potatoes. Place them in a large pan and cover with cold water. Add 3 tablespoons salt and boil for 30 minutes. Drain and place in preheated 450° F. oven and bake about 20 minutes longer. Serve at once. These potatoes will have a frosted appearance due to the large quantity of salt, which dries on the surface when they are baked.

Browned Potato Balls

(for 6–8)

Peel 12 large potatoes and drop in pan of cold water. With potato scooper, make as many little potato balls as possible. Place in cold water until ready to cook. The scraps may be used as a foundation for soup, or cooked and mashed. Melt 4 tablespoons butter in an iron cocotte. Drain the potatoes and pat dry on cloth. Place immediately in the cocotte, place on moderate flame, cover tightly and cook, shaking the cocotte occasionally, for 15 minutes. Remove cover and if the potatoes may be pierced with a fork, continue cooking without a cover, rolling the potatoes around a bit with a wooden spoon until a golden brown all over. Sprinkle with salt and chopped parsley and serve.

Mashed Potato Surprise
(for 6–8)

Wash, stem, and dry 3 dozen medium-sized fresh white mushrooms. Peel and slice them fine. Melt 1½ bars sweet butter in a frying pan, add 1 cup finely chopped onions and cook without browning for 3 minutes, then add the mushrooms and cook, stirring until they form their juice. Continue cooking for 5 minutes longer. Season to taste with salt and pepper, add 2 tablespoons chopped parsley, and cook ½ minute longer.

Peel and cut into 8 pieces 6 large old potatoes, wash, drain, cover with boiling water, cook until they may be pierced with a fork, or for about ½ hour. Drain well, mash, preferably with an electric beater, and add gradually ¾ cup rich hot milk in which you have melted 3 tablespoons butter. Season to taste with about 1 teaspoon salt. Cover bottom and sides of well-buttered, 2-quart-sized Pyrex baking dish with part of the potatoes, making a hollow in the center. Fill the hollow with the mushrooms. Cover with remainder of potatoes. Decorate top with prongs of fork, dot with 1 tablespoon butter, place in preheated, very hot 500° F. oven and bake until lightly browned, or for about 15 minutes.

Potatoes Tarragon
(for 6–8)

First prepare 2 tablespoons chopped parsley and the same of fresh tarragon. Butter copiously a large round Pyrex pie dish. Peel 2 pounds potatoes and slice them thin. Dry on a tea cloth and, working quickly, cover the bottom of the dish with a layer of potatoes, dot with butter, sprinkle with salt and a little coarsely ground black pepper and about ⅓ of the parsley and ⅓ of the tarragon. Repeat the process until the dish is full, using all the potatoes and herbs and about ¼ pound butter in all. Cover the dish with another of the same size and place in preheated, moderate 425° F. oven and bake for about ½ hour, then remove the cover and continue cooking, lowering the temperature to 325° F. and cook until the potatoes are tender and nice and brown on the bottom, or for about

25–30 minutes longer. When ready to serve, loosen the potatoes around the edge and cover with a large round serving platter and turn upside down. The potatoes should come out, but it may be necessary to help them along with a spatula. Serve immediately, garnished or not with a big glob of sour cream and a little freshly chopped parsley.

Chinese Rice
(for 6–8)

Wash 3 cups long grain rice in cold water until the water is clear. Spread the rice evenly over bottom of large saucepan. Add sufficient cold water to reach about ½ inch above the level of the rice. Cover tightly, place on fire and bring quickly to a lively boil. Do not remove the cover, but when the cover begins to jiggle, indicating the lively boil state has been reached, turn the light down as far as it will go and continue cooking slowly for 20 minutes. At this point remove cover and try the rice. If it is done and has absorbed all the water, remove from fire and serve at once. If not done, cover and cook a little longer. Rice cooked this way is not as good left over but there seldom is any left over.

Boiled Scallions with Sauce Hollandaise
(for 6–8)

Buy 8 bunches tender fresh green and white scallions. With a sharp knife, cut off the tops leaving however 5 or 6 inches of the green part attached to the little white bulb onions at the end. Wash carefully, and cut off the little root growing out from the end of the bulbs and peel off 1 layer. Wash them once more and, using thin string, tie them in little bundles, of about 10 to a bundle.

Have ready some Sauce Hollandaise made as per directions on page 140. Place the scallions in a large enamel saucepan, laying them in all in the same direction in a neat pile. Pour over them sufficient boiling water to cover. Place on fire, bring to a boil, add 1 teaspoon salt, cover and cook about 15 minutes or until the white part may be pierced with a sharp fork. Drain thoroughly, and lift carefully onto a flat serving dish, remov-

ing string and arranging them neatly as you would asparagus. Serve at once, accompanied by a bowl of Sauce Hollandaise. For a perfect combination, try these with roast chicken flavored with tarragon, with clear gravy.

Spinach in Cream
(for 6–8)

Wash 3 pounds spinach until you are sure it is free from sand. Then shake it dry. Place on tea cloth and pat even dryer. Remove all the stems and place the leaves in a wooden chopping bowl. Chop with meat chopper until coarsely cut. Don't chop it too fine. Place ¾ cup extra heavy cream in a large enamel saucepan and add the spinach which you have drained dry of any juice that may have formed while chopping. Cover the pan, place it on a hot flame and bring quickly to a boil, shaking the pan occasionally. Cook 4 or 5 minutes at most, stirring lightly with a fork. Remove from fire, season to taste with salt and pepper and serve very hot.

Note: *The spinach should have absorbed all the cream by the time it is done. If by any chance it has not, drain off the juice and reduce by boiling it rapidly until very little is left. Pour back on the spinach, heat and serve at once.*

String Beans with Sour Cream Sauce
(for 6–8)

Wash and cut off the strings of 4 pounds green string beans, leaving them whole. Tie them securely in 6 or 8 bundles. Lay them in a large enamel pan and sprinkle with salt. Pour over them sufficient actively boiling water to cover. Add a tiny pinch of soda. Cover the pan and bring to a boil. Remove cover, skim carefully and cook until tender, but not floppy. Drain and place the bundles on a preheated platter and remove the strings, being careful not to disturb the symmetry of the beans. Pour over them well-seasoned sour cream sauce, sprinkle with 1 tablespoon or more cut chives and serve at once. See next page for Sour Cream Sauce.

Sour Cream Sauce
(for 6–8)

*Prepare 1 tablespoon cut chives and 1 heaping tablespoon grated onions.
Make a cream sauce in the top of a small enamel double boiler in the
usual way, using 2 tablespoons butter, 2 tablespoons flour and 1 cup hot
milk. Cook until well thickened and season highly to taste with salt and
coarsely ground black pepper. Add the grated onion, stir and cover and
continue cooking over hot water for 15 minutes. Just before serving add
1 cup sour cream and stir constantly until heated through. Be careful not
to overheat. Pour over the string beans, sprinkle with chives.*

String Beans to Your Taste
(for 6–8)

*Wash 3 pounds young tender string beans and break off the ends. If you
have a bean X cutter, run the beans through this to French them; otherwise, using a sharp knife, cut off either side, then cut the beans lengthwise twice so that they will be nice and thin.*

*Wash again in cold water. Have ready a pan of rapidly boiling, well-
salted water and drop the beans into this along with a big sprig of parsley.
Cover and bring to a boil again as rapidly as possible. Skim carefully,
then cook until just tender, 10 to 12 minutes maximum. Drain the beans,
remove the parsley and cover them again with cold water. Let them stand
3 minutes, then drain once more and spread them out on a clean dish
towel and pat them dry.*

*In a deep, large pan, place ¼ pound butter. Melt it and add the beans.
Sprinkle generously with some freshly grated nutmeg and add a little
salt and plenty of coarsely ground black pepper. Place pan on moderate
flame and heat for 3 minutes, shaking the pan frequently. At the end
squeeze over the beans the juice from ¼ lemon and add 2 heaping tablespoons freshly chopped parsley. Serve at once.*

Fried Tomatoes with Cream Gravy
(for 6–8)

Slice 8 firm tomatoes in ¾-inch slices. Discard top and bottom slices. Sprinkle both sides with salt and pepper and a very little granulated sugar, then dip each piece both sides in flour. Put them, one by one, into a large heavy frying pan containing plenty of hot butter and bacon drippings in equal quantity, about 4 tablespoons each. Fry the tomatoes quickly on one side, turn over carefully with pancake turner, and place on hot oven-proof platter in the oven, while you fry the rest, adding more butter and bacon drippings if necessary. When all are done, pour 1 cup cream into the frying pan and stir well, season to taste with salt and coarsely ground black pepper, pour over the tomatoes, sprinkle with chopped parsley and serve at once.

Tomatoes Provençal
(for 6–8)

Choose 16 large, perfect, ripe tomatoes. Cut off a slice from the stem end and scoop out most of the pulp. Save the pulp, but discard as many seeds as possible. Sprinkle the tomatoes inside with salt and coarsely ground pepper and turn upside down on a big platter to drain. In the meantime prepare 3 heaping tablespoons chopped parsley, 1 teaspoon finely chopped garlic. Remove crusts from 10 slices white bread and cut in little cubes. Pour over the bread 1 cup consommé. Prepare 6 tablespoons chopped raw onion, and measure out 1 cup toasted bread crumbs. Pour 8 tablespoons olive oil into a large heavy iron frying pan. Open a 2-ounce can of anchovy fillets and add 8 of them to the soaked bread, and rub the bread and anchovies through a coarse sieve. Have ready 2 large rectangular Pyrex baking dishes approximately 12 by 7 by 1½ inches deep. Rub them both lightly with a little olive oil.

Now heat the olive oil in the large iron pan and when very hot place the tomatoes cut side down in the pan so that they do not touch each other, and cook on a low flame for 2 minutes, then turn them over care-

fully with a spatula or pancake turner and cook for 1 minute longer and remove from fire and place them side by side in the 2 oiled baking dishes, cut side up. It may be necessary to fry only half of them at a time, for they must not be crowded. The purpose of doing this to the emptied tomatoes is so that they will retain their shape. When all are prepared and ready for stuffing, proceed as follows:

Place 6 tablespoons olive oil in a small frying pan and cook in it slowly 6 tablespoons chopped onion until it starts to brown lightly. Then add the tomato pulp coarsely chopped, the prepared garlic, 2 tablespoons chopped parsley, and season well to taste with salt and coarsely ground black pepper. Cook slowly for 3 minutes, then remove from fire and add the purée of soaked bread and anchovies. Mix well, and stuff the tomatoes. Sprinkle them liberally with toasted bread crumbs, and trickle a little olive oil over each. Place in preheated, hot 450°–475° F. oven and bake until browned or for about 12–15 minutes. Sprinkle with chopped parsley and serve.

Willa Roberts Plank's Browned White Turnips
(for 6–8)

Peel 12 medium-sized white turnips and slice crosswise very thin. Place 4 tablespoons butter in a pan. Add the turnips and pour over them 2 cups cold water. Cover. Place on fire and bring gently to boil. Simmer until almost all the juice has boiled down or for 15–20 minutes. Add 1½ cups beef consommé and continue cooking for about 15 minutes longer, or until they may be easily pierced with a silver fork. Pour off the juice and save. Place in a small jar with a cover 2 teaspoons of flour, add 2 tablespoons cold water. Shake it violently until smooth and free from lumps. Add this to the turnip juice, place on fire and bring to a boil. This should give you about 1 cup slightly thickened juice. Season to taste with salt and coarsely ground pepper and pour back over the turnips. If time permits, allow them to cool, then reheat when ready to serve, preferably over hot water. Just before serving add 1 teaspoon butter and 2 tablespoons heavy cream. Shake over fire, then place in serving dish. Sprinkle lightly with finely chopped parsley and serve at once.

Caramelized Turnips
(for 6–8)

Wash and peel about 12 large but tender white turnips. With a potato scooper, cut from these as many little balls as possible. Do not discard the remainder of the turnips. They may be cooked separately and mashed in the usual way. Place the balls in a pan of cold water until ready to cook them, at which time drain them well. Melt ¼ pound butter in a large frying pan and add the turnip balls. Cook over low flame for 5 minutes, shaking the pan occasionally, then sprinkle the turnips with 2 teaspoons granulated sugar and continue cooking, stirring frequently with a wooden spoon until they become a pale golden brown all over, or for about 15 minutes. Watch carefully as they burn easily due to the sugar. When brown, pour over them ½ can consommé and cover and cook until the consommé has reduced and formed a nice brown syrupy juice, or for about 10 minutes, at which time add the rest of the can of consommé. Reduce heat even more and cook until the turnips may be pierced with a fork or until they have cooked 30–35 minutes in all. Be very careful not to allow them to cook dry. Add a little hot water if necessary, so that there is still some juice left when they are done. Place in hot serving dish and pour over them the brown juice. Sprinkle with chopped parsley and serve.

Baked Zucchini and Tomatoes
(for 6–8)

Butter a large oval baking dish. Scald 8 or 10 large juicy tomatoes and remove their skins. Place in buttered dish. Wash 1 very large zucchini (Italian squash) or 8 small ones. If you use a large one, peel and cut lengthwise and scrape out the seeds. Slice crosswise in 1-inch thick pieces. The small squash need not be peeled and seeded. Now peel 3 or 4 onions and slice fine. Cover the tomatoes with the onions, sprinkle with salt and pepper. Now add the zucchini, arranging them prettily. Again sprinkle lightly with salt and pepper, and add ½ teaspoon dried sweet basil, crumbled fine, and 2 small bay leaves. Pour over all one can beef consommé, and dot with 2 or 3 tablespoons butter. If you like garlic, bury 1 small clove of it in the dish, or squeeze the juice of one over all, using a garlic press. At the very last, trickle over the surface of all, 4 tablespoons good olive oil. Place in preheated 450° F. oven and bake for about 2 hours, basting frequently with its own juice. Sprinkle with chopped parsley and serve accompanied by crisp French or Italian bread slightly warmed in the oven.

Zucchini with Sauce Hollandaise
(for 6–8)

Peel 18 medium-sized, tender zucchini (Italian squash). Wash, quarter lengthwise, place piled neatly in a pan large enough to hold them flat, sprinkle with about 1 teaspoon salt and pour over them just enough boiling water to cover. Cover with lid, and place on fire and cook rapidly until just tender, or for 7–8 minutes. Drain well. Place in hot vegetable dish, sprinkle lightly with chopped parsley and serve with Sauce Hollandaise served in a separate sauceboat.

Note: *If you prefer, the zucchini may also be cooked with their skins on, but are not quite as delicate in flavor. Scrub them well, cut off both ends, and quarter them. Place in a large enamel saucepan to hold them, add a tiny pinch of soda and 1 scant teaspoon salt and cover with boiling water. Cook rapidly until tender, or for about 14 minutes. Serve in the same way accompanied by plenty of Sauce Hollandaise (see page 140).*

EIGHT

Home For
A
Greedy Person

No one of us, I suppose, save a few confirmed guttersnipes, but intends some day to have a home in the country, a comfortable little house painted white with blue shutters perhaps, and all around it green things growing, trees to shade us, flowers to give grace, hedges for privacy and more prosaically a substantial vegetable garden back of the pergola to provide sustenance for our tables and make us more independent of the greengrocer and the local huckster of uncertain appearance but highly assured prices.

Being one of the many who hope some blissful day to have a home in the country I do not understand why the vegetable garden alone should have the duty of producing food. Why not also the shade trees, the hedges, the shrubbery? In Spain they plant hedges of pomegranates which bear edible fruit attractively and freely. So for my country home I shall take the hint and plant, not pomegranate, but quince, trimmed low and thick with branches interlaced, knowing there will be loveliness of bloom in the spring and later on fruit which in its raw state is so unpalatable that it presents no temptation to predatory children; touched with the magic of fire and sugar these same puckery hard spheres become delicious crimson jelly, quince preserves, quince butter, quince honey and quince conserves, none of which may be ignored by the epicure. The possessor of a quince hedge may well smile pityingly at his neighbor's flourishing privet.

Quince, then, for an along-the-street hedge, but farther back and less accessible to the passer-by I will plan for hedges of blackberry, raspberry and the new improved blueberry, all of which can be trained into tight thrifty green walls and all offer a rich harvest. Currants and gooseberries are also hedge possibilities—if you like them in quantity. I like them both but I'd rather have red raspberries, which with careful pruning and training can be made to serve as a hedge and a home fruit at the same time. No one who likes red raspberries ever had enough of them to eat at any one time, but even a few of the fat red thimbles will add grace to a compote or a plain ice cream. The best way to eat them is to go out to the vines, gather a big handful, tip the head back and put the whole handful in the mouth at once.

For a higher hedge, a screen perhaps or a dividing line, I would plant filberts. The bushes branch at the ground and as they grow, if they're guided into compact shapes, not too high, they make a close useful barrier. Early in the fall the brown nuts will drop out of their clustered ruffled cups, ready to add their special fillip of flavor to the table. Salted filberts, filberts crushed to use in ice cream and puddings and cakes are very very tasty. Many varieties bear nuts freely at an early age so the hedge becomes a free nut store not too long after planting.

People who motor through the East must have noticed a small ornamental tree grown in many small town yards, a tree with a straight bare trunk and a round bushy green head, more like stage shrubbery than a natural growing thing. I don't know the name of this popular tree but I'm quite sure it bears no edible fruit. Did their proud owners but know it they could have little trees quite as decorative and far more useful by planting the Oriental persimmon grafted on native stock; it achieves practically the same roundheaded bushy shape, and in the fall when the great golden persimmons hang on it like apples of Hesperides it is wonderful to see. And oh, how meltingly sweet they are and how expensive if one buys them at fruit stores! Served as a first course chilled with their thin skin cut back in raying petals, or as a dessert with their tops scooped out and a spoonful of orange ice, they are an exotic palate delight. There is one catch to this—persimmons are not hardy in northern states, though they will grow and flourish farther north than fig trees.

No matter where I decide to locate my future home in the country, when I begin to choose its shade trees I will find a whole world of good things to eat. Why plant maples when black walnuts, butternuts, shellbarks and Japanese walnuts will grow just about anywhere and give food as well as shade? If blight-resistant trees are obtainable, add chestnuts to this list and we will make our own *marrons*. In the South the so-called English walnut, the soft- and hard-shell almonds and the wonderful pecan nut can be added to this list, but they do not like the colder climates.

If nut trees do not seem exactly right in my dooryard, I shall plant three apple trees; a Gravenstein both for eating out of hand and making apple pies and applesauce and cider, a Stayman Winesap or a McIntosh or Northern Spy for a crisp tasty winter apple, a Sweet Bough for a juicy fragrant sugary sweet summer eating apple. And I would add, partly because of its foolish romantic name, and partly because of its clear flushed color, a tree of Maryland's Maiden's Blush—which also makes the most perfect apple jelly, amber in color, nectar in flavor.

There must be some pear trees, too, and if space is limited, they may be grown espalier fashion on heavy wires, perhaps to divide the flower garden from the vegetable plot. Such an espalier will make white lace when in flower, and when the fruit is ripe there will be baked pears, preserved pears, pear tarts, and so on as fancy warrants, perhaps even perry, the heady pear cider. Without the labor of making an espalier, it is possible to grow pear trees in a decorative walk, for the pear tree is easy to train in simple formal shape, odd and effective.

Plum trees (think of damsons!), cherry trees, peach trees, nectarine trees, apricot trees, though they do not grow to great size, will give shade for a back-yard terrace and add variety to desserts. Have you ever eaten dead-ripe Oriental plums, peeled, halved and stoned and served with sugar and cream just like peaches? If not, you have a taste thrill yet to experience. And if there's room I'm going to have a couple of mulberry trees which will tempt mocking birds to come and feast and sing their everlasting grace. Note: Don't put mulberry trees over a terrace or a much traveled path, for when the fruit is ripe it will fall and squash and leave purplish spots on stone, cement or tiles.

One of my Southern California friends has in her garden two orange trees, a lemon and an avocado. One of my Florida friends has the same and has added a lime and a mango tree. All of these trees bear excellent useful fruit and in themselves are quite as attractive as eucalyptus or live oak. It's certainly pleasant when you want lime chiffon pie to pick the limes at home!

For my arbor or pergola, or perhaps merely a latticed back porch, there shall be not wisteria and honeysuckle, but three kinds of grapes, one an old-fashioned variety called Croaton, creamy white of skin and without pulp, just a bag of sweet juice, refreshing and delightful; and for the red, either a Catawba for its tang or a high-flavored Delaware and, being conservative in taste, my black grape shall be the old dependable Concord. This last makes an agreeable light wine resembling Marsala. Of course it also makes good jelly, preserves and catsup relish, a rare dish in more ways than one.

For shrubbery about my country home-to-be there shall be few of the usual ornamental bushes, except perhaps lilacs, syringas, a very few azaleas and if the climate permits a pink crape myrtle and an equally pink camellia. Instead, also if the climate permits, I shall plant figs and prune them into bushes and gather ripe figs in the golden summer sunshine. There may also be one native custard apple or papaw because my father liked the fruit, though it affects the average first-time taster very much as does the guava, you either love or hate. And if the greenery of my yard seems monotonous I shall vary it with a purple-foliaged, purple-fruited plum.

Now all this is not an idle scheme. It is quite possible, even on a small lot, to plant for beauty and use simultaneously, to let our trees and shrubs offer us goodly fruits as well as decoration for land and house. Odd and clever things might be done—I once saw peach trees trained espalier fashion over an arbor making a roof of foliage and bearing fruit freely. It took patience, skill and knowledge to achieve this, but not a superhuman amount of them.

The set fashion of mind which accepts only the conventional orchard and vineyard and hedge is doubtful of all other arrangements although fruit and nut trees are delighted to give their best in unusual surroundings if they receive sufficient care. Such trees and bushes have their special beauty, as great or greater than many of the things planted for beauty alone, if we will look to observe it. Imagination—and appetite—might create a whole new fashion in landscape gardening if we will but encourage them.

UNCOOKED FRUIT FOR THE TABLE

Ripe fresh perfect fruit needs no dressing up for the table, not even the usual sugar and cream, but run-of-the-market fruit may be of uncertain age and quality and can therefore use enhancing flavors.

APPLES—Wash and polish, arrange on plate or in bowl lined with green leaves. Service is dessert plate, finger bowl, knife and fork. Cheddar, Bel Paese, Runesten Danish, Poona, Oka, Port Salut or Gruyere cheese, with Bent's or Vermont or other plain crackers, all go well with raw apples.

APRICOTS—Marvelous when completely ripe, acid and flat if green. Serve in bowl of cracked ice, or chill and arrange in basket or bowl. Service is dessert plate, finger bowl, knife and fork. If fruit is not first quality, peel, sprinkle with sugar and a little apricot brandy or apricot liqueur and serve in compote bowl.

BANANAS—Must be dead ripe with dark skins to be at their best. Serve sliced with sugar and cream, or cut in long pieces, roll in ginger syrup and then in grated fresh coconut, and serve with little cakes. Bananas are good in a mixed compote with oranges, pineapple, apricots and raspberries.

CHERRIES—Use only ripe perfect fruit, chill and serve on individual dessert plates piled on a green leaf. Since cherries must be eaten from the fingers, a paper cocktail napkin tucked in with the decorative leaf will save table linen from stubborn stains.

FIGS—Purple or green ripe fresh figs are so delicious they need only be peeled, sliced, dusted with sugar and chilled. Serve with either sweet or sour cream, or whipped sweet cream slightly sweetened and flavored with vanilla. Many people like figs best without any kind of cream, even without sugar.

GRAPEFRUIT—Chill, cut in half, remove center core and run knife around each section of pulp. Add sugar or honey to taste, serve with pointed spoon. To elaborate, pile each half with seeded grapes, or strawberries cut in half, with stoned black cherries, or apricots peeled and cut in small sections. Grapefruit takes kindly to the addition of rum, kirsch, maraschino or mirabelle liqueur, but use sparingly or flavor will be hurt, and if liqueur is sweet go easy on sugar.

GRAPES—Wash, pick off imperfect fruit, and serve piled on a big plate garnished with green leaves, grape scissors on side so each person may clip off his portion. Place cocktail napkin on the dessert plates to keep stains from table linens. Less handsome bunches should be cut into individual portions and served in a deep bowl of cracked ice. It used to be the fashion to have a specially shaped deep glass filled with water at each place to dip the grapes before eating, but few people today have such glasses or can manage the extra service. Should the grapes you buy look stained, wash in strong vinegar, and rinse well before serving.

MANGOES—This luscious fruit should be dead ripe. Peel and slice from the seed carefully, saving the juice. Put in a bowl, add the juice, chill and pass sugar with the sliced fruit though they are better unsugared. If mangoes are served to the family only, put a whole one on each dessert plate, with a sharp dessert knife and fork, add large-sized finger bowls and huge paper napkins, and let everyone peel, cut and gnaw as he likes, and elegance be hanged! For the small fry add an extra paper napkin for a bib.

MELONS—Cantaloupes are chilled and served in unpeeled slices with dessert knife and fork. Cantaloupe Lillian Russell is halves of small cantaloupes, sweet and very ripe, with seeds removed and cavity heaped with vanilla ice cream, sometimes sprinkled with chopped crystallized ginger. Nice for a children's party without the ginger.

Honeydew melons are served in unpeeled slices, chilled, with halves of lime or lemon on the side. Casabas, Canadians, Cranshaws and Spanish Melons are served in chilled generous slices, with lime or lemon halves. To dress them up, serve separately sugar-and-cinnamon mix, crystallized ginger or mint leaves chopped fine, or ground nutmeg, letting each person choose his favorite.

For Melon with Prosciutto as a first course, slice honeydews thin, trim off rind, lay three slices on each dessert plate, and across these three slices, very thin, of prosciutto, Jambon de Parme, or Jambon de Bayonne. Garnish with lemon halves and offer the pepper mill. Dessert knife and fork required.

NECTARINES—see PEACHES.

ORANGES—For breakfast serve small fruit peeled and stuck on fork, if large, cut in half with sections loosened with sharp knife, or whole unpeeled with small knife and fork. For dessert, peel, slice, sugar to taste, cover with fresh grated coconut and chill. Add chopped marshmallows under the coconut if you like them. Plain sliced oranges, sugared and sprinkled with Jamaica rum, Cointreau or Curaçao make a fine compote, but use the liqueur sparingly. Oranges combine well in mixed compotes with bananas, grapefruit, strawberries, pineapple, dates, stewed rhubarb.

PERSIMMONS—The popularity of the luscious large persimmons rises steadily. For first course at luncheon set fruit on stem end, peel down in pointed sections with a sharp knife, so center pulp stands up from flower-like petals. Chill and serve on individual plate with dessert fork and spoon. For dessert, set chilled fruit, unpeeled on stem end and cut out a deep pointed section from the top, just before serving fill with scoop of orange ice. Serve on large platter garnished with green leaves.

PEACHES and NECTARINES—Big perfect ripe fruit should be served whole, chilled, with fruit knife and fork, cocktail napkin at side to avoid linen stains. If fruit is not exceptionally fine in appearance and flavor, peel, slice, and serve with sugar and cream, or without cream but brightened with a sprinkling of fine, chopped, fresh mint, or chopped crystallized ginger, or a dash of peach brandy, kirsch, peach liqueur or maraschino. N.B.: A half of a ripe soft sweet juicy peach put in the shaker with the makings of a bacardi cocktail adds great enchantment to that drink.

PLUMS—There is a subacid quality about some plums which makes them not so good for eating uncooked, although cooked they are fine. The large ripe damsons, and the big green-yellow Orientals, and some of the big red plums are delicious raw. Peel and slice as you would peaches, sprinkle with sugar as you put each layer in the dish. Cover dish and set in refrigerator to chill for an hour or so. Serve with sweet cream. Also you can peel, slice, sugar and dash the plums with kirsch, slivovitz or mirabelle, and serve chilled just so. A few green almonds peeled and put in with the fruit aid the exotic flavor.

PINEAPPLE—Slice in half lengthwise top and all, cut out center core, cut the pulp down the middle almost to the rind, then run the knife deep along each side, inside the rind, so that all the edible part is loose in two long pieces inside the rind. Now slice inch-thick, crosswise, still keeping edible part inside the rind. Sugar to taste, dash with kirsch or maraschino, and chill. Place on tray for serving—a large pineapple will serve at least eight. For a smaller number, cut all the rind off and slice edible part quite thin crosswise, place slices in serving dish with sugar and kirsch or maraschino, chill and stir gently now and then to equalize flavor. Serve as a compote. Any left over bits will go well in a mixed compote of orange, peach, pear, plums, strawberries or raspberries.

PEARS—Fine ripe pears should be washed, dried, and arranged in bowl or basket to display form and color. Serve with dessert knife and fork, and if fruit is very ripe and juicy add dessert spoon. Brie, Pont l'Évêque or cream cheese with hot toasted crackers make the perfect accompaniment to a fine dessert pear.

The huge Comice pears may be served cut in half, unpeeled but cored, the cavity heaped with unsweetened whipped cream, hot chocolate sauce passed separately to dip over the chilled fruit-and-cream. Even a novice cook can do this dessert well. Put nothing alcoholic on raw pears or their subtle flavor will be ruined. Pears not good enough to eat raw should be stewed, baked or used in pastry, with plenty of lemon, sugar and red wine to hide their lack of flavor.

RASPBERRIES—Pick over carefully, never wash unless necessary. Mound fruit on individual plates, serve with powdered sugar and cream, either sweet or sour. Or put fruit in serving dish, sugar lightly and sprinkle with the pure colorless Eau de Vie de Framboise—be sparing, too much leaves a bitter tang. Chill well. A sweet raspberry liqueur, using less sugar, may be substituted for the true Eau de Vie.

STRAWBERRIES—Handle gently, wash only if necessary, cap and pick over carefully taking only ripe, shapely fruit. Mound on individual plates, serve with powdered sugar and cream either sweet or sour. Or serve as a compote, without cream, first sprinkling with sugar and strawberry liqueur, or Cointreau. Chill well. For Strawberries Romanoff the cleaned and capped berries are lightly sugared, then chilled for 2 hours in a mixture of one-half fresh strained orange juice and one-half Curaçao. Serve with heavy cream sweetened stingily, whipped and flavored with vanilla.

WATERMELON—Chill until icy cold. Slice crosswise in 1- or 2-inch slices, cut off rind, cut each slice in half. Serve 1 half-circle slice on a chilled plate with dessert knife and fork. If you want to be lavish, cut open a big melon, scoop out the heart alone in large pieces, serve 2 or 3 of these on chilled individual plates, with dessert knife and fork. A good watermelon needs neither garnish nor seasoning—and above all, please don't cut it up into little balls with the potato scoop and serve in a glass cup, for that is a crime against good eating.

General Directions for Making Jelly

Fruit used for jelly making should be firm and in good condition on the underripe rather than overripe side, but a certain proportion of thoroughly ripe fruit adds greatly to the flavor. The first process is to extract the juice. Look over, wash and stem all fruit, but do not peel apples. Crush berries, currants, grapes and soft fruits to start juice flowing, add a little water. Apples and quinces require water to cover. Cook soft fruits 10 minutes or until soft. Cook hard fruits about 25 minutes. When soft, turn into jelly bag or into a colander lined with several thicknesses of cheesecloth and allow juice to drain, without squeezing but shift the fruit occasionally. The remaining pulp may have water added to cover and be recooked to make a separate second extraction of second quality jelly. Keep this extraction separate from the first, however. The juice should first be measured, then boiled 5 minutes, and it is important to skim it carefully during the process. When the juice has cooked 5 minutes, the required amount of sugar should be added, usually in equal quantities, although some fruits require less. The juice and sugar should then cook together until ready to jell in a deep kettle, of a capacity 4 or 5 times as great as the amount of juice to be cooked, as jelly has a great tendency to boil up and over. The time required for this second cooking varies, but the quicker, the better, is the best rule. A thermometer may be used, which at sea level should register between 218°–221° F., but the good old "sheet" test is the best method, in my opinion. To test, lift a spoonful of the boiling juice about a foot above the kettle and holding the spoon, so that the juice may run out of the side of the spoon, let the juice pour back into the kettle. If the last part of the juice in the spoon forms a thin sheet as it falls off, leaving a clean edge to the spoon, the jelly is done, and should be instantly removed from the fire and poured into sterilized glasses. Be sure to skim the jelly frequently as it cooks, to insure a crystal clear jelly. When the jelly has set and is cold, cover with a ¼-inch coating of hot, melted paraffin or Parawax. Adjust tin lids, label and store in dark, dry place.

Black Concord Grape Jelly
(first and second quality)

Stem slightly underripe Concord grapes, until you have 2½ quarts of them. Wash and drain, and put them in an enamel pan. Mash slightly and bring to a boil, and cook them until juicy and soft, about 10 minutes. Strain through jelly bag, without squeezing, but save the pulp. Measure juice and boil it 5 minutes, skimming it well, then for each cup juice add 1 cup sugar, and cook until it sheets from the spoon, or about 7 minutes. Be careful to skim carefully and constantly. Remove from fire and pour immediately into sterilized glasses. When cold, cover with Parawax and tin covers. Makes about 4 glasses.

To make 2nd quality, put pulp back in pan, and cover again with cold water and cook about 25 minutes, then strain again, squeezing it a bit, if you like. Measure juice, then boil it 5 minutes, skimming carefully, then add equal measure of granulated sugar and boil until it sheets from spoon, or about 7 minutes. Pour into sterilized glasses. When cold, cover with hot Parawax and seal with tin covers.

Red Currant and Black Raspberry Jelly

Put 3 cups washed stemmed red currants in a pan, with 3 cups washed black raspberries. Add ½ cup cold water, bring to a boil and boil 10 minutes. Strain, without squeezing, through cheesecloth or jelly bag. Measure juice and boil it 5 minutes, skimming carefully. Add equal quantity of granulated sugar. Stir until melted and continue cooking 6 or 7 minutes longer, or until it sheets from the spoon. Pour into sterilized jelly glasses. Makes about 5 small glasses. Seal with melted Parawax when cold and set, and cover with the covers.

Red Currant Jelly

Wash and stem 2 quarts red currants, which should give you about 6 cups currants. Add ½ cup water and put them on the fire to boil for about 10 minutes, or until the currants are soft. Drain through cheesecloth or jelly bag, without squeezing. Measure juice. It should give you about 2½ cups juice. Bring to a boil and boil 5 minutes, skimming carefully. Add equal quantity of granulated sugar, cook, skimming constantly until it sheets from the side of the spoon, or about 6 minutes. Pour into sterilized jelly glasses. Makes about 5 small glasses. Seal, when cold and set, with melted Parawax and cover with tin covers.

General Directions for Making Jam

Fruit for jam should also be free from blemishes—and again some under-ripe fruit is desirable. It should be stemmed and washed and drained. Some people cook the fruit before adding the sugar, but I make a syrup of sugar and water in the proportion of 1 cup water to every 5 cups sugar, boil it 5 minutes and pour it over the fruit, then cook it until it sheets from the spoon and the fruit is transparent. Proportionately less sugar is used than for jelly, or about ⅔ as much sugar as you have of prepared fruit. Again the quicker it is cooked, the better. It is also essential to skim it carefully and constantly during the cooking process, also it is wise to stir it frequently with a long wooden spoon. When it is done, I pour it into sterilized jars, adjust new rubber rings, and when cold I cover it with a little hot Parawax, put on covers and seal tight.

Apricot Jam

Take 6 pounds fresh apricots. Split them and remove the pits, putting the halves in cold water as you go along. Next crack open the pits, take out the kernels, put them in a bowl, pour boiling water over them, cover, and allow them to steep 5 minutes, then pinch off the brown skins. Now put 9 cups granulated sugar in a large pan, moisten it with 2 cups cold water, bring it to a boil, skim it well and boil for 5 minutes. Then add the well-drained apricots and continue boiling, skimming carefully, stirring frequently to avoid sticking, and when the juice sheets from the side of the spoon and the jam is thick and transparent, add the blanched kernels and pour or ladle the jam into hot sterilized pint-sized fruit jars, adjust scalded rubbers. When cold, cover with a little hot Parawax, put on the tops and seal tight. It should take about 50 minutes of cooking for the jam to cook to the right consistency, but be careful not to overcook it, as jam thickens when it cools. This quantity should fill 5 pint jars.

Blackberry, Red Raspberry or Black Raspberry Jam

Blackberry or raspberry jam is better if some of the seeds are first re-moved. To do this, mash the fruit well, then pass it through a sieve. Throw away ½ of the remaining pulp, but add the rest to the strained fruit. Measure and for each cup of pulp, put into a pan ⅔ cup sugar. Measure the total sugar and allow 1 cup water to each 5 cups sugar and boil together 5 minutes before pouring it over the first pulp. Cook, skimming carefully and stirring frequently until it sheets from the spoon. Pour into sterilized jars, adjust rubbers. Cover when cold with hot Parawax and covers, and seal tight.

Strawberry Jam

Wash and drain well, and hull 2½ pounds strawberries. Make a thick syrup of 5 cups granulated sugar moistened with 1 cup water boiled 5 minutes. Add the strawberries and cook until the strawberries are trans-parent and the juice sheets from side of the spoon. Stir and skim the jam constantly while cooking. Pour into sterilized jars. Pour a little Parawax over each, and seal tight. Makes 2½ pints.

Wild Strawberry Jam

Wild strawberries are seldom sandy, so it is best not to wash them. Stem them and measure them. For each cup (well packed) of strawberries, put into a pan ⅔ cup granulated sugar. Measure the sugar and for every 5 cups sugar, moisten it with 1 cup water. Boil sugar and water 5 minutes, then pour it over the strawberries. Let it come to a boil, skim carefully and cook 5 minutes. Strain off the juice and cook it until it sheets, then pour it over the strawberries again and cook 5 minutes longer. Pour into sterilized jars, adjust rubbers. When cold, cover with hot Parawax and seal tight.

Gooseberry Jam

Wash berries and with scissors cut off stem and blossom ends. Cut berries in half or quarters if large.

Weigh, and use 1 pound sugar for equal weight of fruit. Start the berries cooking with a little water, to keep them from sticking to the pot. Add sugar in small amounts until it is all absorbed and melted. Cook until the jam is stiff when tried on a saucer. It does not take very long and turns a lovely red color. Pour into sterilized, pint-sized jars and adjust rubbers. When cold, cover with hot Parawax, cover, and seal tight.

It is tart like currant and is good with meat as well as hot biscuits, etc.

Black Cherry Jam

Pit large, black cherries until you have 15 cups of them. Moisten 10 cups granulated sugar with 2 cups cold water, boil it 5 minutes, skimming it carefully. Pour it over the cherries in a big preserving kettle, bring quickly to a boil again, skim carefully and frequently and cook until thick and transparent, about 50 minutes. Pour into sterilized, pint-sized jars and adjust rubbers. When cold, cover with hot Parawax, cover, and seal tight. Makes about 5 pints.

Grape Conserve

Wash and sterilize 4 pint-sized jars. Prepare 1 cup walnuts cut not too fine. Wash, drain and pick off the grapes from 4 pounds Concord grapes. Slip the skins from the grapes, keeping them separate from the pulp. Cut 1 slicing orange in 4, remove any seeds there may be, then put the orange, skin and all, through the coarse meat grinder. Be careful not to lose any of the juice. Boil the grape pulp for about 10 minutes, stirring constantly. Press through a sieve to remove seeds. To the resultant pulp, add 4 cups granulated sugar, 1 cup seedless raisins, the ground-up orange and 1 scant teaspoon salt. Boil rapidly, stirring to prevent burning for about 10 *minutes, or until the mixture begins to thicken. Add the grape skins and boil 10 minutes longer, stirring constantly. Add the cup of chopped walnuts and pour immediately into hot sterilized jars and adjust rubbers. When cold, cover with hot Parawax and cover and seal tight.*

Pickled Watermelon Rind

Cut 5 pounds watermelon rind into 1-inch-wide strips, then cut off all the pink part from the inside and the green rind from the outside. Cut in inch squares. Cover with cold water, adding ½ cup salt to each 2 quarts water, and soak 24 hours in the refrigerator. Drain the watermelon of its brine. Cover with cold water, and drain again. Cover once more with cold water and cook until just tender. Drain thoroughly.

In the meantime, make a syrup of 6 cups white sugar and 1 pound light brown sugar, moistened with 1 quart vinegar and 1 quart water, seasoned with 1 lemon, sliced, 2 sticks cinnamon, broken into little pieces, 2 teaspoons whole cloves, 2 teaspoons Jamaica allspice. When it has boiled down a bit, pour it over the well-drained watermelon rind and continue cooking until transparent. Pour into sterilized pint-sized jars, and adjust rubbers and covers and seal. Makes about 5 pints. It should not be eaten for several months, as it is better after it has ripened in the jar, so to speak.

Quince Preserves

Select 12 perfect, pint-sized fruit jars, preferably ones with glass tops. Wash, place in large kettle, cover with water and bring to a boil to sterilize them. Be sure to sterilize the covers at the same time. Have ready 12 new rubbers.

Wash 12 fine quinces. Peel and quarter them and cut out the cores. Cut the pieces once more lengthwise making 8 pieces of each quince. Place in a large kettle and add enough water to cover the fruit. Place on fire and boil until the pieces are tender through. Drain but save the juice. Weigh the fruit and to each pound fruit measure out 1 pound granulated sugar, placing the sugar in the juice. Boil the juice and sugar together for 5 minutes, then add the fruit and boil steadily until the fruit is transparent and a beautiful red color. Pour in jars, adjust rubbers and seal. Wipe jars clean with cloth wrung out in hot water.

Yellow Tomato Preserves

Wash and dry 1 pound tiny yellow tomatoes. Pour boiling water over them. Allow them to stand 5 minutes, then drain and peel carefully. Place them in bowl, cover with 2 cups granulated sugar and allow to remain overnight. In the morning, drain off the juice. Prepare 24 seeded black raisins, 2 lemons sliced very thin, each slice quartered; also cut up fine 3 pieces preserved ginger, about 2½ ounces. Bring juice to a boil, skim and boil 5 minutes, add prepared tomatoes, ginger, lemon and raisins, and boil 12 to 14 minutes longer, or until thick and transparent. Pour into sterilized jars, and pour a thin coating of Parawax over all immediately and cool. Cover when cold with another layer of melted Parawax, and seal. Makes 2 ½-pint jars and a little over.

Chili Sauce

Peel 12 ripe tomatoes and cut in small pieces. Add 4 green peppers, from which you have removed the seeds, and which you have chopped fine. Also add 2 big onions, peeled and chopped fine, and 4 apples, peeled and cut fine. Put all this into a big enamel pan and add 2½ cups light brown sugar, 1 pint vinegar, 2 level tablespoons salt, 1 teaspoon dry mustard, a pinch of curry powder, 1 teaspoon celery seed, ½ teaspoon ground cloves, ½ teaspoon whole allspice, 1 tablespoon ground cinnamon, a dash of coarsely ground pepper and 1⅓ teaspoonfuls cayenne. Place on fire and cook for 2 hours or until thick and transparent, adding as it cooks 1½ cups more vinegar. Pour into sterilized pint-sized jars, adjust rubbers and seal tight. Makes 4 to 5 pints, depending on size of tomatoes.

Bread and Butter Pickles

Wash young cucumbers, having tender undeveloped seeds, then slice paper thin, until you have 4 quarts. Place them in a big bowl, with lots of chopped ice, sprinkle them with a handful of salt and cover with cold water. Soak for 3 hours, then drain well. Peel and slice very thin, 6 onions. Put the onions and the drained cucumbers in a big enamel pan and pour over them 1 quart pure cider vinegar. Add 1 teaspoon dry mustard, 2 teaspoons mustard seed, 2 teaspoons celery seed and a scant ½ teaspoon ground turmeric powder, also 2 cups granulated sugar. Have ready 4 or 5 quart-sized sterilized hot jars with glass tops and new rubbers. Place the cucumbers on the fire and bring just to a boil, then remove from the fire, and pack the whole to overflowing into the jars, and seal at once. If there should not be enough vinegar to fill all the jars to overflowing, use a little extra vinegar, just brought to a boil in a separate enamel pan.

Red or White Currant Bar-le-Duc

Don't try to make this unless you have infinite time and infinite patience, because the first step is to take the seeds out of a pint of clean, picked-over currants, using a long pin—and it will probably use up the greater part of a whole day. When you have all the currants seeded, and you must take care to crush them as little as possible, put a pint of good plain clear pure honey in a saucepan and let it come to a boil. Drop the currants into the boiling honey and cook them gently for 4 to 5 minutes. Pour into sterilized jars, let cool and seal, or cover with Parawax. You can make gooseberry bar-le-duc the same way, but unless they are very small they will need to be boiled in the honey twice as long as the currants. Use a honey without any fancy flavor.

FOUR SPECIAL FRUIT DESSERTS

Fruit Meringue
(for 6–8)

Butter a 10-inch Pyrex pie plate. Separate the whites from the yolks of 6 eggs. You should have ¾ cup whites. If necessary, add 1 more to make the exact amount. Light your oven and set it at 250° to 275° F. Measure out 1½ cups granulated sugar. Place the whites in a big bowl and add 1 teaspoon cider vinegar and a big pinch salt. Beat with rotary beater until stiff, then add gradually the sugar, 1 tablespoon at a time, beating continuously with the rotary beater. An electric mixer may be used, but I find it safer to start with a hand one. When all the sugar has been beaten in, the whites should be smooth and satiny in texture. Using a tablespoon, fill the pie dish with a 1-inch thickness of the meringue, then pile the rest around the edge, forming a nest, with a 3-inch rim, about the width of a tablespoon. Place in a preheated slow 250° to 275° F. oven and bake for about 50 minutes, or until a light golden brown and until it feels firm to the touch. Remove from oven and place away from draft and cool. When ready to serve, fill the center with raspberries or strawberries or sliced peaches lightly sugared with confectioners' sugar. The top may then be covered with whipped cream, or the whipped cream may be served separately.

Raspberry Gelatine
(for 6–8)

Defrost 2 quarts frozen sweetened raspberries and rub the juice and pulp through a fine sieve. Discard the seeds. This should give you about 3 cups thick juice. Soak 2 envelopes Knox Gelatine in 1 cup cold water for 10 minutes, then add 1 cup boiling water. Stir until gelatine is well dissolved, then add the raspberry juice. Mix and place in 1½-quart-size mold and chill in refrigerator until set. Serve in the same dish without trying to turn it out, accompanied with cream, or, if you prefer, more raspberry juice made in the same way as above, using another quart of frozen raspberries.

Broiled Grapefruit
(for 6–8)

Cut 4 large grapefruit in half crosswise; cut out center core; and run a sharp knife around each section. Place the grapefruit in a shallow pan large enough to hold the 8 halves securely. Fill the center of each with maple sugar cream, or grated maple sugar, and dot each one with 1 teaspoon butter. Light your broiler and place the pan 3½ inches from the flame, and broil until lightly browned, or for about 20 minutes. Serve hot.

Orange Ice
(for 6–8)

Make a syrup with 4 cups granulated sugar moistened with 8 cups cold water. Place on fire and boil 5 minutes. Cool slightly, then add 4 cups strained fresh orange juice, ½ cup strained lemon juice and the grated rind of 4 oranges. Cool and freeze in the usual manner.

NINE

Dinner At Eight, For Eight

Autumn sets the mood for your first dinner party. Everyone's back from the country and you feel that old urge to ask your friends to sit around your table, to eat and drink and make up arrears in personal news—that's the nice way to speak of gossip, my dears—as if you didn't know!

You have beautiful china, linen, glass, silver. You delight in flower arrangements. So far, fine! A beautifully set table strikes the gala note and maintains it.

The catch in dinner parties today is lack of service. Fortunately, there are still trained waitresses-by-the-evening to be had; by all means get one, for good service at table is, to my mind, a requisite of a really enjoyable meal.

But to find a cook is quite another pair of shoes. Maybe you're lucky enough to have one; far more likely, you must prepare the meal yourself or make the main dishes. The dinner described here is planned on the premise that the hostess will do the cooking, or has a cook who isn't of the grand manner when it comes to the range and the saucepans.

This dinner is also planned for guests who do not come on time, which means practically all guests. My experience is that few except those invited for dinner-and-theater ever approximate the hour named in their invitation, so it is wise to have dishes that come to small harm by standing.

COCKTAILS   CANAPÉS   NUTS

MELON WITH PROSCIUTTO

CHICKEN   TAVERNE   ROYALE

TOMATO AND PEPPER MIX   POTATO CHIPS

WATER CRESS AND ENDIVE SALAD

BLUE CHEESE WHIPPED WITH BRANDY   CRACKERS

ICE CREAM LACED WITH RUM

COFFEE

Please don't substitute a soup for the melon because the chicken is soupish. If no melons are available, replace them with oysters baked on the half shell with a sprinkle of minced parsley, chives, a drop of tarragon vinegar and a whiff of garlic. If you don't want oysters, buy small deviled crabs already prepared in their shells and reheat them—or make them yourself.

Assuming that melons can be found, cut the fruit into thin crescents and cut off the rind. Put three crescents of melon on each plate, and across them lay three paper-thin slices of *prosciutto, Jambon de Bayonne,* or Virginia ham whichever is obtainable. Cut slabs off the sides of lemons —they don't squirt when squeezed if cut that way—and put one on each plate. Pass a pepper mill for those of your guests who like this final touch.

The chicken is a simplified version of *Water Zooi* as served at the Taverne Royale in Brussels. For eight people, buy two good-sized stewing chickens. Cut up as for frying, separating the second joint from the drumstick. Put into a pot with three whole carrots, five leeks (leave plenty of their tops), three stalks of celery, a generous inch-cube of salt pork, a bay leaf and a pinch of mace. Cover with warm water, salt lightly, throw in a dozen peppercorns and let come to a boil. Now skim, then lower heat and simmer until tender; it will take an hour and a half to two hours. Fish out the vegetables, and any loose pieces of chicken skin, thicken the broth lightly—don't let the juice be pasty and gravyish. If you have a mixer, put the cooked vegetables into it and reduce them to purée and put back in the broth, but be sure there are no chunks. Pour into your handsomest casserole and keep hot.

For the tomato and pepper mix, butter well a couple of shallow glass pie pans and put in a layer of green peppers, each cut into six sections, seeds and stems removed. Try to get peppers with streaks of red—they look prettier. On each section of pepper place a quarter of a firm tomato (unskinned), add salt and the merest bit of sugar, some chopped chives or a minced scallion and many small dots of butter. Bake in oven about half an hour. Don't overbake this dish, or the tomatoes will lose their shape.

Potato chips are not to be scorned. They supply the crunchiness and neutral taste to set off the tomato-pepper combination. Buy them at the grocery, shake off any superfluous salt, give them a quick oven crisping. If you can't bear potato chips for dinner, you might make small, thin, corn-meal cakes (see recipe for Corn Meal Pancakes, page 125), put them in an overlapping ring on a silver platter, very hot and brittle. It is really important to vary the texture of food.

For the salad, make a plain French dressing and make it bland. Serve with toasted *unsalted* crackers and blue cheese which has been whipped to a thick paste with brandy—Spanish brandy if possible, for the flavor goes well with the cheese.

Now for the sweet. The simplest plan is to buy good vanilla ice cream, put in parfait glasses, leaving a half inch or so to fill with high-flavored, high-powered Jamaica rum. Or, if you feel enterprising enough, you might make a rich coconut ice cream in the refrigerator and add the same rum topping at the last moment.

The drinks for this dinner should be: first, dry Daiquiris, made with one part lime juice and a very very small quantity of honey or Falernum, combined with three parts rum—and get a good rum. There are too many poor rums around and about. Make your canapés as you like, only omit anything with fish or with a fishy taste, for fish is horrible with a Daiquiri. Plain salted almonds will do very well.

With the dinner, serve a medium dry white wine. If there's any Montrachet or Pouilly still in your cellar, either would be wonderful. A Moselle would be excellent, too. Lacking a fine imported vintage, there are many excellent domestic dry wines. Chill properly whatever it may be.

This is a simple dinner to get and a delicious one to eat. It offers a range of flavor and texture. It isn't extravagant, and it isn't wasteful, for should there be any *Water Zooi* left over, it may appear next day covered with a brown crust most successfully impersonating a chicken pie.

Deviled Crabs
(for 6–8)

Procure 16 crab shells. Wash and dry them. Buy 1 pint cooked crabmeat. Pick it over carefully to be sure there is no shell in it, but avoid breaking it up any more than necessary. Make a cream sauce by cooking together for a minute or two without browning, 6 tablespoons butter with 6 tablespoons all-purpose flour. Add gradually 2 cups hot rich milk and stir constantly until it boils and becomes nice and smooth. Season highly with about 2 teaspoons Worcestershire sauce, ¼ teaspoon Tabasco, ¼ teaspoon mace, a little coarsely ground black pepper, and ½ teaspoon salt. Add 1 tablespoon chopped parsley and stir in 2 well-beaten egg yolks. Add the crab meat to the sauce when the sauce has cooled. Melt 4 tablespoons butter and add 1 cup bread crumbs. Stir over low flame until the crumbs begin to brown lightly and are well heated. Fill the shells with the creamed crab meat. Sprinkle the top of each copiously with the buttered crumbs. Place on 2 large cookie sheets, preferably ones with rims, and place the sheets in a preheated, moderately hot 400° F. oven and bake until brown and until the sauce begins to sizzle, or for about 20 minutes.

Coconut Ice Cream
(for 6–8)

You need 3 coconuts. With an ice pick pierce 3 holes in each nut where the 3 soft spots are located. Drain and save the milk. Next break open the coconuts one by one by wrapping in a cloth and giving a few sharp taps with a hammer, resting the nut on the floor or some other hard surface. Use no coconut with black spots inside. When the nuts are all open, separate the meat from the shell in as large pieces as possible, cut off the thin brown outer skin with a sharp knife. Drop the pieces as you prepare them into a bowl of cold water. Next grate all the pieces on a coarse grater. This takes forever but it's worth it.

Put the grated meat in a large bowl, saving out about ¼ cup of it, which is to be sprinkled over the ice cream before serving. To the grated coconut in the big bowl add 4 cups boiling water. Beat thoroughly and work it together with a wooden spoon and let it stand 10 minutes to cool.

Now place a sieve over a bowl and line it with a large clean piece of heavy cheesecloth. Place about ⅓ of the moistened coconut in it, gather up the ends of the cloth and squeeze tight to extract every drop of juice. Repeat the process until all the coconut has been squeezed dry of its own juice and the water which was poured over it. There should be about 4½ cups milky water. Cover the bowl with waxed paper and a plate and place in refrigerator to cool thoroughly. The cream in the coconut will float to the top, just as it does with real milk. Skim it off carefully with a spoon; it should give you about 1½ cups smooth delicious cream. Measure 5 to 6 tablespoons sweetened condensed milk and thin it with 1 cup of the leftover, now very watery-looking, milky water. Add to this the coconut milk which you drained from the 3 coconuts and last of all stir in the coconut cream. You should now have about 5 cups liquid, and if you like add ½ cup more watery milk to stretch the amount a bit.

Freeze very hard by whatever method you prefer, turn out in serving dish, sprinkle the grated coconut which you held in reserve and garnish the dish with limes cut in quarters. A little lime juice is squeezed by each person over the cream before eating.

TEN

Christmas Dinner from a Basket

By June Platt

This year we are having our Christmas dinner in a basket and we will eat it picnic fashion, in front of our own fire! Why? A long story but I'll try to make it short.

Have you ever driven three thousand miles across the continent with two stalwart sons just to go on a picnic in a grove of palms by the sea, on Christmas day? Well we did. It was all my husband's idea. We were in New York and he was in California and we all wanted to be together, so we accepted his invitation (and letter of credit) and set forth, promising to arrive intact and on time on Christmas Eve, and so we did (in the pouring rain, ten minutes ahead of time to be exact), and my husband was there to greet us.

He had gone out the day before, in the glorious sunshine, found the most beautiful private picnic grounds in a grove of palms by the sea and decided it would be fun to take us there for a picnic Christmas Day. He then proceeded to track down the most beguiling picnic basket in town, and filled it bursting full with every fattening delicacy under the California sun, along with plenty of bottles for Christmas cheer. All was ready, red bow on the basket, but—as I said before—it was raining when we arrived (and it was still raining three days later when we tore ourselves away, homeward bound).

It is positive proof of our faith in the California sun that we stubbornly refused all invitations by friends to abandon picnic plans and disrupt their own private family gatherings. Instead we stuck steadfastly to Joe's plan for a private picnic and sat around all day waiting for the sun to come out. It all ended by our having, late in the day, good, but not very Christmasy roast beef sandwiches, produced by the hotel chef, and luke-warm coffee, preceded by far too many bits and pieces from bottles and basket.

But we were all very gay, and so we have decided to try a Christmas picnic again this year from Joe's basket by way of showing our appreciation.

The menu will be: Scotch Mists; celery and olives; cold shrimp, sauce remoulade; cold turkey on Joe's idea of crisp French buttered garlic bread, made with onions instead; hot baked sweet potatoes in their jackets; followed by cookies and festive after-dinner coffee, with chocolate *bouchées*. Finally as a surprise, walnuts in their shells! What's surprising about walnuts? Wait and see.

As far as possible everything will appear neatly packed in the big main picnic basket, but the turkey on a platter will be nestled into a shallow separate basket of its own, breast neatly carved and put back in place, surrounded by plenty of crisp lettuce leaves. I highly recommend a slice of Joe's bread, covered with a leaf of lettuce, topped with a slice of cold turkey breast, spread lightly with mayonnaise, sprinkled with coarsely ground pepper. The sweet potatoes tied up cosily in a big damask napkin will be tucked into the far end of the big basket so as not to add their comforting warmth to the cold shrimp, sauce remoulade, mayonnaise, and whipped butter, each in its respective jar or crock at the other end. Plates will be available and at least one knife and fork will be provided for each of us. These will be neatly rolled up, convent fashion, in big napkins, tied with gay ribbons. Mugs for the hot coffee will be placed on a tray in front of the fire to keep warm. The cookies in their beribboned plastic bags will be passed with the coffee as dessert, followed by the *bouchées* and walnuts.

Scotch Mists
(for 8)

Fill 8 large old-fashioned glasses with finely chopped ice almost to the top. Pour into each 2 jiggers of Scotch. Twist a piece of lemon peel over each, tuck it in and serve.

Boiled Shrimp
(for 8)

Wash 3 pounds of shrimps in cold water. Have ready an enamel pan of boiling water, flavored with salt, whole peppers, a pinch of thyme, a bit of parsley and a few stalks of celery. Drop the shrimp into the boiling water and cook for about 15 minutes or until they have turned pink. Drain and plunge into cold water. Pull off their shells, and with a sharp little knife carefully remove the intestinal vein, which you will find runs along the back from head to tail. As you clean them, dip them into a bowl of cold water and out again to wash off every last bit of black. Place in refrigerator in a covered crock until ready to serve, at which time cover them with the following sauce and serve at once.

Sauce Remoulade

Hard boil 3 eggs. Chop the whites very fine and rub the yolks through a sieve into a bowl. Chop fine 3 tablespoons capers, 3 sweet pickles along with a dozen leaves of tarragon (pickled ones will do). Add to the yolks of eggs 2 tablespoons of French mustard and mix, then add the chopped capers, tarragon and sweet pickle. Also add 1½ teaspoons of grated onion and a little freshly ground black pepper. Now add 1½ cups of mayonnaise and last of all 1½ tablespoons of finely chopped parsley and the chopped egg whites. Taste and add more salt and pepper if necessary. Serve cold.

Crisp French Onion Bread
(for 8)

Slice a big loaf of French bread diagonally in not too thick slices, being careful not to cut all the way through so that it will hold together. Cream ¼ of a pound of butter and spread it between the slices. Place between each slice a very thin slice of white onion. Place on cookie sheet, sprinkle it ever so lightly with a few drops of water. Place in preheated, moderately hot (400° F.) oven and bake for about 10–15 minutes or until thoroughly heated through and until the crust is nice and crisp. Break in half and place in breadbasket lined with a serviette and serve at once.

Baked Sweet Potatoes
(for 8)

Scrub 8 medium-sized sweet potatoes until spotlessly clean. Cut off a tiny piece from the end of each (this supposedly prevents any possibility of their bursting while baking). Place in moderately hot (400° F.) oven and bake until well done, or for about 1 hour. Serve at once with whipped butter made by cutting half a pound of sweet butter into a bowl and creaming it with a spoon, then beating it with a rotary beater, preferably an electric one, until it is very light and fluffy. Place in small butter crock in refrigerator for a few minutes before serving.

Christmas Mincemeat Cookies

First prepare the following ingredients: Slice with a sharp knife shelled almonds until you have 4 heaping tablespoons. Cut seedless raisins in half until you have 4 generous tablespoons. Break up with a fork one 9-ounce package of Borden's NoneSuch Mincemeat. Measure into a sifter 2 cups of flour, ½ teaspoon of soda, 1 heaping teaspoon of powdered cinnamon, 1 teaspoon of powdered cloves. Butter well 2 cookie sheets. Set your oven *at 400° F., and light it. Break 2 whole eggs into a bowl. Beat them slightly. Add 1½ cups of light brown sugar and stir until free from lumps. Sift in the flour and spices and stir well. Add 1 teaspoon of vanilla and 1 generous tablespoon of molasses and 1 tablespoon of melted butter. Stir and add enough boiling water to make the dough on the runny side (about 2 or 3 tablespoons). Last of all, add the nuts and raisins and mincemeat, all very lightly floured. Stir and spread thin over the 2 tins. Don't worry if there does not seem to be enough dough to cover. Spread it very thin. It puffs up and fills in the holes when it bakes. Bake for about 10 minutes in a 400° F. oven, or until you can no longer make a depression in the dough when you poke it with your finger. Be careful however not to burn the cookies. Remove from oven and spread immediately with a thin coating of frosting made by stirring into 1½ cups of sifted confectioners' sugar about 3 tablespoons of hot milk in which you have melted a teaspoon of butter. Flavor to taste with a little vanilla and plenty of almond extract. Cut into squares or diamonds a few minutes after frosting is spread, but do not remove from pan until the cookies are cold and the frosting has set. Place them carefully in a transparent plastic food bag, the kind sold for the refrigerator, one about 12 by 17 inches. Gather the top together and tie with a green satin ribbon.*

Chocolate Bouchées

Wipe clean on a cloth ½ cup shelled almonds and the same amount of shelled hazelnuts. Put them into a heavy aluminum frying pan and sprinkle over them 1¼ cups of granulated sugar. Place pan on a moderate flame and let the sugar melt and caramelize. Poke the nuts occasionally with a wooden spoon and tilt the pan constantly back and forth as the sugar melts. Avoid stirring and don't let the sugar get too brown. When every bit of sugar has melted and the skins on the nuts begin to crack open and the sugar has become a golden brown syrup, remove from fire and pour out immediately onto a lightly buttered cookie sheet, spreading it out with a wooden spoon. Let it become quite cold and brittle. The next step is to reduce the nuts and caramel to a paste. Break the caramel into small pieces and put it through the meat grinder using the coarsest blade. Replace this blade with the medium blade and put the whole through the grinder again. Replace the medium blade with the

finest blade and repeat the grinding process. Now add to the mixture ⅓
of a cup of Baker's semisweet chocolate chips, distributing them evenly
through the mixture, then put it through the grinder for the fourth time,
still using the finest blade. And now that that is done I hate to tell you
but it all has to be gone through again for the fifth and last time. When
this is accomplished, form the mixture into 13 big balls about the size of
golf balls. Why 13? So that you can sample one immediately when they
are done. Place them on a buttered tin in a cool place (but not in the refrigerator) for a couple of hours to harden up a bit, at which time place
2 boxes of Baker's semisweet chocolate chips in the top part of a double
boiler over warm water, registering not more than 120° F. by the candy
thermometer, and stir constantly until the chocolate has completely
melted. This will take a long time, half an hour or so. Do not place the
double boiler over a flame but if the water cools too much, add a little
more hot water to the cooled water. When the chocolate has completely
melted, stir it for a minute longer; then working in a cool room free from
drafts, dip the chocolate-nut balls into the melted chocolate one at a time,
rolling them around with the fingers until coated all over. Then drop
them onto a cookie sheet covered with heavy waxed paper, endeavoring
to make a little curl on top of each. When the chocolate coating has set
wrap them in squares of silver tin foil and place in cool place until ready
to eat, which should be as soon as possible after making.*

Festive After-Dinner Coffee
(for 8)

*An hour or so before dinner place the following ingredients in the top
part of an enamel double boiler: 1 cup of Siboney rum, 3 jiggers of brandy,
1½ jiggers of Cointreau liqueur, 5 level tablespoons of light brown sugar,
a small strip of lemon peel cut very, very thin and the same of orange peel,
2 small pieces of broken cinnamon stick, and 2 whole cloves. Cover and
let stand until ready to use.*

*After dinner make 8 cups of strong drip coffee in the following man-
ner: Scald a large 6-cup earthenware drip coffee pot and place it in a shallow pan of boiling water on a low flame. Measure into the filter* ¾ *of a*

** In this recipe, if Baker's chocolate chips are unobtainable, use 5 pieces Maillard's Triple
Vanilla Sweet Chocolate, cut in little pieces for the nut mixture, and ¾ lb. of the same
for the coating.*

cup of French roast coffee and ¾ of a cup of breakfast coffee, both drip ground. Pour over this 1 cup of rapidly boiling water, cover and allow the coffee to swell a bit, then add boiling water gradually, ½ cup at a time, until the pot is full. Pour this off into the top part of a large enamel double boiler, over boiling water, cover and keep hot while you pour 2 more cups of boiling water through the remaining grounds in the filter. When it has dripped through completely, add it to the coffee in the double boiler. You now should have 8 cups of hot strong coffee.

Now stirring constantly, heat together 3 cups of milk and 2 cups of cream. At this point you will engage in the exciting process of flambé-ing the alcoholic ingredients above. Strictly speaking this should be done in a café brulot bowl but it works beautifully in a big yellow kitchen mixing bowl. If you care to risk doing it in the living room, place the bowl, which should be heated, on a silver tray and have ready a long-handled silver spoon or ladle. Place on a separate tray 8 warmed mugs, each one containing a long stick of cinnamon and a small piece of lemon peel, and two big, hot pitchers, one for the hot milk and one for the coffee.

Place the pan containing the brandy and rum on a low flame and heat it but do not let it boil. Fill one of the big pitchers with the scalding-hot coffee and the other with the milk, straining the milk to be sure there will be no scum. Carry both trays into the living room and place in a safe spot. Dip up a little of the hot liquor with the ladle, light it, and dip the flaming ladle into the bowl which will ignite the whole. At this point turn out all the lights and play with the fire for half a minute or so, then extinguish the flames slowly by pouring the hot coffee into it. When all the coffee has been added and the fireworks are over, ladle the coffee into the 8 waiting mugs filling them about ⅔ full and distribute them. The hot milk should then be passed for anyone who cares to try it. Personally I'll fill my cup right up with it. Serve this with the mincemeat cookies.

Surprise Walnuts

For these you will need 3 pounds of the freshest, biggest, unshelled English walnuts you can find. Also a new large transparent plastic food bag (like the one mentioned above in the cookie recipe), a yard of red satin ribbon, a tube of Duco transparent cement and a collection of tiny pres-

ents. By now you may have guessed that the presents are to be concealed in some of the nuts, then to be mixed with the rest of the nuts, so that when they are served after coffee, gay and festive in their beribboned bag, no one will be aware of the surprise to come. Eventually, unless no one is hungry enough to accept a nut, squeals of delight will be forthcoming, when the first treasure is discovered. After that it is safe to say that all the nuts will be broken, if not eaten. To prepare the treasure nuts, insert a sharp pointed knife in the crack at the round end and give it a little twist. The two halves should separate easily without breaking the shells. When the kernels have been removed, replace them with a treasure and glue the two halves together again using just enough Duco to hold but not enough to have it show.

As to what to put into the nuts, I leave it to your own ingenuity, imagination and generosity. Mine are likely to contain five-and-ten-cent-store rings and earrings, or cuff links, or studs, or stamps, or Indian pennies or at most a St. Christopher medal, or a silver charm, or possibly a neatly folded dollar bill. If, however, you would prefer to fill yours with rubies and emeralds, or thousand dollar bills, I'll be right over and join your party.

Cold Roast Turkey
(for 6–8)

Choose a young plump-breasted hen turkey weighing from 12 to 14 pounds. Clean, singe, wash and dry thoroughly, inside and out. Rub the inside of the bird well with salt and pepper. Place ¼ pound butter inside the bird. Tie it for roasting. Place in a roasting pan and spread with ¼ pound soft butter. Place in a preheated, hot 500° F. oven for about ½ hour or until the breast is a light golden brown, basting occasionally. Now turn the bird over carefully, breast down, and continue roasting until the back is browned, too. Turn breast side up again, and salt and pepper the bird all over and if necessary add more butter. Reduce the oven heat to 350° F. and continue roasting slowly, basting frequently until done, about 3 or 3½ hours for a 12 pound turkey. When done, place on serving platter and make a little clear gravy by adding a cup of boiling water or chicken broth to the butter in the pan and boil down, stirring well until reduced to a thick syrupy glaze. Allow the glaze to stand until the fat rises to the surface, skim off all the fat, and pour the glaze over the breast of the turkey. Cool and serve. It may be placed in the refrigerator, but is better if allowed to cool without refrigeration.

ELEVEN

Menus
For
Moderns

COUNTRY LUNCHEON

TOMATO HALVES BAKED WITH CHEESE

INDIVIDUAL BEEFSTEAK PIES

MIXED GREEN SALAD WITH *FRENCH DRESSING

FRESH FIGS AND GRAPES

BLACK COFFEE

SERVE A GOOD CHIANTI WITH THIS

See Index for Starred Dish

Tomato Halves Baked with Cheese

Take 1 tomato for each person. Cut tomatoes in half crosswise, lay halves face up in a lightly buttered baking dish in which you can serve them. Spread halves lightly with prepared mustard, then salt and pepper heavily. Place 4 small ¼-inch-thick squares of rat cheese on each half, put small dot of butter in center of each half, dust lightly with cayenne. Bake ½ hour in 350° to 375° F. oven. Serve in dish in which they were baked.

Individual Beefsteak Pies
(for 6–8)

Make plain pie pastry as described in chapter on pie, tripling the quantity. Put pastry in refrigerator to chill. Sauté in butter 2 pounds round steak cut into 1-inch squares. When done put in hot pan. Make pan gravy with hot water, salt, pepper and enough beef extract to make generous pint, add 1 tablespoon flour which has been stirred into 1 heaping tablespoon soft butter, and bring to a boil. Pour this gravy over sautéed steak.

Hard boil 4 eggs, take off shells, cut into eighths and add to steak mixture. Now take ½ the pastry dough, roll out thin, line 8 5-inch Pyrex dishes. Fill with egg and steak mixture, and scatter 8 to 10 raisins in each dish. Roll out thin the other half of pastry dough and cover each pie, crimp edge, cut 4 vents in each. Place in preheated hot oven at 450° F., bake until lightly brown, reduce heat to 350° F. and bake 10 to 15 minutes more until well browned. Serve hot in the baking dish, adding sprig of parsley on top if desired.

CITY LUNCHEON

AVOCADO HALVES
SERVED WITH POWDERED SUGAR AND HALVES
OF FRESH LIMES

*HOT SLICED WHITE MEAT OF TURKEY

*JOHNNY CAKE   CRANBERRY RELISH

*SPINACH IN CREAM

COMPOTE OF FRESH PEACHES

*PECAN MACAROONS

BLACK COFFEE

SERVE A LIGHT WHITE WINE WITH THIS, A
GRAVES OR VOUVRAY

See Index for Starred Dishes

Roast Turkey

See recipe for roast turkey (page 187). For luncheon, cut thin slices of white meat only. The turkey may be used hot for dinner the night before, reserving most of the breast for the luncheon.

Cranberry and Orange Relish
(for 6–8)

Wash 2 cups perfect cranberries and dry them. Cut 1 large navel orange in quarters, removing any seeds there might be, but leaving the skin on. Put the cranberries and the oranges through the food chopper, using medium cutter. Add ¾ cup granulated sugar, mix thoroughly and chill for 1 hour and serve.

Compote of Fresh Peaches
(for 6–8)

Peel 15 large, juicy, freestone peaches by immersing them for a second or two, a few at a time, in boiling water. Remove from boiling water and plunge into cold water containing the juice of ½ lemon. The skins should come off easily with the aid of a little knife, leaving fruit whole and unmarred. When all are done, break open 3 of them and extract the peach stones. Break the stones open with a hammer and remove the kernels. With a sharp knife peel off the brown skins.

Now make a syrup by boiling together for 5 minutes, 2 cups granulated sugar moistened with 2 cups cold water. Skim carefully when it first comes to a boil. Add the peaches and the 3 kernels and boil gently until the peaches may be pierced with a fork, but be careful not to overcook them. Five minutes should be sufficient for ripe peaches. Place the 12 whole perfect peaches in a pretty serving dish and pour over them the syrup. Discard the kernels as they were only added for flavor. Replace them with 2 dozen blanched sweet almonds. Cool and chill, before serving accompanied by Pecan Macaroons.

GALA THANKSGIVING DINNER

CHAMPAGNE COCKTAILS

PÂTÉ ON CRACKERS

CREAM OF CLAM AND SCALLOP SOUP

BONED STUFFED TURKEY

*RED CURRANT AND BLACK RASPBERRY JELLY

*MASHED POTATOES
SURPRISE

*CARAMELIZED
TURNIPS

VIENNESE COMPOTE

BLACK COFFEE

HAVING BEGUN WITH CHAMPAGNE, SERVE
MORE OF IT ALL THROUGH THE DINNER

* See Index for Starred Dishes

Cream of Clam and Scallop Soup
(for 6–8)

Order from your fish man, 3 dozen bay scallops, and 2 quarts shelled clams with their juice. When ready to make the soup, strain off the juice from the clams, being careful not to lose any of it. Strain the juice through cheesecloth first rinsed in cold water. Rinse the clams in cold water and put them through the meat grinder using the medium knife. Place the clams and their juice in separate bowls in the refrigerator, while you prepare the following ingredients:

Chop 6 large peeled shallots medium fine, or substitute 3 small white onions. Prepare 1 heaping tablespoon finely cut chives. Measure out 6 level tablespoons flour. Now comes the hard part. Using the sharpest knife you own, proceed to cut the scallops in paper-thin slices (and I do mean paper-thin). Place them in refrigerator while you proceed. Melt 4 tablespoons butter in a small pan, add the chopped shallots and cook slowly until just at the point of browning lightly, at which time add the ground-up clams and let the whole simmer gently while you make a roux in another pan. To make the roux, melt ¼ pound butter in a little pan, then add 6 tablespoons flour, and stir and cook for 1 minute or 2

*without allowing it to brown. Remove from fire and stir in gradually
1½ cups heated thin cream and, when smooth and thick, add part of the
cold clam juice. Stir a bit, then add the clams and shallots; also the rest
of the clam juice and an additional ½ cup cream. Cook gently a few
minutes longer, stirring constantly, then put the whole through a strainer,
using a wooden masher or spoon to press well on the clams to extract all
their juice, but do not try to force them through the strainer. It's the flavor
of the clams you are after. Then discard the clams. You should now have
a perfectly smooth creamy soup. At this point season cautiously with salt
and coarsely ground pepper to taste, and a pinch of nutmeg. Thin to the
desired quantity (8 cups) with about 1 cup hot milk. Place in top part of
a large double boiler, over boiling water.*

*Beat the yolks of 4 eggs, then add a little of the hot soup to the eggs and
stir well, then add it gradually to the rest of the soup, stirring constantly.
When thickened like custard, add the sliced scallops and cut chives and
almost immediately remove from the fire. If you have cut the scallops
fine enough, then momentary contact with the hot soup should have
cooked them sufficiently. Now stir in the strained juice ½ lemon, pour
into hot soup tureen and serve at once.*

Boned Stuffed Turkey

*Right here and now, please, don't look so frightened at the idea of boning
a turkey yourself. It sounds formidable, I know, but it couldn't be easier.
As a matter of fact it takes infinitely more courage to ask the butcher to
do it for you. All you need in the way of equipment is a good sharp knife,
a wooden board, a hammer, a sturdy cleaver or knife and the will to
conquer.*

*Why bother to bone it at all, you say? The answer is that once accom-
plished it reduces the carving process to simple slicing straight across the
bird. No joints to contend with, no messy bones left on the plates, no
waste. It can all be prepared the day before the party, ready for roasting.
No last minute flurry, no confusion and I'll guarantee the bird will bring
forth a mighty burst of applause when he is presented at the table, so
plump, so brown and handsome. Now, here is how it is done.*

First, singe a dressed turkey weighing about 14 pounds, then remove all pinfeathers. Next, working on a wooden board, chop off the tips of the wings, using a strong knife or cleaver and a hammer. Now, wash the bird carefully, inside and out, and dry thoroughly. Split the bird open down the back, like a broiler, and remove all the bones except the drumsticks and small bones in lower halves of wings. What you must not do is to cut through the outer skin and flesh of the breast.

Keeping this always in mind, lay the bird breast down on the board and, starting at the furthermost end of the neck, slit the skin of the neck and back, then cut through the backbone. This accomplished, pull the skin away from the neck, being careful not to tear it, and then chop off the neck, close to the body. Next, cut away the backbone from skin and flesh, and, with caution, cut the rest of the carcass away from the bones, running a sharp knife between the bones and the flesh.

As you come to the joints in wings and legs, break them by bending them backwards before trying to cut through them. Do not attempt to remove the small bones in lower wings, nor the drumsticks. Don't worry if you tear the flesh as you scrape it away from the bones. It's the outside that must remain intact.

Place the bones, as you remove them, in a big enamel pan. When finished, put the boned bird in the refrigerator while you prepare the stuffing. This concoction of ground-up boiled chicken, ham, bread, pecans, celery and seasoning is made in the following manner:

Wash and clean a 5-pound fowl and place it on the bed of turkey bones. Add 5 or 6 whole peeled carrots, 6 well-washed leeks or 6 onions, and 1 bunch washed celery. Pour over the chicken just enough boiling water to barely cover it. Bring to a boil, skim meticulously, cover partially and simmer gently for about 2 hours, or until legs are tender through. Season with salt and pepper when half done.

Next drain the broth from the bones and chicken (saving it of course), and when the chicken is cool enough to handle, pull off all the skin and throw it away. Then pull off all the breast, leaving it as whole as possible and put it aside—for the moment. Now, pull off the rest of the meat from the chicken and any scraps that may have clung to the turkey bones. Put all this, except the breast, through the meat grinder. Now take 3 cups ground boiled or baked ham, including a little of the ham fat. If ham is unobtainable, use a canned substitute or sausage. Soak 16 to 20 slices bread, crusts removed, in 2 cups milk. Break up lightly with a fork and add it to the ground chicken and ham. Also add 1 cup celery chopped fine, 1 cup pecan meats chopped fine, ½ cup parsley, 2 tablespoons grated onion and ½ teaspoon ground black pepper. Mix all together well, moistening it with 3 or 4 tablespoons chicken broth.

You are now ready to stuff the turkey. Spread him out flat, skin down, on the table and sprinkle him lightly with salt and pepper. Cover with layer of stuffing, using about ½. On this lay the whole reserved chicken breast and cover with remaining stuffing. Get someone to hold the two sides of the turkey together again, while you sew him up securely from base of neck to tail, using a poultry or curved upholstery needle and strong, fine, white string. Pull the remaining flap of loose skin from neck down over back and sew it carefully in place. Turn bird breast side up and sew up slit in apron. At this point Sir Turkey will look very flat and odd indeed. It is now up to you to give him a proud shape by pushing his legs up and close to the body, thereby forcing a goodly amount of stuffing up into the breast. Secure the legs and wings close to the body, lacing all with string as you have seen the butcher tie up a boned, rolled roast, but avoid pulling the strings too tight directly over the breast. Now wrap the bird in waxed paper and place in refrigerator until ready to roast the next day.

It will take about 3 hours and 45 minutes to cook the turkey so plan accordingly. Light the oven ahead of time and set control at 500° F.

Cut a large onion in fairly small pieces and brown lightly in 4 tablespoons butter. Add 2 or 3 peeled sliced carrots and place the whole in bottom of large roasting pan. Lay on this bed the turkey, breast side up. Spread over all at least ½ cup soft butter or butter substitute. Place in preheated, very hot oven and roast, basting frequently, until lightly browned or for about 20 minutes, then reduce heat to 450° F. and continue roasting, basting frequently for about 1 hour longer. At this point salt and pepper the bird well all over, cover with top of roaster, leaving vent open and continue cooking, basting occasionally for about 1¼ hours longer. Remove the cover and continue roasting until the bird is rich brown and well done, or for about 1¼ hours longer. Turn cover of roasting pan open side up, close vent, and place turkey in it, transferring it carefully with the aid of a big spoon or firm pancake turner and fork and two extra-strong hands protected against the heat. Now skim off most of the fat from the gravy in the roasting pan and put it back over the turkey. Return the turkey to the oven while you make the following clear gravy:

Add to the remaining brown juice in roasting pan 2 cups chicken broth.

Place on fire and stir well to incorporate all the nice brown bits clinging to sides of pan. Boil down until syrupy, then strain into hot gravy boat; if you prefer, leave the vegetables right in the gravy.

Place the turkey on a hot platter, carefully. Working quickly, cut off and pull out as much of the string as possible. Garnish at tail end with a great big bunch parsley. Serve at once to be sliced at table, accompanied by the hot gravy.

Viennese Compote
(for 6–8)

Procure 1 pound top-quality big plump dried prunes, pitted or not as you prefer. Wash them very carefully and place in large enamel pan. Cover with 1 quart cold water. Add 1 3-ounce can Dromedary orange peel and 1 3-ounce can lemon peel. Also add 1 ounce candied angelica which you have washed in hot water to soften it a bit, then cut crosswise in thin shreds. Place on fire and bring gently to a boil. Cook for ½ hour, being careful that the prunes don't stick and that they don't boil dry. When done they should still have a little juice left. At this point, open 2 11-ounce bottles of Raffetto's Imported Whole Marrons (chestnuts) in heavy vanilla-flavored syrup and add the chestnuts and the syrup to the prunes. Bring to the boiling point and remove from fire. Place in pretty serving dish and when cold, place in refrigerator to chill until ready to serve, accompanied by a bowl of slightly whipped heavy cream, or a bowl of sour cream. Very rich and very good.

TWO AFTER THEATER SUPPERS

I

HOT PIZZA PIE

ASPARAGUS OR STRING BEAN SALAD
WITH EXTRA TART FRENCH DRESSING

FRESH FRUIT BOWL

BEER OR ALE

II

HOT THICK SPLIT PEA SOUP

LOBSTER HUNK SANDWICHES

WHITE HERMITAGE WINE, WELL-AGED,
COLD BUT NOT ICY

Pizza
(for 6–8)

Sometime when you are making Louise's bread (see page 131), plan to have Pizzas for a meal. Have ready before you start the bread, the following mixture: Open 3 large 2-pound 4-ounce cans of Italian peeled plum tomatoes and strain off all of the juice, but do not rub the tomatoes through the sieve. Place them in a bowl and add 2 tablespoons fresh chopped parsley, 1 teaspoon chopped fresh mint, ½ teaspoon dried basil, 1½ teaspoons salt, 1 teaspoon coarsely ground black pepper, 2 teaspoons dried oregano, and 4 cloves garlic chopped fine, and 4 more cloves garlic put through a garlic squeezer. Mix well together. Also grate some fresh imported Parmesan cheese, enough to make ½ cup, and prepare the same amount of finely shredded rat or American cheese. Butter well 2 large flat cookie sheets.

Now make the dough, and when it has risen for the first time and you are shaping the loaves, keep out 2 generous cups of the dough for the Pizzas. Roll this dough ½ at a time out on a pastry cloth, until very, very thin or until approximately 15 by 12 inches. Roll it up on your rolling pin

*and unroll it out onto the cookie sheet. Repeat the process and cover the
second tin.*

*Now pour over each 3 tablespoons good olive oil and spread it over
with a brush. Then cover the entire surface of both Pizzas with the tomato mixture previously prepared. Last of all sprinkle the shredded Parmesan cheese and American mixed together over all. Place in preheated
425° F. oven and bake for 20 minutes or until the crust is a golden brown
around the edge. With a sharp knife cut in pieces and send to table right
on the cookie sheet on trays and eat at once with ice-cold beer.*

Note: *If you do not want to make Louise's bread, substitute hot roll mix,
following directions on box and proceed exactly as above.*

String Bean Salad with Tart French Dressing

*With a sharp knife cut off both sides of 3 or 4 pounds tender string beans,
leaving them whole. Wash and tie them in 8 or 10 bundles, put them in a
saucepan, sprinkle with salt and a tiny pinch of baking soda, and pour
boiling water over them, enough to cover. Stand by, and when the water
comes to a boil again skim very carefully, and cook until the beans are
tender but not floppy—about 10–15 minutes. Drain well. Let the cold
water run over them a second. Place them on a serving platter, neatly in
a row, and remove the strings. Sprinkle with salt, and when cool place
them in refrigerator until ready to serve, at which time be sure there is
no water in bottom of serving platter. Pour over them a good tart French
dressing made of 3 tablespoons vinegar, 6 tablespoons olive oil, salt and
coarsely ground black pepper to taste, and a dash of cayenne or mustard
if you like. Serve.*

Asparagus Salad with Tart French Dressing

*Scrape and wash 2 or 3 bunches fine asparagus, cut off ends and tie in
bunches, top and bottom, with white string. Place head down in cold
water until ready to cook. Plunge into a big enamel pan full of boiling
water, add a tiny pinch of soda and a little salt and cook until tender, but
not floppy—about 15 to 20 minutes. Drain well, place on platter, remove*

strings and cool. Drain off any water in the platter, place in refrigerator and chill until ready to serve. Drain once more to be sure there is no water in the dish and pour over the asparagus the same tart French dressing as for the string bean salad above.

Split Pea Soup
(for 6–8)

Wash ½ small smoked boned daisy ham and cut it in ¾-inch slices. Place in large pan with 2 large onions, peeled and cut up in pieces. Pour over it 2 quarts boiling water. Wash 1 pound split peas and add them to the mixture. Place on fire and bring gently to a boil, skimming it carefully. Cook gently for about 1½ hours, stirring frequently. When it has cooked 45 minutes, add 1½ quarts chicken broth or water, and continue cooking 45 minutes longer or until the peas have disintegrated. Remove from fire and pick out the ham. Cut it into little cubes, discarding all the fat, and replace it in the soup.

When ready to serve, heat over boiling water until scalding hot and season to taste with salt and coarsely ground black pepper. Buttered croutons are good with it, but not essential.

Lobster Hunk Sandwiches

Take the freshest, softest, best-tasting white bread available, cut into slices ½ inch thick, then cut each slice into 4 squares. Between each 2 squares put a rough hunk of cold boiled lobster—no butter on bread, no pepper, no salt, no mayonnaise or other dressing. Both bread and lobster must be the freshest possible, and both should be very, very, very cold. It's a good idea to serve them in a high dish banked in crushed ice.

HOME DINNER

HOT TOMATO BOUILLON (CANNED)

*ROAST PORK SPARERIBS, CHUTNEY OR
SPICED CRAB APPLES (BOUGHT)

FRENCH FRIED SWEET   GREEN PEPPER AND
POTATOES   TOMATO MIX

*TRUDEAU ORANGE MARMALADE PUDDING

BLACK COFFEE

A GOOD CHIANTI, A RED SPANISH MARQUES DE
MURRIETA OR A MODEST BORDEAUX WITH THIS

* See Index for Starred Dishes

French Fried Sweet Potatoes
(for 6–8)

Peel 4 large sweet potatoes, cut in ¾-inch slices, then cut again so as to make ¾-inch sticks. Parboil in salted water 5 minutes. Drain and dry well on a tea cloth. Heat 3 pounds vegetable shortening in a deep fat frying pan, and when it is smoking hot, add a few of the potatoes at a time and cook 2–3 minutes, or until they float to the top and are a pale golden brown. Serve at once.

Green Pepper and Tomato Mix
(for 6–8)

Wash 6 large firm green peppers, remove stems, quarter and remove the seeds. Butter 2 shallow baking dishes and place the quartered peppers in them, smooth side down. Wash 6 fine tomatoes, remove stems, quarter them and place ¼ tomato in each of the green pepper quarters. Sprinkle with salt and coarsely ground black pepper, and scatter over the 2 dishes 1 scant cup finely chopped onion, and ¾ cup raw bacon, cut into little pieces, or the same of raw ham. Pour ½ cup water over each dish and bake in a moderate 400° F. oven until the vegetables are done and the bacon is crisped, or for about 1 hour, basting occasionally. Serve in dish in which it was cooked.

This is capable of many interesting variations. Eggplant can be added in chunks between the pieces of pepper. Bacon and ham can be omitted and butter used instead. A few leftover beans and peas may go in. Flavorings can include favorite herbs. Even grated cheese and a few bread crumbs blend nicely. But the basic green pepper, onion and tomato are essential.

COMPANY DINNER

RIPE OLIVES   CELERY HEARTS

COLD BORTSCH WITH SOUR CREAM

MARYLAND FRIED CHICKEN

*DELICATE CORN   *STEAMED ZUCCHINI,
FRITTERS   HOLLANDAISE

CANTALOUPE HALVES FILLED WITH VANILLA
ICE CREAM (BOUGHT) SPRINKLED WITH
CHOPPED CRYSTALLIZED GINGER

BLACK COFFEE

SERVE WITH DRY WHITE WINE, CHILLED, OR A SOUND
CLARET. IF CANTALOUPES ARE NOT IN MARKET, SERVE
THE ICE CREAM WITH THE CHOPPED GINGER, AND AT THE
VERY LAST MOMENT POUR ON EACH SERVING A TABLE-
SPOON OF BOURBON WHISKY.

* *See Index for Starred Dish*

Cold Bortsch
(for 6–8)

Prepare 2 cups finely chopped raw cabbage, and ½ cup chopped onion. Cook the cabbage 10 minutes in 2 cups boiling salted water. Cook the onions without browning for 3 minutes in 4 tablespoons butter. Drain and save the juice from large can whole beets. Chop the beets fine until you have 2 cupfuls. Add 4 cups chicken broth to the onions and, when it comes to the boiling point, add the cabbage and the water in which it cooked. Now add the chopped beets, 1 cup beet juice, 2 scant teaspoons caraway seed, 1 teaspoon sugar, season to taste with salt and coarsely ground black pepper. Simmer 10 minutes, skimming it carefully. Remove from the fire and add 3 tablespoons lemon juice, ¼ cup dry white wine, another ½ cup beet juice. Chill thoroughly before serving in bouillon cups garnished with a thin slice of lemon and a chunk of frozen sweet cream (made by placing 2 cups heavy unbeaten cream in one of the freezing trays of your refrigerator and letting it remain there without stirring it until barely frozen through, or for about 1½ hours).

Note: *This Bortsch is equally good served hot. Sour cream may be substituted for the sweet.*

Maryland Fried Chicken
(for 6–8)

Buy 2 frying chickens cut into 8 pieces each. Wash and clean, dry and place in a big bowl. Sprinkle over them 1¼ cups bread flour in which you have mixed 2 teaspoons salt, and pepper to taste. Roll the chicken around, then break into the bowl 2 whole eggs, and with your hand turn the pieces of chicken over and over until they are well coated with the egg and flour.

Have ready a big 12-inch iron frying pan in which you have melted ½ pound butter, or use ½ butter and ½ bacon fat. When the butter is sizzling hot, add the chicken and fry slowly until nice and brown on one side, or for about 15 minutes. Turn the chicken over and cook the other side 15 minutes longer. Turn over once more and cook until done or until no juice flows out when you prick the second joint with a fork, or for 5 or 10 minutes longer in all. Remove from pan and keep warm while you add 4 tablespoons flour to the butter in the pan. Stir and cook for 2 or 3 minutes over low flame and add gradually 2½ cups rich milk. Season to taste and serve at once with the fried chicken.

WINTER DINNER

LIMA BEAN AND PEA SOUP

SMALL BROILED TURKEY

SWEET POTATOES WITH   *STRING BEANS SOUR
APPLES   CREAM

CRANBERRY JELLY

*AUNT ELIZA'S PEACH PIE

BLACK COFFEE

SERVE VOUVRAY OR MEURSEULT PREFERABLY, OR
A NOT TOO GRAND RED BURGUNDY

* See Index for Starred Dishes

Lima Bean and Pea Soup
(for 6–8)

This recipe makes about 3 quarts soup but it's so good you won't mind. It may, however, be halved. First, put 4 cups shelled fresh peas and 2 cups fresh shelled lima beans into a deep enamel pan. Add ⅛ teaspoon baking soda, 1 teaspoon salt and 3 cups boiling water. Skim off the foam as it rises to the top and cook about 25 minutes or until the lima beans are done. The peas will be too soft but this does not matter. Do not drain. In the meantime, cook ½ cup chopped onion or the white part of leeks in 4 tablespoons butter for 2 or 3 minutes, stirring constantly to avoid browning. Then add 4 cups hot clear chicken broth, preferably homemade, and cook until the broth has reduced to 3 cups. Add this to the peas and beans and put the whole through a fine sieve or, better still, reduce it to a smooth pulp in your Waring Mixer. Place all this in the top part of a large 3-quart double boiler over boiling water and stir in gradually 1 cup heavy cream. Season to taste with more salt if necessary and plenty of coarsely ground black pepper. Place a small lump butter in a hot soup tureen and pour in the scalding hot soup. Stir until the butter has melted and serve at once.

Note: *Two 12-ounce boxes frozen peas and 1 12-ounce box frozen lima beans may be substituted for the fresh vegetables.*

Broiled Turkey
(for 6–8)

Buy a fine young turkey weighing 8–9 pounds. Have it split down the back as a chicken would be cut for broiling. Clean, singe, and wash and dry it well. Place it cut side up on a flat pan or broiler large enough to hold it. Spread with ¼ pound butter, and sprinkle with salt and coarsely ground black pepper. Place in preheated broiler about 6 inches from the flame, and sear quickly. When it begins to brown, baste it with its own juice, and continue cooking until brown on that side, or for about 20 minutes. Turn, and pour over it another ¼ pound butter, melted this time. Sprinkle this side with salt and more pepper and continue broiling, basting frequently until brown. Reduce the heat and continue cooking, basting frequently, lowering the pan from the flame if it cooks too fast or, if you prefer, transfer the pan to your preheated oven, the temperature set at 350° F. In any event, baste it faithfully with its own buttery juice. The turkey should be done when it has cooked in all about 2 hours. To test, pierce the second joint and if no juice runs out, the bird is done. Transfer it temporarily to another pan and place in hot oven while you make the clear gravy.

Pour off the butter (it may be kept to use again for basting another bird, provided the butter has not been allowed to burn) and add ½ cup water to the broiling pan. Place on fire and stir until it has melted all the nice brown residue in the bottom of the pan, and until it has become thick and syrupy. Place the turkey on a hot serving platter, and pour over it the hot gravy. Garnish with parsley and send to table to be carved and served.

Cranberry Jelly

Wash 1 quart dark red cranberries in cold water, drain them. Put them in a porcelain pan, add a few drops water and bring them very gently to a boil and cook them until every berry bursts. Strain through a colander until all the pulp goes through. Add 2 cups sugar, boil ½ hour, stirring frequently. Wet a mold with ice water, pour in the jelly, and when cool, place in refrigerator until ready to serve, turned out.

Sweet Potatoes and Apples
(for 6–8)

Boil 4 large sweet potatoes until tender, or for about 25 minutes. Remove their skins and slice evenly in ½-inch slices. Core 4 large apples and peel them, then slice crosswise in ½-inch slices, too. Butter copiously a large shallow 12-by-7½-inch Pyrex baking dish. Lay in the dish the sweet potato slices and the apple rings so that they alternate and overlap each other prettily. Dot with ¼ pound butter and sprinkle over them ⅔ cup light brown sugar. Place in preheated 450° F. oven and bake about 40 minutes or until the apples are a golden brown. Baste once or twice with the sugar syrup on bottom of dish, and if it should get too thick, moisten with a tablespoon or so of hot water, so as not to crack the dish. The apples should retain their shape, but be cooked through. This dish is good with pork chops or ham.

ANOTHER GOOD DINNER

*MOZZARELLA IN CARROZA

ROAST LAMB PERSILLÉ

*BROWNED POTATO BALLS

*FRIED TOMATOES WITH CREAM

RHUBARB SHORTCAKE

BLACK COFFEE

SERVE A BÂTARD MONTRACHET, OR A LESS EXPENSIVE
ROSÉ WITH THIS

* See Index for Starred Dishes

Roast Leg of Lamb Persillé

With a sharp knife cut off every bit of lamb fat from a leg of lamb weighing about 8 pounds when trimmed. Insert in the meat, at the shank, 1 clove garlic. Rub the roast all over with another one. Place in a roasting pan, and rub the surface with ¼ pound soft butter. Place in preheated, very hot 500° F. oven and bake for about 15 minutes, basting occasionally or until a light golden brown. At this time, salt and pepper the roast and reduce the heat of the oven to 350° F. and continue roasting and basting frequently for about 2 hours longer or to be exact, 15 minutes to the pound, counting from the time the roast is browned.

In the meantime, prepare a generous cup of fine bread crumbs plucked from the center of a loaf of white bread (do not toast this). Add to it an equal quantity of chopped parsley and, if you love garlic, add 1 small clove well chopped, omit if you don't, and sprinkle lightly with salt and pepper. Fifteen minutes before the roast should be done, transfer it to the top part of your roasting pan, and pour over it the fat, being careful not to include the brown residue. Now cover the entire top surface of the lamb with the parsley and bread crumbs, patting it on gently. Ladle some of the fat carefully over the crumbs, so as not to wash them off, and place back in the oven to continue cooking and until the crumbs are lightly browned. At this time, squeeze ½ lemon over the surface, and it is ready to serve.

In the meantime, add 1 cup water to the original roasting pan and place over low flame and stir well, until all the brown residue has been melted into the water, and until reduced and syrupy. This is the clear gravy to be served with the lamb, which should be placed on a hot platter, garnished with a lemon cut lengthwise in moon shaped pieces, and should be carved at the table.

Serve with this, baked tomatoes (see page 189) and buttered string beans.

Helen's Rhubarb Shortcake
(for 6–8)

Prepare in advance the rhubarb. Buy 2 pounds firm, young, pink rhubarb. Cut off leaves and stem ends. Wash and cut in 1-inch pieces. Place in top part of large 2-quart enamel double boiler, over boiling water. Cover and cook for ½ hour, stirring occasionally. By this time it will have made its own juice. Place pan directly on fire and boil 5 minutes, being careful it doesn't stick, then sweeten to taste with about 1½ cups granulated sugar. Stir and boil another 5 minutes. Remove from fire, cool and chill until ready to use.

Make recipe for Baking Powder Drop Biscuits on page 121, but instead of dropping by spoonfuls onto cookie sheets, spread the dough out onto a large, well-buttered, round layer-cake tin. Place in preheated, hot 475° F. oven and bake about 12–15 minutes or until a light golden brown. Split while hot and spread the bottom half with soft butter, and cover with part of the chilled rhubarb and with plenty of whipped cream. Cover with the top half and spread plenty more rhubarb over the top. Pour over all, at least another cup cream, whipped until stiff. The cream may be flavored with 1 teaspoon vanilla but do not sweeten it. Serve at once.

WINTER DINNER FOR HUNGRY PEOPLE

*ONION SOUP

*ROAST PORK TENDERLOIN

SWEET POTATOES WITH MARRONS GLACÉS

*FRIED APPLES

*STRING BEANS TO YOUR TASTE

*GALETTE WITH MINCEMEAT OR
*CRANBERRY-RAISIN PIE

BLACK COFFEE

SERVE A HEARTY ALE, OR A CHATEAUNEUF OR
CÔTE ROTIE WITH THIS

* See Index for Starred Dishes

Sweet Potatoes with Marrons Glacés
(for 6–8)

Peel, wash, and cut into medium-sized pieces 4 pounds sweet potatoes. Cook until tender in boiling, slightly salted water. Drain well. Add ⅛ pound butter and mash, using a potato masher or electric beater. Moisten gradually with about ½ cup hot thin cream. When nice and fluffy, keep warm in double boiler until ready to serve, at which time fold into them a 13-ounce bottle of French marrons glacés vanillés, syrup and all, having however, first broken the marrons into medium-sized pieces. Be sure the potatoes are very hot before serving. If you like, reserve a spoonful of syrup and marrons and garnish a hole in the center of the mound of potatoes heaped into a hot vegetable dish.

SUMMER DINNER FOR NOT-SO-HUNGRY PEOPLE

MELON REFRAICHI, COLD, À LA MONTAGNÉ

BOILED SALMON WITH EGG SAUCE AND CAPERS

SMALL NEW POTATOES BOILED IN JACKETS

*GREEN PEAS WITH MINT

*BERTA MUELLER'S LEMON PUDDING

BLACK COFFEE

SERVE A CHILLED CHABLIS OR A TANGY WHITE
WINE CUP WITH THIS

* See Index for Starred Dishes

Melon Refraichi, Cold, à la Montagné

You need 2 large Spanish, Cranshaw or Persian melons. Cut a large oval piece from one melon, scoop out seed, then scoop out flesh in large pieces, put into a bowl. Save the melon shell and top piece. Cut open the other melon, take out seed, scoop out flesh in pieces like the other and put in bowl with the other pieces. Now take out a piece or two and experiment. Some people like port wine, some people prefer Cointreau or Curaçao combined with a first-rate brandy, half and half. When you have chosen your wine or liqueur, take 1 scant cup of it, add ½ cup lime juice strained, and sugar to taste—very little sugar is best, and go very scant on that cup of the alcoholic liquid, or it will give a bitter tang. Pour the mix over the melon pieces in the bowl, stir it gently, spoon it all back into the melon shell, put the top on and set in a very cold place in the refrigerator. Stir it gently once or more before serving time. Serve in a big oval dish banked with crushed ice, and decorated with grape leaves.

Hot Boiled Salmon with Hard-Boiled-Egg Cream Sauce

(for 6–8)

Wrap a 5-pound piece fresh salmon (preferably from the center of the fish) in a double piece of cheesecloth and tie the ends with string. Place in a fish boiler, or large enamel pan big enough to hold it, and cover it completely with warm (not hot) court bouillon, made of water and at least 1 cup good dry white wine, 1 teaspoon salt, 2 carrots peeled and sliced, a little parsley, 2 tablespoons vinegar, and 1 large peeled and sliced onion. Place on fire, bring slowly to the simmering point, and simmer for about 50 minutes. In the meantime, make some Hard-Boiled-Egg Cream Sauce in the following manner:

Place 4 eggs in a little pan and cover with cold water. Place on fire and bring slowly to the boiling point, reduce heat and boil the eggs gently for 15 minutes. Remove from fire, plunge into cold water for a few minutes, then crack and remove the shells. Now make a cream sauce. Heat 2 cups rich milk in a little pan. Place 6 tablespoons butter in top part of large enamel double boiler. Melt the butter and add 6 tablespoons all-purpose flour. Cook together for a second or two, stirring constantly with wooden spoon, then add gradually the hot milk, to make a thick smooth sauce. Cut the hard-boiled eggs lengthwise, making 6 pieces of each. Season the sauce to taste with salt and coarsely ground black pepper and thin to desired thickness with about ½ cup cream. Place over boiling water and fold the hard boiled eggs gently into the sauce. Cover and keep warm while you remove the fish from the fish boiler. Place it on a hot fish platter and cut off the ends of the cheesecloth and spread out the cheesecloth. Now working quickly remove all of the skin from top side of salmon. Lift one side of cheesecloth and roll the fish over onto the other side, removing the cheesecloth as you do so. Remove the rest of the skin and decorate the fish platter with plenty of parsley and quartered lemons. Send to table accompanied by the Hard-Boiled-Egg Cream Sauce, and a separate little bowl of capers.

213

SUMMER DINNER WITHOUT MEAT

*SPANISH GAZPACHO

*MUSHROOMS FRIED IN BATTER

*BAKED SWEET CORN   *TOMATOES SWEET AND HOT

COMPOTE OF MIXED FRUIT   *CHOCOLATE FRIANDISES

COFFEE

SERVE THE MARQUES DE MURRIETA WHITE SPANISH
WINE, CHILLED, WITH THIS

* See Index for Starred Dishes

Compote of Fruit
(for 6–8)

First make some syrup in a large pan. Moisten 2 cups sugar with 2 cups water and boil 5 minutes.

Wash 8 perfect pink-cheeked freestone peaches, 8 blue plums, 8 apricots, 8 pears and 8 red plums. Have ready a bowl of cold water containing the juice of 1 lemon. Peel the peaches, by dropping them one by one into boiling water for a second or two, then allowing the cold water to run over them for a second. The peels should then pinch off, leaving the peaches smooth and perfect. Drop them as you peel them into the cold water containing the lemon juice. This is to prevent their discoloration. When all the peaches are done, place them in the syrup and boil just long enough so that they may be pierced with a fork. Remove them from the syrup with a sieved spoon and place them in a large round compotier (fruit dish). Next peel the pears and cut them in two lengthwise and with small potato scooper cut out the core and seeds. Place them one by one in the acidulated water until they are all done, at which time place them in the syrup and cook until just tender, which won't take very long if they are ripe. Remove them carefully one by one and tuck them prettily between the peaches. Now add the apricots, blue plums, and red plums, left whole, to the syrup and cook until the plums pop open. Arrange the apricots symmetrically between the peaches and pears, and the plums, here and there. The juice should then be boiled down until thicker, cooled slightly and poured over all the fruit. Before serving, well chilled, garnish with 2 dozen blanched almonds. To blanch, place the almonds in a little bowl and pour boiling water over them. Let them stand 3 minutes, then plunge into cold water. The skins should pinch off readily. Soak them in cold water in the refrigerator for an hour or so and they will be crisp like green almonds.

A GOOD DINNER

SHRIMP AND OYSTER BISQUE

ROAST GUINEA HEN WITH BLACK WALNUT AND
BREAD STUFFING

*TART CURRANT JELLY   *FRIED CORN MEAL MUSH

*OLD-FASHIONED ASPARAGUS

BANANA CREAM

COFFEE

SERVE WHITE HERMITAGE OF A GOOD YEAR, WITH THIS

* See Index for Starred Dishes

Shrimp and Oyster Bisque
(for 6–8)

For this you need 2 cups shrimp, cleaned and cooked—canned may be used. Also 1 pint shelled oysters. Save out as many of the smallest shrimps as there are people to be served. Now chop very fine the remaining shrimps and the raw oysters, and put in the top of a double boiler with 3 pints milk and any oyster liquor in the measure, also 3 tablespoons chopped onion, ½ cup chopped celery, 2 sprigs parsley chopped, 1 teaspoon salt—or to taste—pinch of mace and some ground black pepper. Cook over boiling water for ½ hour, then press through a sieve.

Melt 5 tablespoons butter, add 5 tablespoons flour, stirring until smooth. Slowly add the sieved mixture, stirring constantly. Let heat gently to be very smooth but do not boil. Put a little shrimp in each soup plate, pour in the soup, dash with cayenne or paprika and serve.

Guinea Hens Stuffed with Black Walnut and Bread Stuffing
(for 6–8)

Peel 1 small onion and cut in two and stick a whole clove in each ½. Place the onion in a little pan, and add to it 1 cup milk. Place on low flame and bring to scalding point. In the meantime, remove the crust from 1 loaf stale white bread, and crumble it into fine crumbs. Add ¼ pound butter, cut into little pieces, then pour over it the scalded milk. Sprinkle with salt and pepper and grate over all ½ a whole nutmeg. Also add ¾ cup black walnut meats, broken into small pieces. Toss the whole lightly together using a fork.

Clean 2 fine plump guinea hens, sprinkle them lightly inside with salt and pepper, then stuff them well with the bread mixture, burying ½ onion in the center of each. Sew up the cavities using thin string. Place side by side in a small roasting pan, and dot with ¼ pound butter. Place in preheated 500° F. oven and roast until well browned, basting frequently. In about ½ hour, reduce the heat to 375° F. and add to the basting butter in the pan, several stalks of celery and 1 large carrot cut into small pieces. Continue basting frequently and roast until well done, or for about 1½ hours in all.

When done, transfer the birds to another pan and pour over them some of the fat from the roasting pan, then place back in oven to keep hot while you make a gravy by adding to the remaining vegetables and juice in the pan, 2 scant teaspoons Torex (beef extract) dissolved in 1 cup boiling water. Stir well, and reduce by simmering until nice and syrupy. Remove the strings used for tying up the birds, and the ones used for sewing up the cavities, and place birds on a warm platter. Carve and garnish with parsley and serve accompanied by the gravy from which you have skimmed off all the remaining fat. Grape Conserve (see page 169) adds a superlative touch, or currant jelly may be served as a substitute.

Banana Cream
(for 6–8)

Soak 1 package Knox Gelatine in ¼ cup cold water for 5 minutes. Pour over it 1½ cups boiling water. Add ¼ cup granulated sugar and stir until dissolved, then cool. Rub 3 ripe bananas through a sieve and add to the cooled gelatine water. Stir well and fold in 1 cup heavy cream whipped until stiff. Place in mold which you have rinsed in cold water and chill until set and firm. Run knife around the edge and turn out onto pretty serving dish. Serve with or without a garnish of sliced fruit or berries.

OLD-FASHIONED HEARTY DINNER

*CORNED BEEF AND CABBAGE WITH CORN
MEAL DUMPLINGS

*HOT SWEET POTATO CAKE-BREAD

*SUSIE'S MUSTARD PICKLE

BAKED PEARS AND CREAM

*ELECTION CAKE

COFFEE

* *See Index for Starred Dishes*

Baked Pears
(for 6–8)

Wash 8 Italian brown pears and place them in a deep baking pan, close together so that they will stand up. Place 1 cup light brown sugar in a pan and moisten with 1½ cups water. Add 3 tablespoons butter and bring to a boil. Pour over the pears. Add 1 inch vanilla bean, or a few strips of thinly cut lemon peel. Cover the pears with chef's foil and bake in moderate 375° F. oven for about 1 hour or until the pears may be pierced with a fork. Baste frequently. Serve hot, with cream or with a little vanilla ice cream.

DINNER WHICH WILL WAIT FOR LAGGARD GUESTS

HOT OR COLD MADRILENE (CANNED)

ROAST SQUAB CHICKEN STUFFED WITH BROWN RICE

*BRAISED CELERY

*EMMY REYNOLDS'S LEMON MOUSSE

PECAN OR HAZELNUT MACAROONS

BLACK COFFEE

SERVE A CHILLED TRAMINER, MEURSEULT OR VOUVRAY
WITH THIS

* See Index for Starred Dishes

Roast Baby Squab Chickens Stuffed with Brown Rice
(for 6–8)

Clean, singe, wash and wipe dry inside and out, 8 small plump baby squab chickens, weighing about 1 pound each.

To prepare the stuffing, wash 1 pound (or 2 cups) brown rice in a sieve until perfectly clean by allowing the cold water to run through it. Have ready a big pot containing 5 quarts actively boiling water salted with 2 tablespoons salt. Add the rice gradually so that the water never stops boiling. Cook, stirring occasionally, until the rice tastes just barely done, or for about 40 minutes. Have ready 2 quarts boiling water, and when the rice is done, drain it in a colander and pour through it the 2 quarts boiling water. Shake well, and return the rice to the pot in which it cooked. Place on asbestos mat over very low flame, cover and steam for about 5 minutes.

In the meantime, prepare 1 cup finely chopped Bermuda onions and the same of chopped hearts of celery. Cook these in ⅛ pound butter for about 5 minutes, stirring constantly or until they just begin to brown. Now melt an additional ⅛ pound butter in a fairly large pan and add to it the cooked vegetables and the rice. Stir lightly until well mixed.

Season to taste with coarsely ground pepper, a little salt and 1 tablespoon Gumbo Filé Powder (procurable at food specialty shops). Also add 3 tablespoons chopped parsley. Mix thoroughly but lightly with a fork, and allow to cool before stuffing the prepared little birds.

When ready to stuff the birds, sprinkle them lightly inside with salt and a little pepper and, using a teaspoon, stuff them nice and full. Close the opening by sewing or use a sturdy toothpick. Wipe clean with damp cloth and place side by side in a large roasting pan, on a bed of 1 cup carrots cut into small pieces. Pour over them ½ pound melted butter. Place in preheated 450° F. oven and roast, basting frequently, for about 40 minutes. Ten minutes before they will be done, transfer them to the top part of the roasting pan, and make some clear gravy by adding 1 cup chicken broth to the pan in which they were roasted. Stir well and reduce until syrupy. Strain into a small pan, discarding the carrots. Remove excess fat and heat before serving with the birds placed on a hot platter surrounded by crisp water cress.

Pecan or Hazelnut Macaroons
(for 6–8)

Put ½ pound shelled hazelnuts or shelled pecans (about 2 cups) through the nut grater, which should reduce them to a powder. If any large bits slip through, remove them by sifting through a coarse sieve. Mix into this 3 well-rounded tablespoons pastry flour. Beat the whites of 3 eggs stiff, then beat in gradually generous cup (½ pound) powdered sugar. Fold in the powdered nuts and flavor with 1 teaspoon vanilla. Drop by small teaspoonfuls onto 2 unbuttered cookie sheets and place in preheated, slow, 300° F. oven and bake for 20–25 minutes. Loosen immediately from pan with a spatula. Makes about 3 dozen small macaroons.

TWELVE

Gourmet, My Eye

The plump lady at the luncheon party waved away the cigarette offered with the *apéritif* of dry Madeira. "I am a gourmet," she said. "A gourmet does not smoke just before eating."

That was the only time I ever heard anyone actually claim to be a gourmet. Usually it is a tribute offered, not an attribute asserted; and the lady not only named herself as a gourmet but offered a definite rule for being one. There it was: "A gourmet does not smoke before eating." That's what *she* thought. It started me collecting other definitions and I found many, most of them mere comic trivia like this one. Here are some of them verbatim:

"He is a great gourmet—he is simply mad about *Crêpes Suzette*."

"She is a wonderful gourmet—everything you eat at her house is flavored with herbs."

"A real gourmet always rubs the salad bowl with garlic."

"An extraordinary gourmet, his favorite breakfast is *Pâté aux truffes,* French bread and a pint of champagne."

"Uncle Doremus was a true gourmet; he could tell the liver wing of a chicken by taste."

"I couldn't ask him to dinner that night for he is a gourmet and we were having corned beef and cabbage."

"That restaurant at The Hague where they served asparagus in gourmet style, flavored with nutmeg . . ."

"A perfect gourmet always lets his wild ducks hang until their heads drop off." And another about wild duck: "No gourmet will eat wild duck unless blood follows the carving knife."

"White wine vinegar is the only kind a gourmet ever uses."

"A gourmet never cuts fruit except with a silver knife."

"She had the gourmet instinct about coffee; she won't drink it unless it is fresh roasted, fresh ground, and fresh made."

And everyone has heard of those English gourmets who say reproachfully to the club waiter: "Come, come, Hawkins, you've given me the '64 port, not the '47."

The war with its shortages and rationing pushed such marks of gourmetism into oblivion. Uncle Doremus forgot all about the liver wing of the chicken and devoured meat balls and was mighty glad to get them. The gentleman who couldn't be invited to corned beef and cabbage would, those days, simply beg to be allowed to stay and partake if he caught a whiff of this delicious combination. And not so long ago in the devastated Hague, people were eating tulip bulbs, two a day and one potato being their allotted portion, and if there was any asparagus about they didn't refuse it because of lack of nutmeg.

As for *Crêpes Suzette,* I have said before and will here repeat that this much-touted dish has little but snob value. The pancakes are made in the kitchen by an undercook and then paraded out to a special table where, with chafing dish and an array of liqueurs, they are recooked and folded and flambéed with much chi-chi by an expert headwaiter and the result is often a row of nondescript, leathery little morsels for which the diner is expected to pay an extra tip.

That chap who rubs the salad bowl with a clove of garlic, well, it's fine if he and his family and friends like garlic. A great many worthy people loathe it. Either way it's no mark of distinction in taste, only a difference. And since I once knew a gourmet who had his wild ducks hung till their heads dropped off I will merely report that the odor drove his family as far down the table as they could remove themselves; also he had more than one aftermath of ptomaine.

To examine more of the gourmet definitions: that business of flavoring with herbs can be overdone until the food tastes and smells like medicine. If people want to eat medicine that is all right with me, but I prefer food that tastes like food and not like something the doctor ordered. As for white wine vinegar, yes, it's very good when used in the right proportion, but so also are cider vinegar, red wine vinegar and lemon juice.

If such expert nuances were real, they do not necessarily make gourmets any more than are the desert chieftains gourmets who consider the eye of a roasted sheep a rare and delectable tidbit and maintain that a black sheep's eye is more toothsome than a white sheep's eye. To each race, its favorite food. I have always liked the story of Arnold Bennett, who declined some specially prepared terrapin with the candid comment: "It looks like a nawsty dish."

After all, individual preferences in taste are only individual preferences in taste and not marks of personal distinction or superiority. Consider, please, the torrid arguments that rage perennially in our public press over whether or not clam chowder should be made with tomatoes; consider the screams of outrage that arise from each side of the eternal controversy about cinnamon in apple pie; and the venomous brawl over whether the mint in a julep should be crushed or uncrushed. As for that lady who couldn't drink anything but fresh-roasted, fresh-made coffee and the people who can't season food except with salt and pepper ground from their respective hand mills—are they superior beings or just fussbudgets? What do you think?

France is so generally called a nation of gourmets that I consulted Larousse as to the disputed word. A dictionary should be able to speak with authority. Well, Larousse says: *"Gourmet, n.m. qui se connait en vins, en bonne chère; Lucullus est reste le type des fins gourmets. Dégustateur."*

I knew Lucullus would get dragged into this somewhere so I tracked him down in an encyclopedia. His fame as a gourmet was omitted entirely but he is given this revealing comment: "Lucullus was a great general in all but one respect: His soldiers did not love him; he was perhaps the only enlightened governor Roman Asia ever had." Another encyclopedia remarks with caution that Lucullus was said to have lived luxuriously. Montaigne contributes the item that Lucullus loved to make himself conspicuous in battle by rich armor and accouterments of particular color and luster, and lauds him as an orator. So much for Lucullus, that typical fine gourmet. Since his life span was from 110 B.C. to 57 B.C. his food was so enormously different from ours today that we have no standards by which to judge his gourmetism. He remains a legendary figure, but his name has given us the adjective "Lucullan," and even those soldiers who didn't love him cannot rob him of this meager fame. Maybe he feasted on ortolan tongues while his troops munched Roman K-ration.

Now putting Lucullus out on the side lines, I like the part of Larousse's definition which defines a gourmet as one who knows wines and food, with the inference that such knowledge is both general and particular and would surely include the everyday items as well as the luxurious rarities. Continuing food shortages, high prices, and the scarcity of cooks have made us all far more conscious of how good, how very good the plainest dishes may be. Bread has come up in the world to a place far above cake and patisserie, and is important for flavor and nourishment as never before. The dull potato baked to mealiness and enlivened with a spoonful of cream, salt and sweet paprika is an epicure's pleasure. As one born in the South I shout the praises of the products of corn, but especially corn meal and what can be made from it. There is nothing better than corn-meal mush for a winter supper and there are hundreds of muffins, griddle cakes, pones, puddings, johnny cakes, corn sticks and spoon breads, all of them wonderful. And we rediscover how exquisite are ripe red raspberries or a big blushing ripe peach untouched by sugar! When there was scant butter to make rich sauce we learned all over again the true taste of asparagus and how well-steamed broccoli stands alone. Thick peasant soups are back, filled with everything we can find in the icebox and for hot days there is the Spanish *gazpacho,* that refreshing iced soup filled with the tiniest bit of raw onions, carrots, tomatoes, green peppers, celery, cucumber, parsley, chives, basil and savory, touched with olive oil and lemon—it is like half-eating, half-drinking a whole cool vegetable garden. The Spaniards show high imagination about soup—they make one called *jigote,* a strong beef broth with chopped raisins and croutons in it that is marvelous! That gourmet we were talking about, the one who knows food, never has to eat stupid meals.

But let's be clear on this—eccentricities of taste or strong individual preferences have little to do with gourmetism. Taste is an elusive, variable quality, it changes with each individual, it cannot be captured in rules or in graphs, or in tabulations. Time, place, education, nationality, custom and tradition shape it. It cannot be paraded as a virtue or even a noble component of character.

A palate sensitive to flavor is an agreeable adjunct to daily living;

recognition and use of a wide range of the elements of good cheer make for variety and interest at table; but to go high-hat because of a predilection for tomato in chowder or decayed duck is vanity and ignorance. All God's chillun ain't gourmets because of a craving for a pâté-and-champagne breakfast or uncrushed mint in the julep! The real gourmet remains the man—or woman—who knows food and wine and employs them wisely. He is not greedy nor puffed up like a soufflé with the knowledge he possesses. He considers eating and drinking one of the pleasures of life but not life's aim or purpose. Above all he will never exalt his own taste choosings as a sign of superiority to those who differ with him!

Index
of
Recipes

Adelaide Heilner's Seawood Canapé, 80

After-Dinner Coffee, Festive, 185

Aimée Evans's Mozzarella in Carroza, 81

Aimée Evans's Orange Bread, 131

Allentown Potato Doughnuts, 134

Amanda Kerr's Blackberry Mush, 98

Amanda Kerr's Pancakes with Blackberries, 96

Ambrosia, Orange, 44

Apple (Dried), and Raisin Pie, 33

Apple (Green) Custard Pie, 61

Apple Pie, made with Applesauce, 61

Apples, 161
   Fried, 46
   Sweet Potatoes and, 207

Applesauce, Apple Pie made with, 61

Apricot Jam, 167

Apricot Pie, 59

Apricot Pudding, Won Kim's, 97

Apricots, 161

Apricot Turnovers, Mary Palmer's, 94

Arline's Rich Waffles, 124

Artichokes, Boiled, with Sauce Hollandaise, 140

Asparagus, Old-Time Style, 141

Asparagus Salad
   with Tart French Dressing, 199

Baked Corn, 144

Baked Potatoes
   Sweet, 183
   White, 148

Banana Cream, 216

Banana Cream Pie, 73

Bananas, 161

Banbury Tarts, 69

Bannocks, Indian Meal, 127

Bar-le-Duc
   Currant, Red, 172
   Currant, White, 172

Batter Cake, Corn Meal, 125

Beans
  Lima, Boiled, 141
  Marrow, Purée of Dried, 18
  String
    Salad of, with Tart French Dressing, 199
    to Your Taste, 152
    with Sour Cream Sauce, 151
Beef, Corned
  Hash, with Caramelized Onions, 34
  Dinner, with Corn Meal Dumplings, 33
Beef Patties, Broiled, 31
Beefsteak Pie, Individual, 190
Beef Stew, 46
Beets, Raw, Sautéed, 142
Beignets, Soufflés, 112
Berta Mueller's Lemon Pudding, 97
Biscuits
  Baking Powder, 121
  Beat (Maryland), 15
Bisque, Shrimp and Oyster, 215
Blackberries, Amanda Kerr's Pancakes with, 96
Blackberry Jam, 168
Blackberry Mush, Amanda Kerr's, 98
Blackberry Pie, 66
Black Cherry Jam, 169
Black-Eyed Peas, 38
Black Raspberry Jam, 168
Black Walnut and Bread Stuffing, Guinea Hen with, 215
Blanchard's, Mlle., Tomatoes and Rice, Lenten, 87
Blueberry Muffins, 122
Blueberry Pancake Pies, 95
Blueberry Tart, 63
Boiled Potatoes, Baked in their Jackets, 148

Bortsch, Cold, 203
Boston Brown Bread, 128
Bouchées, Chocolate, 184
Braised Celery, 144
Brandade of Salt Codfish, 111
Bread
  Aimée Evans's, Orange, 131
  Boston Brown, 128
  Corn, Custard, 126
  French Onion, Crisp, 183
  Irish, 133
  Louise's Portuguese, 131
  Nut, 132
  Oatmeal, 132
  Onion, Crisp French, 183
  Orange, Aimée Evans's, 131
  Portuguese
    Louise's, 131
    Sweet, 129
  Spoon, 126
  Sweet Portuguese, 129
  Togus Loaf, 127
Bread and Butter Pickles, 172
Bread-Cake, Sweet Potato, 133
Bretonne, Crêpes, Madame Le Douzen's Café de France, with Hazelnut Butter, 113
Brioche, Large, 128
Brown Bread, Boston, 128
Brown Rice, Squab Chickens Stuffed with, 218
Butter, Hazelnut, Crêpes Bretonne with, 113

Cabbage, Red, Glorified, 142
Cake
  Batter, Corn Meal, 125
  Corn, Spider, 37
  Cup, Date, Mrs. Wolfe's, 92
  Election, 93
  Johnny, 125

Cake (*continued*)
  Orange, Katherine Emmet's, 92
  Pound, 16
  Short, Rhubarb, Helen's, 209
  Sponge, 17
Canapé, Seawood, Adelaide Heilner's, 80
Carrottes à la Nonne, 143
Catsup, Grape, Old-Fashioned, 48
Cauliflower, Boiled, 143
Celery, Braised, 144
Cheese Custard Pie, 72
Cheese, Tomato Halves Baked with, 189
Cherries, 161
Cherry, Black, Jam, 169
Cherry Pie, Sour, Latticed, 60
Cheese Popovers, 89
Cheese Tartines, Hot, 90
Chess Pie, 70
Chicken
  Fricassee with Dumplings, 41
  Fried, Maryland, 204
  Hot Paté of, 20
  Pie, 39
  Roast, 107
  Sautéed, 23
  Squab, Roast Baby, Stuffed with Brown Rice, 218
  Water Zooi, 176
Chiffon Pie, Lime, 66
Chili Sauce, 171
Chinese Rice, 150
Chocolate Bouchées, 184
Chocolate, Friandises of, Willa Roberts Plank's, 108
Chocolate Pie, 73
Chops, Pork, Fried, 43
Chowder, Halibut, Peggy's, 49
Clam and Scallop Soup, Cream of, 193

Clam Pie, Dr. Walter Taylor's Favorite, 48
Coconut Cream Pie, 74
Coconut Ice Cream, 178
Codfish, Salt, Brandade of, 111
Coffee, After-Dinner, Festive, 185
Cole Slaw with Hot Boiled Dressing, 32
Compote
  of Fresh Peaches, 192
  of Fruit, 213
  Viennese, 197
Concord Grape, Black, Jelly, 165
Conserve, Grape, 169
Cookies, Christmas Mincemeat, 183
Coquilles Saint Jacques, 108
Corn, Baked, 144
Corn Bread, Custard, 126
Corn Cake, Spider, 37
Corned Beef
  Dinner (Boiled), 33
  Hash with Caramelized Onions, 34
Corn Fritters, Delicate, 145
Corn Meal
  Batter Cake, 125
  Dumplings, 33
  Muffins, Basic, 124
  Mush, Fried, 127
Corn Sticks, 126
Crab Cakes, Minny Cover's, 89
Crabs, Deviled, 178
Cranberry and Orange Relish, 191
Cranberry Jelly, 206
Cranberry Pie, 62
Cranberry Raisin Pie, 62
Cream, Banana, 216
Cream Gravy, Fried Tomatoes with, 153
Cream, Rice, Sweet, Julia Hunt's, 98

Cream, Sour, Sauce, 152
Cream, Spinach in, 151
Crêpes Bretonne, Madame Le Douzen's Café de France, with Hazelnut Butter, 113
Cupcakes, Date, Mrs. Wolfe's, 92
Currant
  Red, Bar-le-Duc, 172
  Jelly, 166
  White, Bar-le-Duc, 172
Custard Corn Bread, 126
Custard Pie
  Apple (Green), 61
  Cheese, 72
Custard Sauce, Stewed Pears with, 35

Date Cupcakes, Mrs. Wolfe's, 92
Delicate Corn Fritters, 145
Deviled Crabs, 178
Dinner, Corned Beef Boiled, with Cornmeal Dumplings, 33
Doughnuts
  Potato, Allentown, 134
  Raised, 135
Douzen's, Madame Le, Crêpes Bretonne, 113
Dressing
  Boiled
    Grandmother Schaffner's, 88
    Hot, Cole Slaw with, 32
  French, Tart, 199
Drexel's Mushroom Fritters, 86
Dumplings
  Baking Powder, 42
  Chicken Fricassee with, 41
  Cornmeal, 33

Eggs, Hard-Boiled, with Grandmother Schaffner's Boiled Dressing, 88

Election Cake, 93
Eliza's, Aunt, Peach Pie, 15
Emmet's, Katherine, Orange Cake, 92
Emmy Reynolds's Lemon Mousse, 99
Evans's, Aimée
  Mozzarella in Carroza, 81
  Orange Bread, 131

Festive After-Dinner Coffee, 185
Figs, 161
Fish Cakes, 38
France, Café de, Crêpes Bretonne, 113
French Dressing, Tart
  Asparagus Salad with, 199
  String Bean Salad with, 199
French Fried Onions, 32
French Fried Sweet Potatoes, 201
French Onion Bread, Crisp, 183
French Toast, 137
Friandises of Chocolate, Willa Roberts Plank's, 108
Fricassee, Chicken, with Dumplings, 41
Fried Apples, 46
Fried Chicken, Maryland, 204
Fried Oysters, 13
Fried Tomatoes, with Cream Gravy, 153
Fritters
  Corn, Delicate, 145
  Mushroom, Drexel's, 86
Fruit, Compote of, 213
Fruit Meringue, 173
Fruit, Uncooked, for the Table, 160 ff.

Galette with Blazing Mincemeat, 68
Gazpacho, 83

Gelatine, Raspberry, 173
Gingerbread, 94
Glorified Red Cabbage, 142
Gooseberry Jam, 169
Gooseberry Tart, Deep Dish, 64
Grape Catsup, Old-Fashioned, 48
Grape Conserve, 169
Grapefruit, 161
  Broiled, 174
Grape Jelly, Black Concord, 165
Grapes, 161
Gravy, Cream, Fried Tomatoes with, 153
Green Pepper and Tomato Mix, 201
Guinea Hen
  Hot Paté of, 20
  Stuffed, with Black Walnut and Bread Stuffing, 215

Halibut Chowder, Peggy's, 49
Hash, Corned Beef with Caramelized Onions, 34
Hazelnut Butter, Crêpes Bretonne with, 113
Hazelnut Macaroons, 219
Heilner's, Adelaide, Seawood Canapé, 80
Helen's Rhubarb Shortcake, 209
Hollandaise, Sauce, 140, 156
  Artichokes (boiled) with, 140
  Green, 143
  Scallions (boiled) with, 150
  Zucchini with, 156
Huckleberry Pie, 65
Hunt's, Julia
  Marguerites, 91
  Sweet Rice Cream, 98

Ice Cream, Coconut, 178
Ice, Orange, 174

Indian Meal Bannocks, 127
Individual Beefsteak Pie, 190
Irish Bread, 133

Jacques, Saint, Coquilles, 108
Jam
  Apricot, 167
  Blackberry, 168
  Cherry, Black, 169
  General Directions for Making, 167
  Gooseberry, 169
  Raspberry
    Red, 168
    Black, 168
  Strawberry, 168
  Wild, 168
Jellied Pickles, Maryland, Mixed, 100
Jelly
  Cranberry, 206
  Currant, Red, and Black Raspberry, 166
  General Directions for Making, 164
  Grape, Black Concord, 165
Johnny Cake, 125
Julia Hunt's
  Marguerites, 91
  Sweet Rice Cream, 98

Kale, 38
Karl Pfeiffer's
  Potage Chantilly, 82
  Tomatoes Sweet and Hot, 87
Katherine Emmet's Orange Cake, 92
Kerr's, Amanda
  Blackberry Mush, 98
  Pancakes with Blackberries and Wine and Lemon Sauce, 96
Kim's, Won, Apricot Pudding, 97

Lamb
  Roast Leg of, Persillé, 208
  Saddle of, 17
  Stew, 42
Lasagne, Amalfi, Mary Elizabeth
  Taylor's à la Mrs. Pistone, 84
Lemon Meringue Pie, 67
Lemon Mousse, Emmy Reynolds's,
  99
Lemon Pudding, Berta Mueller's, 97
Lemon Snow Pudding, 35
Lenten Tomatoes and Rice, Mlle.
  Blanchard's, 87
Lima Bean and Pea Soup, 205
Lima Beans, Boiled, 141
Lime Chiffon Pie, 66
Lobster
  Armoricaine, à l', 109
  Boiled, Cold, with Mayonnaise,
    106
  Hunk Sandwiches, 200
Lorraine, La Quiche, 105
Louise's Portuguese Bread, 131

Macaroons
  Hazelnut, 219
  Pecan, 91, 219
Mangoes, 162
Marguerites, Julia Hunt's, 91
Marrons Glacés, Sweet Potatoes with,
  210
Marrow Beans, Purée of Dried, 18
Marte's Heavenly Squash, 85
Maryland Beat Biscuits, 15
Maryland Fried Chicken, 204
Maryland Jellied Mixed Pickles, 100
Mary Palmer's Apricot Turnovers, 94
Mashed Potato Surprise, 149
Mayonnaise, 106
  Lobster, Cold Boiled with, 106
Melba Toast, 137

Melon Refraichi, Cold, à la Mon-
  tagné, 211
Melons, 162
Meringue, Fruit, 173
Milk Onion Soup, La Providence,
  83
Milk Toast, 136
Mincemeat Cookies, Christmas, 183
Mincemeat, Galette with Blazing, 68
Minny Cover's Crab Cakes, 89
Mint, Green Peas with, 147
Mix, Green Pepper and Tomato,
  201
Mousse, Lemon, Emmy Reynolds's,
  99
Mozzarella in Carroza, Aimée
  Evans's, 81
Mueller's, Berta, Lemon Pudding, 97
Muffins
  Blueberry, 122
  Corn Meal, Basic, 124
  Egg, Basic, 122
  Raspberry, 123
Mush
  Blackberry, Amanda Kerr's, 98
  Corn Meal, Fried, 127
Mushroom Fritters, Drexel's, 86
Mustard Pickle, Aunt Susie's, 5
Mutton, Saddle of, 17

Nectarines
  See Peaches
Nonne, Carrottes à la, 143
Nut Bread, 132

Oatmeal Bread, 132
Onion Bread, Crisp French, 183
Onion Pie, 145
Onions, Caramelized with Corned
  Beef Hash, 34
Onions, French Fried, 32

Orange Ambrosia, 44
Orange Bread, Aimée Evans's, 131
Orange Cake, Katherine Emmet's, 92
Orange, Cranberry and, Relish, 191
Orange Ice, 174
Orange Marmalade Soufflés, Dr. Francis Trudeau's Favorite, 99
Oranges, 162
Oriental Sauce, 100
Oyster Bisque, Shrimp and, 215
Oyster Pie, 47
Oysters, Fried, 13

Palmer's, Mary, Apricot Turnovers, 94
Pancake Pies, Blueberry, 95
Pancakes, 123
Pancakes, Amanda Kerr's, with Blackberries, 96
Parsnips, Mashed, 146
Parsnip Stew, 146
Partridge, Wrapped in Grape Leaves and Bacon, 19
Pastry, Plain, for One Pie, 58
Paté, Hot
  Chicken, 20
  Guinea Hen, 20
  Pheasant, 20
Peaches, 163
  Fresh, Compote of, 192
Peach Pie, 59
  Aunt Eliza's, 15
Pears, 163
  Baked, 217
  Stewed, with Custard Sauce, 35
Peas
  Black-Eyed, 38
  Green, with Mint, 147
  See also Pois, Petits

Pea, Soup, Lima Bean and, 205
Pea (Split) Soup, 200
Pecan Macaroons, 91, 219
Peggy's Halibut Chowder, 49
Persimmons, 162
Pfeiffer's, Karl
  Potage Chantilly, 82
  Tomatoes Sweet and Hot, 87
Pheasant, Hot Paté of, 20
Pickled Watermelon Rind, 170
Pickle, Mustard, Aunt Susie's, 5
Pickles
  Bread and Butter, 172
  Jellied, Maryland, Mixed, 100
Pie
  Apple (Dried) and Raisin, 33
  Apple (Green) Custard, 61
  Apple, Made with Applesauce, 61
  Apricot, 59
  Banana Cream, 73
  Beefsteak, Individual, 190
  Blackberry, 66
  Black Walnut, Butterscotch, 70
  Cheese Custard, 72
  Cherry, Sour Latticed, 60
  Chess, 70
  Chicken, 39
  Chiffon, Lime, 66
  Chocolate, 73
  Clam, Dr. Walter Taylor's Favorite, 48
  Coconut Cream, 74
  Cranberry, 62
  Cranberry Raisin, 62
  Custard
    Cheese, 72
    Green Apple, 61
  Huckleberry, 65
  Lemon Meringue, 67
  Lime Chiffon, 66
  Onion, 145

Pie (*continued*)
  Oyster, 47
  Peach, 59
    Aunt Eliza's, 15
  Plain Pastry for One, 58
  Pumpkin, 68
  Raisin, Cranberry, 62
  Shoo-Fly, 71
  Sour Cherry, Latticed, 60
  Squash, 68
  Sweet Potato, 71
Pies, Blueberry Pancake, 95
Pineapple, 163
Pistone, Mrs.
  See Lasagne
Pizza, 198
Plank's, Willa Roberts
  Browned White Turnips, 154
  Friandises of Chocolate, 108
Plums, 163
Plum Tart, 64
Pois, Petits, à la Française, 147
Popovers, 123
  Cheese, 89
Pork
  Chops, Fried, 43
  Roast Loin of, 36
  Spareribs, Roast, 37
Portuguese Bread
  Louise's, 131
  Sweet, 129
Potage Chantilly, Karl Pfeiffer's, 82
Potato Balls, Browned, 148
Potato Doughnuts, Allentown, 134
Potatoes
  Baked Sweet, 183
  Baked White, 148
  Boiled and Baked in Their Jackets, 148
  Mashed, Surprise, 149

Potatoes (*continued*)
  Sweet
    and Apples, 207
    Baked, 183
    French Fried, 201
    with Marrons Glacés, 210
  Tarragon, 149
  White, Baked, 148
Poundcake, 16
Preserves
  Quince, 170
  Tomato, Yellow, 171
Providence, La, Milk Onion Soup, 83
Pudding
  Apricot, Won Kim's, 97
  Lemon, Berta Mueller's, 97
  Lemon Snow, 35
Puff Paste, 58
Pumpkin Pie, 68

Quiche Lorraine, La, 105
Quince Preserves, 170

Raisin, Apple (Dried) and, Pie, 33
Raisin Cranberry Pie, 62
Raspberries, 164
Raspberry, Black
  Jam, 168
  Jelly, 166
Raspberry Gelatine, 173
Raspberry Muffins, 123
Raspberry, Red, Jam, 168
Red Cabbage, Glorified, 142
Red Currant Bar-le-Duc, 172
Red Raspberry Jam, 168
Relish, Cranberry and Orange, 191
Remoulade, Sauce, 182
Reynolds's, Emmy, Lemon Mousse, 99
Rhubarb Shortcake, Helen's, 209

Rice

  Brown, Squab Chickens Stuffed with, 218

  Chinese, 150

  Cream, Julia Hunt's Sweet, 98

  Tomatoes and, Mlle. Blanchard's, Lenten, 87

Roast Chicken, 107

Rolls, Pocketbook, 14

Roquefort, Tartines of, 90

Saint Jacques, Coquilles, 108

Salad

  Asparagus, 199

  String Bean, 199

Sally Lunn, 134

Salmon, Boiled (Hot) with Hard-Boiled-Egg Cream Sauce, 212

Sandwiches, Lobster Hunk, 200

Sauce

  Chili, 171

  Custard, Stewed Pears with, 35

  Hard-Boiled Egg Cream, 212

  Hollandaise, 140

    Green, 143

  Oriental, 100

  Remoulade, 182

  Sour Cream, 152

  Wine and Lemon, 96

Scallions, Boiled, with Sauce Hollandaise, 150

Scallop and Clam Soup, Cream of, 193

Schaffner's, Grandmother, Boiled Dressing, Hard-Boiled Eggs with, 88

Scones, Scotch, 121

Scotch Mists, 182

Seawood Canapé, Adelaide Heilner's, 80

Shoo-Fly Pie, 71

Shortcake, Rhubarb, Helen's, 209

Shrimp Bisque, Oyster and, 215

Shrimp, Boiled, 182

Soufflés Beignets, 112

Soufflés, Orange Marmalade, Dr. Francis Trudeau's Favorite, 99

Soup

  Clam and Scallop, Cream of, 193

  Lima Bean and Pea, 205

  Milk Onion, à la Providence, 83

  Split Pea, 200

Sour Cherry Pie, Latticed, 60

Spareribs, Roast, 37

Spider Corn Cake, 37

Spinach in Cream, 151

Split Pea Soup, 200

Spongecake, 17

Spoon Bread, 126

Squab Chickens, Roast Baby Stuffed with Brown Rice, 218

Squash, Marte's Heavenly, 85

Squash Pie, 68

Stew

  Beef, 46

  Lamb, 42

Strawberries, 164

Strawberry Jam, 168

String Beans

  Salad of, 199

  to Your Taste, 152

  with Sour Cream Sauce, 151

Stuffing, Black Walnut and Bread, Guinea Hen with, 215

Susie's, Aunt, Mustard Pickle, 5

Sweet Portuguese Bread, 129

Sweet Potato Bread-Cake, 133

Sweet Potatoes

  and Apples, 207

  Baked, 183

  French Fried, 201

Sweet Potatoes (*continued*)
  with Marrons Glacés, 210
Sweet Potato Pie, 71
Sweet Rice Cream, Julia Hunt's, 98

Tarragon, Potatoes, 149
Tartines
  Cream Cheese, Hot, 90
  Roquefort, 90
Tarts
  Apple, 24
  Banbury, 69
  Blueberry, 63
  Gooseberry, Deep Dish, 64
  Plum, 64
  Taylor's, Dr. Walter (Favorite Clam Pie), 48
  Taylor's, Mary Elizabeth, Lasagne Amalfi à la Mrs. Pistone, 84
Toast
  French, 137
  Melba, 137
  Milk, 136
Togus Loaf, 127
Tomatoes
  Baked
    Cheese and, 189
    Zucchini and, 155
  Fried, with Cream Gravy, 153
  Provençal, 153
  Rice and, Mlle. Blanchard's Lenten, 87
  Sweet and Hot, Karl Pfeiffer's, 87
  Yellow (Preserves), 171
Tomato Mix, Green Pepper and, 201
Trudeau's, Dr. Francis, Favorite Orange Marmalade Soufflés, 99

Turkey
  Boned Stuffed, 194
  Broiled, 206
  Roast, 191
    Cold, 187
Turnips
  Caramelized, 155
  White, Browned, Willa Roberts Plank's, 154
Turnovers, Apricot, Mary Palmer's, 94

Veal, Blanquette of, 45
Viennese Compote, 197

Waffles, Arline's Rich, 124
Walnut (Black) Stuffing, and Bread, 215
Walnuts, Surprise, 186
Watermelon, 164
  Rind, Pickled, 170
Water Zooi, 176
White Currant Bar-le-Duc, 172
White Potatoes, Baked, 148
Wild Strawberry Jam, 168
Willa Roberts Plank's Friandises of Chocolate, 108
Wine and Lemon Sauce, Pancakes with Blackberries and, 96
Wolfe's, Mrs., Date Cupcakes, 92
Won Kim's Apricot Pudding, 97

Yellow Tomato Preserves, 171

Zooi, Water, 176
Zucchini, Baked, Tomatoes and, 155
Zucchini with Sauce Hollandaise, 156